Jack C. Richards & Chuck Sandy
with Margareth Perucci

An upper-level multi-skills course

Passages

Teacher's Manual

CAMBRIDGE
UNIVERSITY PRESS

1

PUBLISHED BY THE PRESS SYNDICATE OF THE UNIVERSITY OF CAMBRIDGE
The Pitt Building, Trumpington Street, Cambridge, United Kingdom

CAMBRIDGE UNIVERSITY PRESS
The Edinburgh Building, Cambridge CB2 2RU, UK   http://www.cup.cam.ac.uk
40 West 20th Street, New York, NY 10011–4211, USA   http://www.cup.org
10 Stamford Road, Oakleigh, Melbourne 3166, Australia
Ruiz de Alarcón 13, 28014 Madrid, Spain

First published 1998
Fourth printing 2000

Printed in the United States of America

Typeface Baskerville Book   *System* QuarkXPress®   [AH]

A catalog record for this book is available from the British Library

ISBN 0 521 56472 7 Student's Book 1
ISBN 0 521 56470 0 Workbook 1
ISBN 0 521 56468 9 Teacher's Manual 1
ISBN 0 521 56466 2 Class Audio Cassettes 1
ISBN 0 521 56464 6 Class Audio CDs 1
ISBN 0 521 56471 9 Student's Book 2
ISBN 0 521 56469 7 Workbook 2
ISBN 0 521 56467 0 Teacher's Manual 2
ISBN 0 521 56465 4 Class Audio Cassettes 2
ISBN 0 521 56463 8 Class Audio CDs 2

Book design, art direction, and layout services: Adventure House, NYC

Contents

Introduction

Passages is a two-level multi-skills course for upper-intermediate to advanced-level students of North American English. It provides an ideal follow-up for students who have completed a beginning to intermediate course, and is carefully coordinated to function as a sequel to *New Interchange*, one of the world's most successful English courses for adult and young adult learners.

The course covers the four skills of listening, speaking, reading, and writing, while giving systematic attention to grammar and vocabulary. *Passages* develops both fluency and accuracy in English through a topic-based syllabus. The topics are of high interest to students and provide many opportunities for personalization and discussion, promoting the development of both linguistic and communication skills.

Course Length

Each level of *Passages* provides material for 60 to 90 hours of class instruction. In situations where more time is available, the Teacher's Manual provides Optional Activities to extend each unit. Classes with shorter semesters can reduce the amount of time spent on Reading, Writing, Optional Activities, and the Workbook.

Course Components

Student's Book
The Student's Book contains 12 eight-page units with 4 four-page reviews after every three units. There is also a set of Grammar Extensions at the back of the book.

Teacher's Manual
The Teacher's Manual contains detailed suggestions on how to teach the course, unit-by-unit notes, numerous suggestions for optional activities, answers to all Student's Book exercises, and transcripts of the listening activities. Answers to Workbook exercises are found at the back of the book.

Workbook
The Workbook provides a variety of exercises that develop students' proficiency with the grammar, reading, writing, and vocabulary in the Student's Book. The Workbook can be used in class or assigned as homework.

Class Audio Cassettes or CDs
The Class Audio Cassettes or CDs are for use in the classroom or language laboratory. They contain the recordings for the listening exercises. Although the speakers primarily model North American accents, nonnative varieties of English are also used where appropriate. Exercises that are recorded are indicated with the symbol 🔊.

Review Tests

A package of four review tests is available to enable the teacher to evaluate students' progress and to determine if any areas of the course need further study. There is one achievement test following every three units of the Student's Book. The test booklet is accompanied by an audio cassette for the listening sections; all tests may be photocopied for class use. Test answer keys as well as complete information on administering and scoring the tests are included in this booklet.

Unit Organization

Each unit of the Student's Book is organized around a central topic or theme and is divided into 2 four-page lessons (Lessons A and B). These lessons complement each other by treating the unit topic from two different perspectives. For example, Unit 9 in Student's Book 1 is entitled "Putting the mind to work." The first four-page lesson, "Exploring creativity," focuses on the topic of creativity and jobs. In this lesson, students describe jobs that require creativity, take a quiz, and find creative solutions to difficult problems. In the second four-page lesson, "Ideas that work," products and services that have changed our lives are highlighted. For this lesson, students explain why new products are invented and choose inventions that have had a great impact on society.

The following unit structure is used throughout the course:

Lesson A

page one: Presentation activities introduce the topic of the first lesson through listening and oral work.

page two: Grammar exercises provide controlled practice leading to communicative activities that utilize the structures and language being taught.

page three: Fluency pages provide further listening practice and oral work.

page four: Writing exercises teach practical writing and composition skills.

Lesson B

page one: Presentation activities introduce the topic of the second lesson through listening and oral work.

page two: Grammar exercises provide controlled practice leading to communicative activities that utilize the structures and language being taught.

page three: Fluency pages provide further listening practice and oral work.

page four: Reading passages develop reading skills and stimulate discussion.

Approach and Methodology

Passages seeks to develop both fluency and accuracy in students at the upper-intermediate to advanced level of proficiency. The course assumes that students have studied English for a number of years and have a good foundation in general language skills. *Passages* extends students' communicative competence by developing their ability to:

• expand the range of topics they can discuss and comprehend in English
• extend their knowledge and use of grammar

- broaden their knowledge and use of vocabulary
- speak English fluently (i.e., express a wide range of ideas without unnecessary pauses or breakdowns in communication)
- speak English accurately (i.e., use an acceptable standard of pronunciation and grammar when communicating)

To teach these skills, *Passages* uses a communicative methodology that centers around:

- presenting topics that extend students' oral and grammatical skills
- providing students with opportunities to carry out communicative tasks that require an exchange of information and negotiation of meaning
- developing students' control of grammar and conversational language through activities that present and model language patterns, and then provide opportunities to practice them in authentic communicative contexts

At the same time, the topic-driven syllabus provides a rich source of information and language that allows for a great amount of student personalization and response in each lesson.

Exercise Types

The following exercise types are used throughout *Passages:*

Exercise Title	Description
Starting Point	These exercises often present real-world information (e.g., quizzes, facts, short texts). They begin each lesson and are designed to generate students' interest in and reaction to the topic that forms the basis of the lesson.
Discussion	These exercises consist of discussion tasks, ranking activities, class surveys, and other activities that encourage an exchange of information.
Listening	These exercises develop a variety of listening skills, such as listening for general ideas, listening for specific information, and inferencing. The listenings are based on authentic recordings of interviews and discussions with native and second-language speakers of English. They have been edited and recorded for clarity.
Grammar Focus	The grammar exercises seek to: • illustrate how structures and grammar items the students may have previously encountered can be used in more complex ways • expand students' grammatical knowledge and usage in both speaking and writing

Reading	Readings are adapted from a variety of authentic sources and edited for clarity. Pre-reading and post-reading tasks allow students to fully utilize each reading passage and to develop reading skills such as skimming, scanning, and making inferences. They also stimulate class discussion.
Writing	Each unit contains one page of writing activities. In Level One, students learn about using topic sentences, identifying main ideas and supporting details, and organizing paragraphs. They move from writing short paragraphs to composing a three-paragraph composition.
Vocabulary	Vocabulary exercises develop students' knowledge of lexical sets, synonyms and antonyms, as well as idioms and collocations.
Grammar Extensions	Grammar Extensions are located at the back of the book. They expand on the grammar introduced in each unit and can be used to deepen students' understanding of the structures being taught.

Review Units

Review units recycle the teaching points from the three preceding units. Each review unit has two pages of exercises focused on accuracy, followed by two pages on fluency.

General Guidelines for Teaching Passages

The unit-by-unit notes in the Teacher's Manual give detailed suggestions for teaching each exercise. On a more general basis, however, the following guidelines and general procedures can be used.

Beginning a New Unit
- Introduce the theme of the unit by asking questions and eliciting information about it. If you wish, bring in some realia related to the theme to use as a springboard for a class discussion. Such realia might include photos or pictures, a short newspaper or magazine article, or a personal item. Warm-ups should be brief and should serve to lead students into the lesson.
- After introducing the topic, explain and write on the board what the students will study in the lesson. You may also wish to lead students through the plan of the lesson as presented in the Plan of Book 1 on pages xiv–xvii.

Teaching the Exercises in a Unit

Starting Point

The exercises in each Starting Point serve to build interest in the theme of the lesson and to activate students' background knowledge about the topic. Often the material in the Starting Point provides models of the main grammar focus of the lesson. It is not necessary, however, to draw students attention to this. Models are provided to show how the language of the lesson is used in a natural context.

- Introduce the topic by asking questions or by leading a class discussion. Use this time to elicit key vocabulary (or present it) from the exercises and to ask for students' opinions about the information they are going to look at. Remember to build on students' own interests and background knowledge.
- Books open. Lead students through the information. Go over any problems with comprehension as they arise. Have students complete the task and compare with a partner or around the class.
- Bring the class back together, and have selected students or volunteers share answers or opinions with the class.
- If you wish, use students' answers or opinions as the basis for a class discussion.

Listening

It is essential that students are aware of the skill they are practicing in a particular listening exercise, so be sure to bring this to the students' attention before they listen.

- Books closed. Set the scene and explain the situation. If you wish, brainstorm with students to predict what language they are likely to hear.
- Books open. Explain the task and lead students through the activity, making sure they know what information they need to complete it. Remind students that they are listening in order to complete a specific task.
- Play the audio program once. Have students listen for general comprehension and complete whatever information they can.
- Have students ask about unknown vocabulary or comprehension problems that have arisen. Point out any additional key vocabulary that is essential for the task.
- Replay the audio program. Have students complete the task as they listen.
- Have students compare answers with a partner or around the class. Then ask if anyone needs to listen again to complete the task. Replay the audio program as necessary.
- Go over the answers with the class.
- If you wish, replay the audio program a final time so that students may check their completed work.

Grammar Focus

Although grammatical accuracy is an integral part of proficiency, it is important to remember that grammar is always a means to an end rather than an end in itself. Second-language learners do not usually develop grammatical proficiency by studying rules. They generally acquire new grammar by using the language in situations where it is needed. This means the grammar should always be practiced communicatively. However, since language learning also involves testing out hypotheses about how the language works, some students more than others will rely on grammatical explanations.

Avoid turning any lesson into a grammar class. Lead students into the practice activities for the new grammar points as quickly as possible. Then use the students' performance on these activities to decide if further clarification is necessary. Whenever this is the case, remember that there are additional grammar exercises in the Workbook that can be used as a follow-up.

- Lead students through the information and examples in the boxes. When appropriate, remind students of earlier encounters they may have had with the grammar points.
- When possible, try to get students to explain the grammar point; elicit the rules from the students.
- Give students additional examples to illustrate the grammar point where necessary. If appropriate, have students come up with additional examples of their own.
- If you wish, model how to do the first item in the task. Then have students complete the rest of the task on their own. Often an activity can be completed orally as a class before students complete it individually or in pairs.
- Have students compare answers with a partner or in groups. Encourage them to discuss and revise their work.
- To check students' answers and to give feedback, have selected students or volunteers read one of their answers aloud. Alternatively, have students write one of their answers on the board. Work with the class to revise answers as necessary.

Vocabulary

The vocabulary activities in *Passages* have been carefully designed not only to give students the lexical tools they need to complete a task or tasks, but to help them develop the vocabulary range typical of students at this level. Vocabulary exercises in each unit develop students' knowledge of lexical sets, synonyms and antonyms, as well as idioms and collocations.

Texts throughout the course, such as the Reading passages, were taken from authentic sources and therefore often present vocabulary beyond the students' productive range. Students should recognize that in most language-learning situations, they will encounter vocabulary they do not know. It is important to remind students that they do not need to understand every word. In addition, when students encounter an unknown word, they can often guess its meaning from the situation or context. Where it is necessary, try to pre-teach new vocabulary, but make sure to focus only on key vocabulary.

If you wish, have students keep a vocabulary notebook over the duration of the course to write down new words as they encounter them. For the most part, discourage the use of dictionaries during class; instead, get students in the habit of underlining or jotting down unfamiliar words as they encounter them so that they may look them up later and keep a record of them.

- Encourage students to guess the meaning of a new word by first looking at all the other words surrounding it and then considering the general meaning of the phrase or sentence in which it is located. Encourage students to ask themselves: How does this new word fit into the general idea of the context here?
- Where necessary, provide the meanings of words through definitions, mime, synonyms, antonyms, examples, or translation. It is not necessary to give long explanations as the majority of adult students will already understand the concept of the new word (or know the equivalent word) in their native language.

Discussion Activities

The Discussion activities in *Passages* are designed both to practice new structures and vocabulary as well as to give students opportunities to express their ideas and opinions about the themes and topics in a lesson. The focus of a fluency activity should be on doing the activity itself rather than on its completion. Encourage students to go beyond giving simple answers. Have them ask and answer follow-up questions to get more information from their partner(s). Ask them to give reasons and examples to support their answers and opinions. Remind students that fluency activities give them a chance to use all the language tools they have at their disposal and not just the language being practiced in a lesson.

Pair Work
- Divide the class into pairs. If there is an odd number of students, form one set of three.
- Explain the task and go over any sample language.
- If appropriate, model the activity with one or two students. Call on a pair of students to do the task as a further model if necessary.
- When appropriate, encourage students to ask and answer follow-up questions and to provide reasons to support their answers and opinions.
- Set an appropriate time limit. Then have students practice in pairs. Move around the class to provide help as necessary and to keep students on task.
- Bring the class back together before students quiet down completely. It is not a good idea to keep the entire group waiting while a few students finish.
- **Optional:** Have students change partners and do the task again, if appropriate.
- Call on pairs of students or volunteers to share answers or opinions with the class. Provide feedback and lead a class discussion when appropriate.

Group Work
- Divide the class into small groups of three or four, or larger groups of five or six, whichever seems more appropriate for the task.
- Explain the task and go over any sample language. If you wish, model the activity with one or more students.
- Set a time limit.
- Have groups carry out the task on their own as you circulate to provide help as needed and to keep groups on task. Again, encourage students to ask and answer follow-up questions and to give reasons to support their answers.
- When things begin to quiet down, bring the class back together. There are several ways in which to check students' answers or ideas:
  1. Have each group select a spokesperson, and have this person report the group's answers or ideas to the class.
  2. Have each group present only its most interesting or most original idea.
  3. Have two groups compare answers, and have one group report the other group's answers to the class.

Writing

Writing is a complex process involving a number of skills, so the aim of each writing exercise is to learn and gain practice in only one particular skill. While issues such as grammatical accuracy and spelling are important, they should not be the main point of the writing lesson. Encourage students to write for each other and to give each other feedback on their work. Above all, writing is a communicative act, and the writing exercises in *Passages* provide tasks that lend themselves well to discussion and the sharing of ideas.

If you wish, maintain a portfolio of each student's writing over the course of the semester. It is sometimes difficult for students to see the progress they are making, and a portfolio of collected writing can provide the means to identify improvement over time.

- Go over the information in the box at the top of the writing page. Provide additional information and examples as necessary to illustrate the focus of the writing lesson.
- Explain the first task, and have students complete it silently or in pairs.
- Have students compare answers with a partner, and then go over them with the class.
- Follow these steps for each additional task leading up to the writing activity itself.
- The writing task may be done in class or it may be assigned for homework. If it is done in class, set an appropriate time limit, and have students work silently to write their paragraphs or compositions.
- As students write, circulate to help with vocabulary and ideas. Do not focus too much attention on accuracy at this point. Instead, help students to put into practice the focus of the writing lesson.
- When most students seem finished, lead students through the post-writing task. Then, when appropriate, have students exchange paragraphs or compositions with a partner to carry out the task.
- Circulate to help and to answer questions. Encourage students to give suggestions to improve their partner's paragraph or composition.
- If you wish, have students revise their writing based on their partner's ideas and recommendations.
- **Optional:** Have a few selected students or volunteers read their paragraph or composition to the class. Alternatively, post some or all of the students' writing on a bulletin board.

Reading

Each reading text in *Passages* was chosen both for the way the topic relates to the theme of the lesson and for the reading strategies and skills that the text necessitates. The reading syllabus, then, does not move in linear fashion from beginning to end; rather, each reading page provides a self-contained lesson. A pre-reading task draws students into a text, activates background knowledge, and often draws students' attention to particular features of a text. Post-reading tasks have students look back at a text to find reasons to support their answers, draw inferences, or bring their knowledge of the text's topic into play. In addition, the reading texts are meant to serve as a springboard for discussion, and teachers are encouraged to use them as source material for further group or class discussion.

Reading passages may be assigned for homework if necessary.

- Books closed. Before students read the passage, introduce the topic of the reading by asking questions about the topic and soliciting answers and opinions.
- Books open. Have students look at any pictures in the text and any titles and subtitles. If you wish, have them predict what sort of information and vocabulary they are likely to find in the text.

- Go through the pre-reading questions with students, and have them discuss the questions in pairs or groups. If you wish, have selected students or volunteers share answers or opinions with the class.
- If you wish, pre-teach any key vocabulary you feel students are unlikely to know and would be unable to infer from context.
- Encourage students to read for meaning and to guess the meaning of unknown words from context. Explain that if an unknown word is not key to understanding the meaning of the passage, they can underline it and check the meaning in a dictionary after they read.
- Have students read the text silently. Remind students that they are reading to complete a task or to compare their ideas with those of the author. Discourage students from using monolingual dictionaries as they read. Circulate to provide help as necessary.
- If you wish, have students underline answers or differences between their ideas and the author's ideas as they read.
- When most students seem to have finished, have students compare answers to the pre-reading questions with a partner before going over them with the class.
- If you wish, have students ask questions about new vocabulary or comprehension problems that arose as they read.
- Lead students through the post-reading task or questions. Then have students work individually or in pairs to answer the questions.
- Have students compare answers with a partner before going over them with the class.

From the Authors

It has been our goal with *Passages* to provide stimulating subject matter that will make both teaching and learning an enjoyable and enriching process, while at the same time providing students with the tools they need for effective communication outside the classroom. We hope that you enjoy *Passages* and look forward to hearing your comments on the course.

Jack C. Richards
Chuck Sandy
Margareth Perucci

Authors' Acknowledgments

A great number of people contributed to the development of *Passages*. Particular thanks are owed to the following:

The insights and suggestions of the teachers who **reviewed** and **piloted** *Passages* in these institutes helped define the content and format of this edition: Karen Eichhorn, **ELS Denver**, **Regis University**, Denver, Colorado, USA; Amy Saviers, **Junshin Daigaku**, Nagasaki, Japan; Liliana Baltra, **Instituto Chileno-Norteamericano de Cultura**, Santiago, Chile; Maribel Lozano, **Universidad Anahuac**, Anahuac, Mexico; Gary D. Klowak, **CIMA**, Mexico City, Mexico; Mary Oliveira and Vera Burlamaqui Bradford, **Instituto Brasil-Estados Unidos (IBEU)**, Rio de Janeiro, Brazil; Marilda Amaral Ramalho de Castro, **Instituto Cultural Brasil-Estados Unidos (ICBEU)**, Belo Horizonte, Brazil; Gisleine Mantovani Brancher, **Instituto Cultural de Idiomas**, Caxias do Sul, Brazil; Gloria Delbim, Rosa Erlichman, Odila Jambor, **União Cultural Brasil-Estados Unidos (UCBEU)**, São Paulo, Brazil; Julia Burks, Richard Lynch, and Marjorie Manley, **AUA Language Center**, Bangkok, Thailand; Blanca Arazi, **Instituto Cultural Argentino Norteamericano (ICANA)**, Buenos Aires, Argentina; Jennifer Eick, **ITESM**, Monterrey, Mexico; Jay Melton, **Kumamoto Kenritsu Daigaku**, Kumamoto, Japan; Steven S. Cornwell, **Osaka Jogakuin Junior College**, Osaka, Japan; Julie Posinoff, **International Center for American English**, La Jolla, California, USA; Orlando Carranza R., Rubi Montejo Gamarra, Rosa Namuche, and Helen E. Kelly de Pando, **Instituto Cultural Peruano Norteamericano**, Lima, Peru; Jennifer Porter, **Language Studies International**, San Diego, California, USA; Kevan Klawitter, **Intensive English Language Center**, **California State University**, Bakersfield, California, USA; David Bernard Wirtz and Stephen P. Van Vlack, **Sookmyung Women's University**, Seoul, Korea; Daniel Francisco Acosta Garza and Candelaria Cantú Martínez, **Centro de Idiomas, Faculdad de Filosofía y Letras, U.A.N.L.**, Monterrey, Mexico; Demetri Liontos, **Lane Community College**, Eugene, Oregon, USA; Donevan Hooper, **Tokyo Foreign Language College**, Tokyo, Japan; Steve Jacques, **Intercultural Communications College**, Honolulu, Hawaii, USA; Linda D. Forse, **The Language Institute**, Brownsville, Texas, USA; **Senac-Serviço Nacional de Aprendizagem Comercial**, Curitiba, Brazil; and the many teachers around the world who responded to the *Passages* questionnaire.

The **editorial** and **production** team: Suzette André, Sylvia P. Bloch, John Borrelli, Kathleen Caratozzolo, Mary Carson, Karen Davy, Tünde Dewey, Deborah Goldblatt, Deborah Gordon, Emma Gordon, Pauline Ireland, James R. Morgan, Kathy Niemczyk, Kathleen Schultz, Howard Siegelman, Rosie Stamp, and Mary Vaughn.

And Cambridge University Press **staff** and **advisors**: Mary-Louise Baez, Carlos Barbisan, Kate Cory-Wright, Riitta da Costa, Peter Davison, Elena Dorado, Cecilia Gómez, Koen Van Landeghem, Alejandro Martínez, Nigel McQuitty, Carine Mitchell, Chuanpit Phalavadhana, Dan Schulte, Ian Sutherland, Chris White, and Janaka Williams.

Plan of Book 1

xiv

DISCUSSION	LISTENING	WRITING	READING
• Finding out what personality traits you have in common with your classmates • Studying personality profiles • Talking about how you have changed or how you would like to change • Comparing families • Talking about rules in your family	• Three young people describe how they have changed • Two people compare similarities and differences between their families	• Identifying the main idea in a paragraph • Writing a paragraph about your most positive or negative quality	• "Upside-Down Families": Families where the children have too much control
• Making suggestions to improve schools • Explaining how school prepares young people for life • Stating your goals for the future • Discussing different ways to learn something	• Two young people explain how they developed personally at college • Three people describe the strategies they used to learn something new	• Choosing topic sentences • Writing a paragraph about your educational beliefs	• "Home Schooling: A Growing Trend": Advantages and drawbacks of educating children at home
• Explaining why you'd like to visit a particular city • Choosing the right city for a particular purpose • Deciding which city is best to live in • Evaluating your hometown • Discussing quality-of-life issues	• A TV show introduces two exciting cities • Two foreign students explain what they like about their host city • Two New Yorkers talk about life in their city	• Creating topic sentences • Writing a paragraph about a place you know	• "Get Yourself Lost": The best way to enjoy sight-seeing in a new place
• Discussing personal energy levels • Classifying activities that raise or lower your energy level • Giving advice on a radio call-in program • Talking about sleeping habits • Interpreting dreams	• Three people describe methods they use to lower stress • Two people describe their dreams and try to figure out what they mean	• Choosing the best topic sentence • Writing a paragraph about times of day, daily schedules, or relaxation	• "Ten Keys to a Better Night's Sleep": Tips on fulfilling a basic human need
• Talking about what's average • Discussing what makes you typical or unique • Talking about future concerns • Explaining your personal concerns	• Three teenagers compare themselves to other people their own age • Three people describe their different approaches to solving problems	• Identifying supporting statements • Developing a paragraph with supporting statements	• "Statistically Speaking": The living arrangements, education level, and beliefs of the average American
• Discussing conversational styles and habits • Giving advice for awkward social situations • Determining appropriate topics for small talk • Deciding if it's appropriate to tell secrets • Reporting news about your classmates	• Several people make small talk at a party • Three people tell some interesting news	• Keeping a journal • Writing your reaction to a good piece of news	• "Don't Be a Bore!": How to be a good conversationalist

	FUNCTIONS	GRAMMAR	VOCABULARY

DISCUSSION	LISTENING	WRITING	READING
• Telling stories about uncomfortable situations • Talking about personal experiences • Creating a story with your classmates • Studying the different sections of a newspaper • Presenting a news story of local interest	• Two people describe personal dilemmas • An actress describes her most embarrassing moments • A radio broadcast highlights the top news stories of the day	• Putting events in order • Writing a narrative paragraph	• " 'Nutty' News": Humorous news articles about some strange events
• Talking about values you've learned • Describing personal memories and regrets • Giving advice to young people on getting the most out of life • Stating personal beliefs	• An interviewer asks people about personal values • Three people describe their role models	• Choosing a thesis statement for a multi-paragraph composition • Writing a composition about a significant time in your past	• "It's Not So Bad to Be Middle-Aged": Some of the rewards of middle age
• Describing jobs that require creativity • Taking a creativity quiz • Finding creative solutions to difficult problems • Choosing inventions that have had a great impact on twentieth-century life • Explaining why new products are invented	• Three employees explain how their jobs are creative • Three people devise imaginary inventions	• Choosing new paragraph beginnings • Writing a composition about someone who is creative or unique	• "Silly Questions, Brilliant Answers": The strange history of three successful products
• Complaining about everyday annoyances • Comparing styles of complaining • Finding solutions to problems in your community • Stating consumer complaints • Giving advice on avoiding consumer problems	• Two people describe irritating situations • Two friends compare the problems in their neighborhoods	• Writing a letter of complaint	• "Getting What You're Entitled To": How to exercise your rights as a consumer
• Giving advice on moving overseas • Comparing customs between North America and your country • Imagining the experience of living abroad • Telling how a trip you took could have been better • Explaining your travel preferences	• Three young people talk about the positive and negative aspects of living abroad • Three travelers describe personal mishaps	• Planning a composition • Brainstorming ideas and organizing an outline • Writing a composition about traveling or living abroad	• "Smooth Talking": Overcoming the language barrier when traveling abroad
• Describing controversial issues • Giving opinions about current issues • Giving reasons for behavior • Explaining how you would solve personal dilemmas	• Three people explain what issues they think are important • Two people describe being confronted by an ethical dilemma	• Presenting persuasive evidence to a specific audience • Writing a paragraph about a public concern	• "Little Lies": Common "lies" we tell in everyday life

In this unit, students use gerunds and noun clauses after *be* to talk about themselves and their families. They also practice describing personal changes and expressing likes and dislikes.

 Lesson A *What kind of person are you?*

 Tell me about yourself.

starting point These activities introduce the theme of personality traits and preview the grammar.

A

1 Books closed. Ask Ss what the words *talkative, serious,* and *friendly* describe when talking about personality traits. Ask Ss for other examples of words describing personality traits. Write the answers on the board. Ask Ss to raise their hands if any of these words describe them.

2 Books open. Explain that Ss are going to take a personality quiz. Ask where personality quizzes are commonly found (answer: magazines). Have Ss read the ten statements in the quiz silently while you circulate, answering vocabulary or comprehension questions. Write the vocabulary items that Ss asked about on the board, and check that Ss understand the following:

> **to avoid** to make an effort not to do (something)
> **(can't) stand** (very difficult) to tolerate
> **to accomplish** to finish something successfully
> **definitely true** true all of the time
> **generally true** true most of the time
> **definitely not true** never true

3 Suggest that Ss circle any new words they come across for self-study.

4 Have Ss work alone to complete the quiz, adding two more items of their own.

B Pair work

Books open. Explain that Ss will compare their quiz results with a partner. Have Ss form pairs to compare answers and discuss differences.

C Group work

1 Books open. Explain that Ss are now going to use the statements in the quiz and their own examples to explain the meaning of the adjectives in the exercise.

2 Check that Ss know the meanings of the adjectives, especially the following:

> **ambitious** having a strong desire to achieve success
> **reserved** shy and unwilling to talk about feelings
> **sympathetic** showing that you understand and care about others

3 Pronounce the words that might cause Ss difficulty. Suggest that Ss circle any new words. Then have each pair of Ss from Exercise 1B join another pair. Tell Ss to match each of the ten adjectives to a statement in the personality quiz.

4 Have Ss read the example sentence in the speech balloon, and explain that they should use this sentence pattern when giving their answers. Check answers by going through the list of adjectives one by one, with selected Ss providing answers.

Answers

> An adventurous person is the kind of person who is interested in visiting unusual places. (10)
> An ambitious person is the kind of person who loves to accomplish goals. (9)
> An impatient person is the kind of person who can't stand waiting for people. (3)
> An organized person is the kind of person who likes to make a daily schedule. (4)
> A practical person is the kind of person who loves finding solutions to problems. (5)
> A reserved person is the kind of person who avoids showing others what he/she is feeling. (2)
> A romantic person is the kind of person who enjoys walking on the beach at sunset. (1)
> A sociable person is the kind of person who likes to have lots of friends. (8)
> A sympathetic person is the kind of person who doesn't mind listening to people's problems. (7)
> A talkative person is the kind of person who enjoys spending hours on the phone. (6)

Optional activity 1: *My personality*

Time: 10 minutes. Ss further practice using descriptive adjectives and talking about their personalities.

1 Books open. Ask Ss to check (✓) the two adjectives from Exercise 1C that most closely describe their own personality. Then have Ss write new example sentences to illustrate the meaning of each adjective they chose.

2 *Pair work* Ss take turns explaining their adjectives to a partner, like this: "I'm reserved. I'm the kind of person who avoids situations where I have to talk a lot."

3 Ask several Ss to share one of their answers with the class.

Optional activity 2: *Class survey*

Time: 10 minutes. Ss use the personality quiz in Exercise 1A to identify the various personality types in their classroom.

1 *Group work* Books open. Take a class survey of the personality quiz. Have Ss raise their hands to show their responses as you call out "definitely true," "generally true," and "definitely not true." Tally the responses on the board. You can also categorize the responses by tallying them as male or female.

2 Put Ss into small groups to discuss the results on the board (e.g., Were they surprised to see that there were so many "romantics" in the class?).

What do you have in common?

discussion In this activity, Ss find out about each other's personality traits and practice using expressions for agreeing and disagreeing.

Pair work

1 Books open. Explain the task and point out the sample dialog and the phrases in the box. Model the phrases to illustrate correct stress and intonation, and have Ss repeat after you.

2 Have Ss work in pairs to find two personality traits they have in common and one they don't. Ask selected pairs to share their answers with the class.

Optional activity: *Chain reaction*

Time: 10 minutes. Ss practice using phrases of agreement and disagreement.

1 Conduct a chain drill around the class. One S starts by saying, for example, "I'm reserved. It takes me a long time to feel comfortable talking to someone about my thoughts or feelings," and then quickly says another S's name.

2 The S whose name is called either agrees, using a phrase from the box and giving an example (e.g., "So am I. I'm . . .), or disagrees using a rejoinder and giving an example (e.g., "I'm not at all like that. I'm . . .). He or she then says the name of another S.

3 Continue the chain around the class until someone makes a mistake. Then have Ss begin again with a new starter sentence. For large classes, divide the class into two or more groups to do the activity.

Gerunds

grammar focus The grammar box presents the use of gerunds after selected verbs and the gerund as the object of a preposition. The exercises give Ss practice in expressing likes and dislikes using gerunds and infinitives.

> **Grammar notes** Gerunds and infinitives often perform the role of nouns in sentences. What they name are activities, rather than things or people. They are usually introduced by verbs that describe mental processes or verbs of perception (e.g., *like, love,* and *enjoy*).
>
> The verbs *enjoy, dislike, don't mind,* and *avoid* are always followed by a gerund, whereas *like, love, hate,* and *can't stand* can be followed by either a gerund or an infinitive.
>
> Other common verbs that are followed by gerunds include *finish, give up, can't help, imagine, keep, miss,* and *suggest.*
>
> Other common verbs that can be followed by either a gerund or an infinitive include *start* and *try.*

A gerund always follows *interested in* as the object of the preposition. Some other common prepositions that are followed by a gerund are *look forward to, be used to, be accustomed to, keep on, be afraid of, be sorry about,* and *feel sure of.*

1 Books open. Discuss the information in the grammar box, and model the example sentences. Explain that the verbs in the left-hand column are always followed by a gerund (a verb ending with *-ing*), whereas the verbs in the right-hand column are followed by either a gerund or an infinitive (*to* + a base-form verb). Point out that many Ss make mistakes because they don't know which verbs are followed only by gerunds and which can be followed by a gerund or infinitive.

2 **Optional:** Books closed. Solidify the grammar point by conducting a quick drill. Call out the verbs in the grammar box one by one, and ask Ss to say whether it's followed only by a gerund or either by an infinitive or a gerund. Then have Ss make short sentences with each verb.

A Pair work

1 Books open. Ss work alone to write a sentence explaining how they feel about each of the eight things, as you circulate to offer help and check for accuracy. Then put Ss in pairs to compare and discuss their answers. Encourage them to ask and answer follow-up questions, such as "How often do you talk on the phone with friends?" or "What kind of junk food do you like to eat?"

2 Ask several Ss to share one or more of their sentences with the class.

B Pair work

1 Books open. Read the instructions and go over the model sentences with the class, pointing out that the second sentence in each model gives additional information. Tell Ss to give explanations for their sentences about themselves.

2 Ss work alone to write statements about themselves using each of the verbs in the grammar box. Then ask Ss to form new pairs to compare and discuss their answers. They should ask at least three questions about the statements their partner wrote.

Optional activity: *Who am I really?*

Time: 10 minutes. Ss are given additional practice using gerunds and infinitives to talk about themselves.

1 *Pair work* Books open. Ss work individually to write two true and two false statements about themselves using the verbs in the grammar box. Then they take turns reading their sentences while their partner asks questions to determine which sentences are true and which are false.

2 Ask selected Ss to read one of their sentences aloud. The class guesses with a show of hands whether it is true or false. Ask a couple of Ss to give reasons for their answer.

discussion   These activities consolidate the use of adjectives, gerunds, and infinitives to describe personalities.

A

1 Books closed. Ask the class if they have ever read personal ads in newspapers or magazines, and what kind of information these ads usually contain (answer: personality profiles). Explain that personal ads are used by people who want to meet someone, usually for romantic purposes. Ask Ss if people in their country use personal ads as a way of meeting.

2 Books open. Explain the task. Have Ss read the four personality profiles. Check that Ss understand the following words:

> **avid** extremely eager or interested
>
> **dedicated** giving a lot of time and effort to an activity
>
> **fan** a person who has a great interest in someone or something
>
> **incurable** something that cannot be healed or changed

3 Suggest that Ss circle any new words. Tell Ss to read the profiles again and answer the questions. Then put Ss in pairs or groups to compare and discuss their answers.

Optional activity: *The personals*

Time: 5 minutes. Ss add to the text using the vocabulary for personality traits, and gerunds and infinitives.

1 *Pair work* Books open. Put Ss in pairs, and tell them to add at least one more appropriate personal quality to each personality profile.

2 Have pairs join another pair to compare their additions. Tell them to explain to each other why they think their addition is appropriate.

B Class activity

1 Books open. Explain the task and have Ss individually write their own personality profile (without their names on it and without letting anyone else see it). Collect the papers and put them in a bag. Each S pulls one paper from the bag and thinks about who the profile describes.

2 Tell Ss to ask questions similar to the one in the speech balloon. Ss should sit down once they have been matched to their own profile and once they have found the person who wrote the profile they picked.

3 Once all Ss are seated again, ask them if any of the profiles surprised them, and if so, why.

listening

In these activities, Ss first discuss personality changes over time and then listen to three people talk about how they've changed and would like to change.

A Group work

1 Books closed. Introduce the topic by giving an example of how you've changed in the last five years and why. Then ask one or two Ss to give an example to share with the class.

2 Books open. Ask Ss to discuss the two questions in groups of four or five. Circulate, giving help as needed.

3 Have Ss report back to the class about some of the personal changes their groups discussed.

B

1 Books open. Have Ss read the instructions and look at the chart.

2 **Optional:** Pre-teach any of the following vocabulary items that you think will be helpful for your Ss:

> **homebody** a person who enjoys spending a lot of time at home
> **to settle down** to stop moving around and live permanently in one place
> **corporate headquarters** the main offices of a company
> **benefits** extra allowances provided by an employer, such as paid vacation days, bonuses, and health insurance
> **to commute** to travel to and from work [also used as a noun]
> **self-employed** working for yourself
> **in terrible shape** in poor physical condition

Alternatively, wait until after the first listening to see if Ss need help with any of these vocabulary items.

3 Suggest that Ss listen to the audio program once without attempting to complete the chart. Play the audio program.

4 Before playing the audio program again, explain that Ss are to write in note form. Point out that there is not enough time to write more than just a few key words. If necessary, model this by playing the first segment of the audio program while you make notes on the board. (Ss can construct sentences from their notes later on.)

5 Replay the audio program. Have Ss complete the chart as they listen. Then ask Ss to compare answers with a partner. Go over the answers with the class, replaying the audio program if necessary.

Answers

	Luis	Celine	Diana
Used to be	single, enjoyed going out, was a lot more sociable	in a large company, was very ambitious	more reserved, hardly exercised, rarely spent time outside, was in terrible shape
Change	got married, became more of a homebody	became self-employed	more talkative, started exercising frequently
Reason	was tired of going out all the time, ready to settle down	got tired of the job, didn't like commuting	worried about health

Transcript

Listen to how Luis, Celine, and Diana have changed in the last five years. Why did they decide to change? Complete the chart.

Luis: Well, I guess the biggest change in my life over the last five years is that I got married. I used to be single, and now I'm not! I used to enjoy going out with friends every weekend – you know, I was a lot more sociable. Now, I'm more of a homebody – I like to stay at home, watch TV – that kind of thing. It's not so bad. I guess you could say that I grew up – I was tired of going out all the time and ready to settle down and start a family.

Celine: For me the change has been with my work. I used to work in a large company. I worked in their corporate headquarters downtown in the accounting department. It was a great job – good money, decent benefits. When I first started at that company, I was very young and very ambitious. But after a while, I got tired of it. I was so unhappy there, and the commute was killing me! But one evening two years ago, I attended a seminar on working for yourself – you know, being self-employed and starting your own company. So I quit my job and gave it a try. It was scary at first, but after a little while I could see it was going to work out just fine for me. I couldn't be happier.

Diana: Gosh, five years ago I was a completely different person. You wouldn't have recognized me if you'd seen me then! I talk a lot now, but I was more reserved then. And I hardly exercised at all. I never played any sports and rarely spent time outside. I was in terrible shape and worried about my health. But all that changed when I met my friend Judy. See, she convinced me to start slowly, you know, by walking every morning before work and swimming twice a week. Well, now I spend most of my free time outside – hiking, swimming when the weather's good, playing tennis or racquetball – those kinds of things. I'm in pretty good shape now and feeling wonderful.

c

1 Books open. Explain the task. Play the remainder of the audio program once completely through while Ss write their answers on the chart. Again, emphasize that Ss are to write key words only.

2 Replay the audio program to give Ss the opportunity to check their answers before having Ss compare with a partner. Go over the answers with the class, replaying the audio program if necessary.

Answers

	Luis	Celine	Diana
Wants to change	be more practical about wasting money and not buy things he doesn't need	be better organized at work and hire an assistant	be a better mountain climber, become mentally and physically stronger, and go climbing in the Himalayas

Transcript

Listen again. What does each person still want to change?

Luis: Well, my wife is always saying that I'm not very good with money, not practical at all. She's always teasing me about my spending habits, but she's right. When I see something I want, I just go and buy it, even if it is something I don't really need. I guess I waste a lot of our money. We're expecting our first child in December, and now that there's going to be three of us, well, I think I do need to be more careful.

Celine: Working at home has been a real struggle. It's been a lot harder than I imagined. I needed to be more organized, that's for sure. So, I've decided to hire a part-time secretary – you know, someone who can come in a couple of times a week and help out with the phones, the filing, and just clean up in general. I'm so busy that sometimes I kind of let things get out of hand – the office gets really messy! I sure could use some help.

Diana: Well, I started mountain climbing a year and a half ago, and I just love it. Well, the next step for me is to concentrate on that sport and see where I can go with it. I'd love to someday – say, five or ten years from now – go mountain climbing in the Himalayas. They have some of the highest and most beautiful mountains in the world. That would be a real adventure! But before I do anything like that, I have to practice, practice, practice! And I have to get stronger – mentally as well as physically.

Optional activity: *Who has changed the most?*

Time: 10 minutes. Ss evaluate the changes of the three speakers' lifestyles.

Pair work Books open. Tell Ss to rate Luis, Celine, and Diana by the amount of change in their lives, giving a 1 to the person whose lifestyle they think has changed the most. Then put Ss in pairs to compare and discuss their ratings. Ask them to discuss which of the three people they think they are the most similar to.

How have you changed?

discussion In this activity, Ss discuss how they've changed in the last five years and what they want to change about themselves now.

A

Books open. Explain the task and lead Ss through the sample language in the box. Point out that in the United States and Canada, change is usually considered something positive and a part of self-improvement. Have Ss individually complete the chart. Circulate to provide help as needed.

B Pair work

1 Books open. Explain that Ss will now take turns asking and answering questions about each other's charts. Point out B's follow-up question in the sample dialog and how it encourages A to give more information.

2 Put Ss in pairs to do the activity. Make sure that Ss don't simply show each other their charts but rather discuss them. Circulate to help Ss with appropriate and useful follow-up questions.

3 **Optional:** Have Ss who finish early discuss whether they found filling in the chart easy or difficult, and why.

Optional activity: *Class reunion*

Time: 10 minutes. Ss role-play attending a class reunion in the future to describe how they've changed.

1 *Class activity* Books closed. Tell the class to imagine that it is ten years from now: How might they have changed? Tell Ss to think about their own personal goals for the future.

2 Have the class stand up and move about the room, greeting at least five classmates as old friends and talking about how they've changed in the last ten years.

3 When the class sits down again, ask Ss if any of their classmates' changes were particularly surprising, and if so, ask them to identify the classmate and describe the change.

Main ideas in paragraphs

writing In this activity, Ss learn that an English paragraph has one main idea and that all information in the paragraph must relate to that main idea.

A

1 Books closed. Ask Ss what they know about writing paragraphs in English. Try to elicit the information that appears in the box at the top of the page.

2 Books open. Explain the task and check that Ss understand the meaning of the following:

> **frustrating** annoying
> **to misplace** to lose something because you can't remember where you put it
> **clutter** mess; untidiness

3 Have Ss silently read the two paragraphs, find the main ideas, and underline them. Then ask Ss to compare answers with a partner.

Answers

> **First paragraph**: My most positive quality is that I'm very practical.
> **Second paragraph**: My most negative quality is that I'm an extremely disorganized person.

B

1 Books open. Explain the task and have Ss silently read the two paragraphs again to find and cross out any information that is not related to the main idea.

2 **Optional:** As this task may be more difficult than the task in Exercise 7A, you may want to work with Ss on the first paragraph, and then let Ss do the second paragraph on their own.

3 Have Ss compare with a partner before going over the answers with the class.

Answers

> **First paragraph:** His computer is a powerful one.
> **Second paragraph:** My sister is very neat.

C

1 Books closed. Have Ss individually make a list with phrases describing their most positive and most negative qualities.

2 **Optional:** Ss add a personal example to illustrate each quality in their list.

3 Ask a few Ss to share their answers with the class. Explain that these could each be the main idea of a paragraph.

D

1 Books open. Explain the writing task, reminding Ss that they should write only one paragraph about either their most positive or their most negative quality.

2 **Optional:** Ss choose the quality they want to write about. Then they make a list of some examples to illustrate that quality before they begin writing.

3 Books open or closed. Have Ss work individually to write their paragraphs. Remind them to make sure that each sentence is related to the main idea.

E Pair work

This is a peer-editing activity that gives Ss the opportunity to read each other's paragraphs and make suggestions for improving them. If peer-editing is new to the Ss, remind them that their comments should be interpreted as helpful rather than critical, and that someone else's comments and questions will help to show them where their writing is not clear.

1   Books open. Explain the task and read the two questions. Give some examples to illustrate the second question, pointing out that the answers to this question should give the writer more ideas about his or her topic.

2   Books open or closed. Have pairs exchange paragraphs and try to improve each other's paragraphs by answering the two questions. They should discuss one paragraph at a time.

3   Circulate to help and make sure Ss are editing properly. Encourage them to ask and answer follow-up questions. It can be helpful to show Ss how they could include the answers to the follow-up questions in their paragraphs.

 Every family's different.

 Let me tell you about my family.

starting point   These activities introduce the theme of families and preview the grammar.

A Group work

1   Books closed. To introduce the topic, you may wish to bring in several photos of your own family or of families from magazines. Ask Ss to identify family members in each photo and to say what they think might be special or unusual about each family.

2   Books open. Explain the task and have Ss read the phrases under each picture and the sentence in the speech balloon. Check that Ss understand the meaning of the following:

> **nuclear family** a family consisting of two parents and their children, but not including aunts, uncles, grandparents, etc.
>
> **bicultural family** a family where the parents are from two different cultures

3   Put Ss in groups of four or five to discuss the questions.

4   **Optional:** Ss compare their families with those pictured and decide which one is most similar to theirs.

5   **Optional:** Write answers on the board to make a class chart of advantages and disadvantages of each family type.

B Pair work

1 Books open. Explain the task. Have Ss read the questions individually and put a check in the boxes by the questions they want to discuss. In pairs, Ss take turns asking and answering their questions. Circulate and encourage Ss to ask and answer follow-up questions.

2 When things begin to quiet down, ask several Ss to share one or more answers with the class. Lead a class discussion.

How are their families different?

listening In these activities, Ss first listen to two people talking about their families and how they are different. Then they work in pairs to discuss which family is most similar to their own.

A

1 Books open. Explain the task and go over the chart, making sure Ss understand what information is needed. Emphasize that Ss are to write in note form.

2 Check that Ss know the meaning of the following:

> **close-knit family** a family whose members have good relationships with each other
> **spread out** far apart
> **leftovers** food that has not been eaten

3 Play the audio program completely, and have Ss individually work to fill in the chart. Then ask them to compare answers with a partner. If necessary, replay the audio program for Ss to complete the chart and check their answers. Go over the answers with the class. (*Note:* Ss are asked to come up with two differences between Paul's and Andrea's families. Encourage them to write down more than two, if possible.)

Possible answers

Paul	Andrea
family lives nearby	family doesn't live nearby (inferred)
not close-knit	close-knit
smaller family (three brothers)	larger family (six kids)
rarely get together as a family	tries to get home as much as possible
mother cooks meals at home	family eats meals in restaurants

Transcript

Paul: So, Andrea, you going home for the holidays?

Andrea: I sure am. I've booked a flight for tomorrow afternoon and I can't wait!

Paul: That sounds great.

Andrea: What about you? Going home, too?

Paul: I haven't decided yet. I'm still debating. . . .

Andrea: Haven't decided? Oh, you're never going to get a flight out of here. I'm sure all the seats have been reserved by now. It's the holiday season, after all!

Paul: Well, it's not such a big deal for me. My family only lives about a hundred and fifty miles from here. I usually drive or take the train. It's a short trip.

Andrea: You don't sound very excited about it.

Paul: Well, we're not really a very close-knit family. I have three brothers, and they're spread out all over the place. One lives on the East Coast and the other on the West Coast. I even have a brother in Montreal!

Andrea: Oh, wow! What does he do?

Paul: Translation work. It's kind of strange, but we rarely get together as a family anymore.

Andrea: Well, I try to get home as much as possible. We're a big family – there are six of us children – so it's always a lot of fun.

Paul: Six kids?

Andrea: Yep. And we're all really close. You should see it – most of us are married, too, so it makes for a very crowded house over the holidays.

Paul: I can imagine.

Andrea: Of course, there are too many people to cook dinner for. It's a real headache for my parents. So we end up going out to dinner a lot. It's pretty crazy.

Paul: Well, at my house my mother loves to cook. So, when all of us do get home – which isn't that often – she always cooks big, homemade meals. We have leftovers for days!

B Pair work

1 Books open. Explain the task. Then put Ss in pairs to discuss the questions. Remind Ss to explain the reasons for their answers.

2 Ask selected Ss to share their answers with the class.

Optional activity: *Unusual and typical families*

Time: 5–10 minutes. Ss talk about atypical families in their own cultures and compare them to families in the United States or other cultures they are familiar with.

1 *Group work* Books closed. Ask Ss to think about what would constitute an unusual family in their culture (e.g., large/small family, divorced parents, nuclear/extended family, adult children living far away from/with their parents, working mothers). Have Ss write down a few ideas on a sheet of paper.

2 Put Ss in groups of four or five to compare notes about unusual families.

Noun clauses after be

grammar focus The activities in the grammar focus present and practice the use of noun clauses after *be*.

> **Grammar notes** A noun clause is a group of words that functions together as a noun. Every noun clause has at least a subject and a predicate.
>
>   Noun clauses are dependent clauses (they cannot function independently as sentences) that fill noun phrase slots in a sentence, such as direct object or subject. The introductory word *that* does not have any meaning in the sentence, and its role is to signal the beginning of a noun clause.

Books open. Look at the grammar box, and point out that *that* in noun clauses after *be* is optional. Emphasize the use of the prepositions *of* after *advantage* and *disadvantage, about* after *best thing* and *worst thing,* and *with* after *problem.*

A

1   Books open. Explain that Ss should first work alone to complete each sentence with their own information. Circulate to check for accuracy, and provide help as needed. Check that Ss know the meaning of:

> **supportive** being helpful and sympathetic to someone

2   Put Ss in pairs to compare answers, and encourage them to ask and answer follow-up questions to explain their ideas.

3   Ask a few Ss to read one or more of their sentences aloud, and write down the most interesting ones on the board.

Possible answers

> 1. An advantage of having an extended family is (that) you always have someone to take care of young children.
> 2. The worst thing about being a parent is (that) you worry a lot about your children.
> 3. The best thing about having a nuclear family is (that) it's less crowded in your house.
> 4. A disadvantage of being an only child is (that) you don't have other children to play with.
> 5. The worst thing about living near your parents is (that) they can drop by without calling first.
> 6. A problem with being the oldest child is (that) you have to look after your younger brothers and sisters.
> 7. The best thing about having a supportive family is (that) you have people you can talk to.

B

1   Books open. Ss first complete the sentences on their own. Then they compare their answers with a partner. Have Ss choose the sentence of their partners that they think is the most interesting.

2   Go over the answers with the class by having selected Ss read their partner's most interesting sentence aloud. Write these sentences on the board.

Answers

1. An advantage of being the most talkative person in your family is (that) you get a lot of attention.
2. A disadvantage to being the youngest in your family is (that) you are treated like a baby.
3. An advantage to being a twin is (that) you always have someone around who understands you.
4. An advantage to having young parents is (that) they have lots of energy.
5. A disadvantage to working in the family business is (that) you never get away from the family.
6. A problem with living alone is (that) you have to pay all the rent.
7. A disadvantage to having a large family is (that) you have to share things with your brothers and sisters.

C

1   Books closed. Ask Ss at what age most children stop living with their parents. Explain that in the United States and Canada, it is not uncommon for teens to go to a college far away from their parents' home. Many others who do not go on to college move out of their parents' homes to live in apartments with friends.

2   Books open. Have Ss read the instructions and the survey answers, and then list their two advantages and disadvantages.

3   **Optional:** Put Ss in groups to discuss their advantages and disadvantages, and ask a spokesperson from each group to share some of their ideas with the class.

   Your place in the family

discussion   In these activities, Ss have another opportunity to talk about their families and practice the grammar and vocabulary of the lesson.

A

1   Books open. Explain the task and have Ss read the eight statements. Check that Ss know the following:

> **frankly** openly and honestly
> **strict parents** parents who set many rules and insist on the rules being followed
> **to follow in someone's footsteps** to do the same thing as someone else who came before you

2 Have Ss work alone to check (✓) the statements that are true for them.

3 **Optional:** Ask selected Ss to read one of the statements they checked and to provide an example to illustrate it (e.g., "My parents were very strict when I was a child. They wouldn't let me go out on weekdays."). Have other Ss ask follow-up questions and provide examples of their own.

4 Take a tally of the number of answers for each statement, and put the totals on the board to form the basis of a class discussion.

B Group work

Books open. Explain the task. Then put Ss in groups of four or five to talk about the advantages and disadvantages of the statements they checked.

Optional activity: *Family survey*

Time: 15 minutes. Ss think of their own survey questions and use noun clauses to discuss the results.

1 *Group work* Books open or closed. Put Ss in groups of four or five, and ask them to write a yes-no question about an aspect of family life. Ss stand up and circulate around the class, asking their classmates their question.

2 Ss return to their groups and discuss the results of their survey. Have Ss list the advantages and disadvantages of the topic of their question.

Describing parents and children

vocabulary These vocabulary activities present some more adjectives to describe personalities and provide practice in using them to describe family members.

A

1 Books open. Have Ss read the instructions and the list of adjectives, helping out with stress and pronunciation when needed. Check that Ss understand the following:

> **mischievous** naughty
> **sensible** reasonable, practical

2 Check that Ss understand the meaning of *neutral* in this instance, giving an example, such as "Jim is very talkative." Point out that if you were trying to study with Jim, *talkative* would be a negative trait, whereas at a party, *talkative* would be a positive trait. Have Ss work alone to decide whether the words are positive, negative, or neutral.

3 Have Ss compare answers with a partner, and encourage them to give reasons to support their decisions. Remind Ss that several of the words will be viewed differently by different people. Go over the answers with the class, having Ss give reasons for their answers.

Possible answers (*Note:* These answers are culturally dependent.)

> **Positive** active, adventurous, generous, innocent, patient, responsible, sensible, supportive
> **Negative or neutral** frank, inexperienced, mischievous, strict

B

1 Books open. Explain the task and have Ss work alone to fill in the charts. Then put Ss into pairs to compare answers. Encourage Ss to give reasons or examples.

2 Bring the class back together, and have several pairs share their answers with the class.

Possible answers

Parents	Children
generous, patient, responsible, sensible, strict, supportive	active, adventurous, frank, inexperienced, innocent, mischievous

Optional activity: *Teachers and students, siblings, and parents*

Time: 5 minutes. Ss use adjectives that describe personality to talk about other categories of people.

Books open. Repeat the same procedure as in Exercise 5A, but this time have Ss decide which adjectives describe teachers and students, brothers and sisters, or mothers and fathers.

C

1 Books open. Explain the task and have Ss work individually to make their lists, while you circulate to help.

2 **Optional:** Allow students to use an English-English dictionary for this activity.

Possible answers

Adjectives	Opposites
active	inactive, lazy
adventurous	careful, cautious
frank	reserved
generous	stingy, cheap
inexperienced	experienced
innocent	worldly, experienced
mischievous	well behaved
patient	impatient
responsible	irresponsible
sensible	impractical
strict	relaxed, easygoing, lenient
supportive	unsupportive

D Pair work

1 Books open. Explain the task. Ask Ss to silently select an adjective to describe each of their family members and think of reasons for their adjective selections.

2 **Optional:** Have Ss write their adjectives with the name of the appropriate relative on a slip of paper.

3 Lead Ss through the model dialog. Put Ss in pairs to talk about their own family members. Encourage them to ask and answer follow-up questions.

Optional activity: *Guessing game*

Time: 5 minutes. Ss are given more practice with adjectives that describe personalities.

Books open. Ask selected Ss to silently choose one of the adjectives and either explain its meaning to the class, give an example, or provide a word with the opposite meaning. However, Ss must not use the word itself. Others guess the adjective.

---

 6 **Family rules**

discussion In this activity, Ss talk about rules they followed in their families when they were growing up.

Group work

1 Books closed. Ask Ss what kinds of tasks they perform at home. Then ask if they have family rules they have to follow, and whether or not they like these rules. Have a couple of Ss call out a family rule, and then ask a follow-up question about that rule.

2 Books open. Explain the task and clarify that Ss are to write lists of rules related to the topics given. Go over the language in the speech balloons. Check that Ss understand the following:

> **household chores** jobs around the house, such as cleaning the
>   dishes and vacuuming the carpet
> **disputes** arguments
> **to settle disputes** to resolve arguments

3 Put Ss in groups of four or five to discuss the topics and add more topics. Each group makes a list of rules that are shared by their families.

Optional activity: *The strictest family rules*

Time: 10 minutes. Ss write their own family rules.

1 *Group work* Books closed. Have Ss, working in small groups, write a list of five very strict family rules that they'd never want to follow or be able to follow (e.g., *You're not allowed to watch TV on the weekend.*).

2 Have groups take turns reading their list of strict rules to the class. Then the class votes on the strictest set of rules.

reading This text introduces the topic of family discipline. Ss make predictions and then read the article to check their answers.

A Pair work

1 Books open. Tell Ss that reading is easier when they give some thought to the topic of the passage before starting to read it. (A good way to do this is to look at the title and predict what might be contained in the text.)

2 Put Ss in pairs to discuss the pre-reading questions.

3 Have Ss silently read the text to compare their ideas with the author's. Suggest that as Ss read they underline up to five unfamiliar words they feel they need to know to understand the text.

4 Bring the class back together, and go over any vocabulary items Ss need clarified.

5 Put the Ss back in pairs to discuss the pre-reading questions again.

6 **Optional:** Have Ss check their own comprehension by closing their books and working in pairs to write a definition of an upside-down family. Then ask several pairs to share their definition with the class.

B Pair work

In this post-reading activity, Ss work in groups to draw inferences from the reading.

1 Books closed. Explain that to do this task, Ss will be making *inferences,* using what they know about the author's ideas to make good guesses.

2 Books open. Have Ss read the statements. Do the first one together. Elicit or provide the explanation that the author probably wouldn't agree that children usually don't challenge authority because as stated in this article: "Challenging authority is a normal part of child development."

3 Put Ss in pairs to decide which statements the author is likely to agree with. Encourage Ss to say why or why not.

Answer

The author would agree with statements 3 and 4.

Optional activity: *Making inferences*

Time: 5 minutes. Ss are given additional practice in making inferences.

Pair work Books open. Write the following statements on the board, and then have pairs decide whether the author would agree or disagree with them, and why.

1. Children want to feel equal to parents.

2. Many parents think they are helping their children by trying to be a friend.

3. Children want parents to make rules.

Answers

The author would agree with statements 2 and 3.

C Group work

In this activity, Ss personalize the ideas in the reading.

1   Books open. Go over the two questions with the class, and then put Ss in groups to discuss them. Encourage Ss to discuss the reasons for their opinions and to relate their opinions to ideas in the article.

2   Ask a group spokesperson to share the highlights of their discussion with the class.

This unit introduces the topics of education and learning. It focuses on the language of making suggestions, using the modals *should* and *ought to* in both the active and passive. It also highlights the use of infinitives and gerunds to talk about how to do things.

How can schools be improved?

Schools in the United States

starting point   In these activities, Ss read about schools in the United States and compare them with schools in their own countries.

A

1   Books closed. Introduce the topic by writing the phrase *Schooling in the United States* on the board, and elicit from Ss anything they know about the topic. Write their ideas on the board. Also ask "What would you like to know about schooling in the United States?" Have Ss call out questions, and write these on the board.

2   Books open. Ss silently read the facts about schools in the United States to see if their ideas are included or their questions are answered. Go over any new vocabulary, including the following:

> **compulsory** required
> **typical** normal
> **annual tuition** money paid for one year of classroom instruction

> **Culture note**   All states have their own public universities and colleges in addition to private universities and colleges. Although public universities and colleges are funded by local taxes, there is still a need for students to pay tuition fees. Many students get student loans from banks and the government to help them pay the tuition. Tuition at private universities and colleges is more expensive because those schools depend almost entirely on tuition fees and donations.

3   Have Ss check (✓) the two facts they find most surprising and compare with a partner. Then ask them to share their answers with the class.

Optional activity: *Schooling similarities*

Time: 10 minutes. Ss discuss similarities between schooling in the United States and schooling in their own countries.

Class activity Books open. Have Ss individually look through the Facts About U.S. Schools. Bring the class back together to discuss these similarities, and write down the information that is the same for their country.

B Pair work

1 Books open. Explain the task and go over the sample answer. Then have each S work to write four statements about schooling in his/her own country that would be of interest to someone from another country.

2 Circulate to provide help as needed. When most Ss have finished, put them in pairs to compare statements. After five minutes or so, have each pair share their most interesting statements with the class.

3 **Optional:** Write Ss' statements on the board, and then have the class help you correct grammatical or lexical errors.

Optional activity: *Fact sheets*

Time: 10 minutes. Ss further personalize the information about schooling.

Group work Books closed. Have groups of four or five Ss prepare a fact sheet about schools in their country. Ask each group to present their facts to the class while you list them on the board. Use them to generate a class discussion.

How can we make education better?

discussion   In these activities, Ss discuss and evaluate recommendations for improving education in their own country.

A Pair work

1 Books closed. Ask the class "How do you think education can be improved in your country?" (e.g., "I think the school day should be longer/shorter."). Ask students for suggestions, and write them on the board.

2 Books open. Explain the task and lead Ss through the suggestions in the box. Go over any new vocabulary. Check that Ss understand the following:

> **multimedia center** a library with computers and audiovisual equipment in addition to print material

3 Have pairs discuss each suggestion and then choose the two they would recommend. Encourage them to think of several reasons to support their recommendations.

B Group work

1 Books open. Combine the pairs into groups of four or five, and have them share their recommendations and give reasons to support them.

2 Have each group's spokesperson present the most important recommendation to the class with their reasons. Write them on the board to use as the basis for a class discussion.

Should *and* ought to *in the active and passive*

grammar focus Ss use *should* and *ought to* in the active and passive to give suggestions.

> **Grammar notes** In the active form, the modals *should* and *ought to* are followed by the simple form of the verb (e.g., People *should go* to the dentist regularly.).
>
> In the passive form, the modals are followed by *be* + the past participle (e.g., Teachers *should be paid* better.). The passive is used primarily when the action is more important than the "doer" or agent of the action, or when the agent is unknown. In other situations, it is usually better to write the sentence in the active form.
>
> *Should* can be used in both the affirmative and negative; however, in American English *ought to* is usually used in the affirmative only.

A

1 Lead Ss through the information in the grammar box, and model the example sentences. Provide additional examples, if needed.

2 Explain the task and then have Ss individually complete each sentence using the active or passive form of *should* or *ought to* and the correct form of the verb in parentheses. (*Note:* Answers can be affirmative or negative.)

3 Go over the answers with the class.

Answers

> 1. Computers *should(n't) be/ought (not) to be purchased* for all students.
> 2. Schools *should(n't)/ought (not) to install* computers, videos, and CD-ROMs in their language labs.
> 3. Class credit *should(n't) be/ought (not) to be given* for foreign travel.
> 4. Science *should(n't) be/ought (not) to be taught* by famous researchers via television.
> 5. Physical education classes *should(n't) be/ought (not) to be made* optional.
> 6. Students *should(n't)/ought (not) to take* classes in all subject areas.
> 7. Students' grades *should(n't) be/ought (not) to be based* on class participation.
> 8. Schools *should(n't)/ought (not) to limit* class size to ten students.

B Pair work

1 Books open. Explain the task and go over the sample language. Have Ss check (✓) the ideas they agree with.

2 Put Ss in pairs to discuss and explain why they agree with the ideas they checked. Also ask Ss to discuss why they are not in favor of the ideas they disagree with.

3 After five to ten minutes, have selected pairs share their reasons for agreeing or disagreeing with one or more of the statements. Lead a class discussion.

Optional activity: *English class makeover*

Time: 10 minutes. Ss are given more practice using modals to make suggestions.

1 *Group work* Books open or closed. Have groups of four or five prepare five statements about the way things should be or ought to be in your class.

2 Circulate and provide help as needed. Have group representatives present their recommendations to the class. The class should then vote on the recommendations they like the best.

Maintaining educational standards

discussion These activities give additional practice using *should* and *ought to* to make suggestions and giving reasons to support them.

A Pair work

1 Books open. Explain the task and have Ss silently read the four opinions. Ss check (✓) the ones they agree with. Then put Ss in pairs to compare answers and share their reasons.

2 **Optional:** Ask pairs to think of an advantage and disadvantage for each of the four opinions. Then have pairs share their ideas with the class.

B Group work

1 Books open. Go over the model dialog. Combine the pairs to form groups of four, and have them discuss their answers. Encourage a lively exchange of opinions by telling Ss to try to persuade their group members of their own opinions.

2 Ask several Ss to share an answer with the class. Lead a class discussion.

Optional activity: *Educational consultants*

Time: 10 minutes. Ss have an opportunity to further explore the topic and get more practice using *should* and *ought to* to make suggestions.

1 *Pair work* Books open or closed. Pair Ss of similar backgrounds, where possible. Tell them to make a short list of ideas for improving education in their home countries. Students can use their suggestions from earlier in the lesson, if they wish.

2 Remind Ss to use *should* and *ought to* whenever possible.

3 Have representatives from each group share their suggestions with the class.

discussion These activities expand the topic of education and learning to include personal development and social skills.

A

1 Books closed. Ask Ss what else they learn at school besides academic subjects (e.g., learning how to follow rules). Call for suggestions and write them on the board.

2 Books open. Explain the task and have Ss read the nonacademic skills listed in the box. Check that Ss know the following vocabulary:

> **confidence** a strong belief in your own abilities
> **independent** not controlled by other people

3 Have Ss individually work to add two more nonacademic skills to the list. Then have selected Ss share a skill with the class.

B Pair work

1 Books open. Have Ss read the four discussion questions. Answer vocabulary questions as needed.

2 Give Ss a few minutes to think about their own answers to the questions before putting them in pairs to discuss them. Encourage Ss to give reasons to support their answers.

3 Have selected Ss share their answers with the class. Lead a class discussion.

Optional activity: *Missed opportunities*

Time: 10 minutes. Ss rank the skills they didn't learn in school from least important to most important.

Group or pair work Books open. Write on the board a list of important skills Ss felt they did not learn at school (responses to question 4). Put Ss in groups or pairs to rank the importance of each skill listed. Tell them to support their ranking with reasons.

C Group work

1 Books open. Explain the task and lead Ss through the sample language in the two balloons. Check Ss' comprehension of the following:

> **extracurricular activities** activities, such as sports and drama clubs, that happen outside of the required courses
> **course offerings** classes that students can register for at school or college

2 Ask Ss how many of them are involved in extracurricular activities at school. Also ask Ss to list different types of classroom equipment and teaching methods. Then put Ss in groups to discuss their recommendations.

3 Have each group share one or more of their recommendations with the class.

6 What they learned in school

listening

This activity practices listening for specific information.

A

1 Books closed. Set the scene by explaining that Ss will hear two college Ss talking about some of their nonacademic learning experiences.

2 **Optional:** Pre-teach any of the following vocabulary that you think will be helpful for your Ss:

> **dormitory** a building on a college or university campus where students live
> **property** something owned by someone
> **to respect** to be considerate of other people and their possessions
> **suffering** becoming worse
> **tight quarters** a small, crowded living space

3 Ask Ss to listen for Carol's and Michael's learning experiences while at college, but to not write anything down yet. Play the audio program once.

4 Books open. Go over the chart. Remind Ss that they are to complete the chart with notes rather than sentences. Replay the audio program. Ask Ss to complete the chart with the information they hear. Explain that the information may come in a different order from the way it is presented in the chart, and that Michael describes two experiences from which he learned the same thing.

5 Have Ss compare charts with a partner. Then replay the audio program, if needed, before going over the answers with the class.

Answers

	College experience	What they learned from it
Carol	never lived away from parents before/ leaving friends behind lived in a big dormitory shared a room with two other girls	how to get along with others how to respect other people's opinions and property how to get along living in tight quarters
Michael	used to stay up late watching TV, didn't eat well, went to class unprepared grades were suffering	how to manage time better how to be more responsible

Transcript

Listen to Carol and Michael talking about experiences they had when they went away to college and what they learned from those experiences. Complete the chart.

Carol: Well, I went away to college when I was seventeen. I'd never lived away from my parents before, and I was really looking forward to it. But I was also scared because I was leaving my friends behind, and I didn't know anyone when I first arrived. I lived in a really big dormitory and shared a room with two other girls. I guess the thing I learned the most was how to get along with others – you know, how to respect other people's opinions and property – stuff like that. At home I'd always had my own room. This was the first time I'd had to live with other people in the same room.

We were all really different – I mean, our personalities and lifestyles were completely opposite in some ways! Anyway, at first it really caused problems, but we learned how to get along living in those tight quarters. Three seventeen-year-olds living in one room – can you imagine? I'm surprised we survived it at all.

Michael: I think, for myself, the hardest thing was learning how to manage my own time better. I used to stay up late watching TV a lot, didn't eat well, often went to class unprepared, and things like that. My grades were really suffering, and I could hardly keep my eyes open in class! It was a drag! Somehow, midway through the semester, I changed and started to do well.

Organizing my time was a real challenge. In high school, I didn't have to worry – I had the same schedule every day, and at night my parents were pushing me to study. But it's different when you go away to college. You have to learn to take responsibility for your actions. No one is going to tell you what to do. You have to figure it out yourself.

Optional activity: *Details, details*

Time: 10 minutes. This activity requires Ss to listen carefully to answer comprehension questions.

1 Books closed. Write the following questions on the board:
   1. How old was Carol when she went away to college?
   2. Why was dormitory life so difficult for Carol?
   3. How many roommates did Carol have?
   4. What did Michael do that caused him problems?
   5. What did Michael's parents do for him?

2 Tell Ss to note down answers to the questions while they listen to the audio program one more time.

3 Replay the audio program. Then put Ss in pairs to compare answers before going over the answers as a class.

Answers

1. Seventeen.
2. Carol had never shared a room before.

3. Two.

4. Stayed up late. Went to class unprepared. Didn't eat well.

5. They pushed him to do his homework.

B Pair work

1 Books open. Put Ss in pairs to discuss the question.

2 Ask selected Ss to share their answers with the class.

Optional activity: *Valuable lessons*

Time: 10 minutes. This activity provides Ss with the chance to talk about their own school experiences.

Pair work Books closed. Ss individually take notes about an experience they had at school from which they learned a valuable lesson. Then have Ss form pairs and take turns telling each other about their experiences.

Identifying topic sentences

writing These activities provide additional practice with main ideas and topic sentences.

1 Books closed. Ask the class for the difference between a topic and a topic sentence. Solicit answers from selected Ss, and provide the following explanation, if necessary: A topic is what a paragraph is generally about (e.g., school). A topic sentence states an aspect, belief, or opinion about the topic (e.g., Schools ought to be improved.).

2 Books open. Have Ss read through the information about topic sentences in the box. Provide additional explanation, if necessary.

A

1 Books open. Explain the task and have Ss read through the three possible topic sentences. Then ask Ss to silently read the paragraph and decide which topic sentence most clearly states the paragraph's main idea.

2 Have Ss compare answers with a partner, with each S giving the reason for his/her choice. Then ask several Ss to share their answers and reasons with the class.

Answer

The best topic sentence for this paragraph is *Students should have access to the Internet.* Both of the other possible answers contain ideas that are not supported in the paragraph.

B

Books open. Explain the task and then have Ss read the paragraph again to cross out any information that doesn't explain the main idea. Have Ss compare answers with a partner before going over the answer with the class.

Answer

> Ss should cross out the sentence *I belong to an Internet discussion group on computer games* because this fact does not explain why *Ss should have access to the Internet.*

C

1 Books open. Explain the task and have Ss silently choose the sentence they agree with. Then circulate to ask Ss which topic sentence they chose and why. Encourage Ss to give reasons for their opinion.

2 **Optional:** Put Ss in pairs, and have them discuss the reasons why they support the belief stated in the topic sentence they chose. Ask each S to share at least three reasons for his/her opinion.

3 Books open or closed. Have Ss write their paragraphs.

D Pair work

1 Books open. Put Ss in pairs, and explain the task. Remind Ss of the value of peer editing (see Unit 1, Lesson A, Exercise 7E). Then have pairs exchange paragraphs.

2 Ss silently read their partner's paragraph before writing a title for it, crossing out any sentences that do not relate to the main idea.

3 Ask Ss to return their partner's paragraph and to discuss the title they gave it and the reasons why they crossed out any sentences.

4 Encourage pairs to discuss the ideas presented in their paragraphs and to ask and answer follow-up questions.

5 **Optional:** Have Ss tell the class the title of their partner's paragraph and summarize the ideas presented.

 Lesson B *What's the best way to learn?*

 Learning strategies

starting point These activities introduce the theme of learning strategies.

A

1 Books closed. Introduce the topic by asking Ss if they know any proverbs or sayings in their own languages that have to do with learning.

2 Books open. Explain the task and have Ss read the four statements about learning. Check that Ss understand the following vocabulary items:

> **ignorance** a lack of knowledge
>
> **power** the ability to control or do things

3 Put Ss in pairs or groups to work out a paraphrase or explanation for each of the four statements and to discuss which they agree with and why.

4 Ask several Ss to share an answer with the class. Lead a class discussion.

B Pair work

1 Books closed. Brainstorm with Ss on the best ways to learn a foreign language and to learn about literature. Write all suggestions on the board.

2 Books open. Explain the task and then have Ss read through the five statements to see if the ideas they came up with are included. Put a check (✓) beside the ones on the board that are also listed in the book.

3 Have Ss read the model dialog and then form pairs to discuss the statements they agree with and to add two more statements of their own. Encourage Ss to be creative.

4 **Optional:** Have pairs join to form a group of four. Then have groups share their ideas for learning and choose the most creative one to present to the class. After the ideas have been presented, ask the class to vote on the most creative one.

What's their learning strategy?

listening In these activities, Ss listen to three people talking about what they are learning and the strategies they use to improve their learning.

A

1 Books closed. Put Ss in small groups to discuss something they want to learn and how they want to learn it. Have selected Ss share an answer with the class.

2 Set the scene by telling Ss they will hear three people talking about what they're currently trying to learn and the strategies they are using. Then play the audio program. Ask Ss to call out the information they understood.

3 **Optional:** Teach any items from the following vocabulary list that you think will be helpful for your Ss:

> **discouraged** less confident and enthusiastic about something
> **beforehand** earlier
> **embarrassing** something that makes you feel uncomfortable or ashamed
> **to pick (something) up** to learn something, such as a skill
> **community center** a building for a community's educational and recreational needs
> **to wander off the topic** to talk in an unfocused way

4 Books open. Play the audio program again, and ask Ss to complete the chart with the information they hear. Remind Ss to fill in the chart with notes rather than sentences.

5 Play the audio program a third time so that Ss can check their answers. Then put Ss in pairs to compare answers. Check Ss' answers around the class.

Answers

	How they are trying to learn	Problems they are having
Frank	study group with friends	some people come unprepared, or forget their notes, or don't read the chapter beforehand
Regina	reading the manual	too much information to remember not enough time to study the manual
Sonia	taking a class at the community center	class is too difficult other Ss are better the teacher is not very good/wanders off the topic

Transcript

Listen to Frank, Regina, and Sonia talking about something they're trying to learn. What strategies are they using? What problems are they having?

Frank: I'm having some trouble with chemistry this year. It's hard. The teacher acts like we're so smart – that we ought to have no trouble learning it. I find the textbook confusing, and then I get discouraged. Well, some of us got together and formed a study group. It seems to work OK most of the time – we compare notes and then go over the discussion questions in each chapter. The only problem is that sometimes one of my friends will come to the study group unprepared. He'll forget his notes or he won't have read the book beforehand. That really bothers me! I guess those guys who don't prepare are going to have a hard time on the final exam!

Regina: I'm trying to learn this new computer program at school. It's kind of embarrassing – most of the other kids have already picked it up, and I just can't get it. There's this software manual at school – I borrowed the book and took it home to read, but it didn't seem to help. There was simply too much information for me to remember. My problem is that I don't have enough time to sit down and learn it properly. I'm not sure what to do next.

Sonia: I'm going to France next summer, so I want to learn as much French as I can. So, I started taking a French class at the local community center. Well, the great thing is the class is free. The problem is it's not very easy. Well, you see, it's supposed to be a beginning-level class – no way! I'm telling you, most of the people in there – they already knew how to speak French when they started the class. They can say basic conversational phrases, and they know how to pronounce the words. I am a complete beginner! I did not know one word of

French when I started this class! So I always feel lost – even from day one, I had no idea what was going on. Now, the teacher is nice, but he's not very good. He gets off the topic, and he'll get stuck on some tiny, little point for like half an hour at a time. But you know, I really shouldn't complain because after all, this class is free!

B Pair work

1   Books open. Explain the task and have pairs think of other suggestions for Frank, Regina, and Sonia.

2   After five to ten minutes, ask some volunteers to share their ideas with the rest of the group. Write these ideas on the board.

Optional activity: *Role play*

Time: 10 minutes. Ss use their charts and their suggestions from Exercise 2B to role-play a conversation among Frank, Regina, and Sonia.

1   *Group work* Books open. Put Ss in groups of three. Tell them to take on the roles of Frank, Regina, and Sonia. If necessary, change male and female names to fit the groups.

2   Ss tell their group members what they are trying to learn, how they are doing it, and what problems they face. Explain that group members should ask follow-up questions and offer their own suggestions. Encourage Ss to be in character as much as possible.

3   Have selected groups perform their role plays for the class.

Infinitives and gerunds to talk about how to do things

grammar focus

Ss practice describing how to do things using either the infinitive or *by* + gerund.

> **Grammar notes** Both *be* + infinitive or *be* + *by* + gerund can be used to talk about ways to do things (e.g., A good way to learn a foreign language *is to make* friends with a native speaker.).
>
> In these types of sentences, the infinitive or gerund phrase (e.g., *to make friends with a native speaker*) is a subject complement that functions as an adjective because it describes the subject of the sentence (e.g., *A good way to learn a foreign language . . .*).
>
> A gerund always follows the preposition *by*.

1   Books open. Review the language in the grammar box, and model the sentences.

2   Write an example of each structure on the board, and remind Ss of the form of a gerund and an infinitive. Also remind Ss that you cannot combine the two forms at the same time (e.g., you cannot say "to making" or "to living").

A Pair work

1 Books open. Explain the task and lead Ss through one or two items. Explain that more than one answer is possible for each. Check that Ss understand the following vocabulary:

> **to run a business** to manage a business
> **current events** news about recent events, such as politics and sports

2 Have Ss individually match each activity on the left with a way to learn it on the right. Then have Ss read the sample language in the balloon before getting in pairs to discuss and give reasons for their answers. Have selected Ss share an answer with the class.

Possible answers

> 1. The only way to learn how to drive a car is to practice doing it with a personal instructor at your side.
> 2. A good way to learn about history is to read as much as possible about the subject.
> 3. The best way to learn how to run a business is by talking to people who were successful at it.
> 4. The only way to learn how to fly a plane is by taking a course from an expert.
> 5. A good way to learn a musical instrument is to practice doing it by yourself.
> 6. The best way to learn advanced math is by following a set of rules or instructions.
> 7. The only way to learn a new dance is by watching someone do it, and then doing the same thing.
> 8. A good way to learn about current events is to read as much as possible about the subject.

B Pair work

1 Books open. Explain the task and give your own example to illustrate it. Then have pairs tell each other about how they learned something successfully and why they think they were successful in learning it.

2 Have selected Ss share their experience and advice with the class.

In order to *and* so that

grammar focus This grammar focus presents the expressions *in order to* and *so that* to give a reason or purpose for doing something.

1 Books closed. On the board write *I am studying English in order to . . .* , and underneath that write *get a good job.* Ask Ss to call out their own reasons for learning English, and write them on the board.

2 Then write *I took this class so that I could . . .* , and have Ss call out their reasons. Write them on the board.

3 Books open. Lead Ss through the language in the grammar box, and model the example sentences. Explain that you have to use a verb in its base form (without *to*) to complete sentences with *in order to,* and a subject pronoun (*I, you, he . . .*) followed by *can, could, will,* or *would* to complete sentences with *so that.*

4 Explain the task and go over the first sentence. Then have Ss work silently to complete each sentence with a reason or purpose of their own.

5 Have Ss compare answers with a partner. Then go over the answers with the class by asking Ss to provide their answers for each of the sentences. Write them on the board.

Possible answers

> 1. One way to learn a foreign language is to live in a country where it's spoken so that you can get practice using it every day.
> 2. If I wanted to learn to use a computer, I'd sign up for a class so that I wouldn't have to read a manual.
> 3. I'd like to purchase my own computer in order to work at home.
> 4. If you don't know how to drive, it's best to go to a driving school so that an experienced teacher can show you what to do.
> 5. It might be fun to enroll in a cooking class in order to learn how to cook Chinese food.
> 6. I would like to take a math class in order to brush up on my skills.

Optional activity: *Nonsensical sentences*

Time: 10 minutes. Ss are given extra practice with statements of purpose using *so that* and *in order to.*

1 *Class activity* Books closed. Divide the class into two equal groups, A and B.

2 Have Group A write the first clause of three purpose statements and Group B write the second clause of three purpose clauses (beginning with *in order to* or *so that*). Neither group should look at what the other group has written.

3 Have members of Group A take turns reading their statements and members of Group B take turns completing it with theirs. (Ss normally come up with funny things.) Then have Ss switch groups.

My future goals

discussion   In this activity, Ss think of their own learning goals.

Pair work

1 Books open. Explain the task and have Ss read the sample dialog.

2 Have Ss individually make their lists. Then put Ss in pairs to tell each other about their goals and their plans for achieving them. After five minutes or so, have selected Ss tell the class one of their goals.

Helping others learn

discussion In this activity, Ss are given additional practice using gerunds and infinitives to discuss the best ways to do things.

Group work

1 Books open. Explain the task and have Ss read the sample language. Then put Ss in groups of four or five to choose one of the situations and discuss the best ways to help someone learn or prepare for the activity.

2 Have selected groups present their ideas to the class.

Optional activity: *Situation exchange*

Time: 10–15 minutes. Ss are given more practice using gerunds and infinitives to discuss the best ways to do things.

Group work Books open. Have each group write out a situation. Then have groups exchange situations and discuss the best ways of helping someone learn the activity. Groups later share their ideas with each other.

 Reach the top!

vocabulary This activity focuses on collocations that are related to personal goals.

A

1 Books closed. Write the verbs *achieve, complete, fulfill, reach,* and *realize* on the board, and go over the meaning of each with the class. Then ask Ss if they can think of a noun to go with each verb. Have Ss call out answers, and write these on the board.

2 Books open. Explain the task and go over the nouns at the top of the chart, clarifying meaning as necessary. Then have Ss individually complete the chart by checking the possible collocations before comparing with a partner.

3 Go over the answers with the class.

Answers

achieve a goal	complete a task	fulfill a dream	reach a goal	realize a dream

B Pair work

1 Books open. Explain the task and have Ss read the sample language in the speech balloon. Note that each sentence can be completed with a phrase that begins with either the infinitive form of a verb (with *to*) or a gerund.

2 Put Ss in pairs to compare and discuss their answers. Ask several Ss to share their answers with the class.

Learning alternatives

discussion   **Pair work**

This activity presents some new vocabulary associated with methods of learning.

1   Books closed. Present the following three situations: learning to write children's books, learning how to play a musical instrument, and learning how to be a hairdresser. Ask Ss to think of different ways in which they could learn these things.

2   Have Ss match each type of course to the correct definition. Then have Ss compare answers with a partner before going over the answers as a class.

Answers

| **1.** c | **2.** e | **3.** a | **4.** b | **5.** d | **6.** g | **7.** f |

3   Model the language in the balloons. Then put Ss in pairs to discuss the benefits of each of the seven ways of learning something, as well as experiences they may have had with any of these types of instructions.

Optional activity: *Course listings*

Time: 10–15 minutes. Ss further practice discussing the topic of the unit by providing an appropriate subject for each type of course listed.

Group or pair work Books open. For each of the seven types of courses listed, have pairs or groups think of one activity or subject that can be easily learned using this method. Then have groups or pairs share their answers with the class. Lead a class discussion.

9   Learning at home

reading   This article is about the growing trend in home schooling in the United States. The exercises practice predicting, reading for gist, and relating ideas to real-world knowledge.

> **Culture note** Although laws vary from state to state in the United States, all parents have the option to teach their children at home rather than send them to school. Various programs exist to help parents meet state-mandated curriculum goals, but some parents prefer to design their own classes and curriculum. In most states, home-schooled children must be registered with either the state or the local Department of Education.

A   Pair work

1   Books closed. Introduce the topic by writing the title of the article on the board. Check Ss' understanding of *trend*. Ask "What do you think home schooling is? Why might it be a growing trend?" Brainstorm with Ss and write all responses on the board.

2 **Optional:** Write the two pre-reading questions on the board. Have Ss discuss the questions in pairs.

3 Books open. Have Ss silently read the article to compare their ideas to those presented in the text.

4 Go over words from the following list if they seem to be obstructing Ss' comprehension of the text:

> **model students** students who are excellent in their studies, attitude, behavior, etc.
> **achievement tests** tests that measure how much someone knows about a
> specific subject
> **to miss out** to not have the opportunity to do something
> **option** choice
> **to rank** to be rated at a certain level in comparison to others
> **self-directed** self-motivated
> **sophomore** a student in his or her second year of high school or college
> **to interact** to communicate and work together with other people

B Group work

1 Books open. Explain the task and have Ss read the four discussion questions. Give Ss a few minutes to think about the answers to the questions, highlighting or underlining parts of the text if they need to, before putting Ss in small groups to discuss them.

2 Bring the class back together, and have selected Ss share one or more answers with the class. Lead a class discussion. (*Note:* The answers for question 1 are listed below. For questions 2–4, answers will vary.)

Optional activity: *Home-schooling debate*

Time: 15 minutes. Ss further discuss the ideas presented in the article.

1 *Group and pair work* Books closed. Divide the class into two groups to debate the advantages and disadvantages of home schooling. Assign Group A to debate in favor of home schooling and Group B against home schooling.

2 Pair up Ss in their own groups to list as many reasons as they can to support their assigned belief.

3 Put pairs from Group A together with pairs from Group B to discuss their ideas. Then bring the class back together, and have several Ss share their most convincing ideas with the class.

Answers

Advantages of home schooling	Disadvantages of home schooling
Parents can do a better job of educating children at home.	Ss have fewer chances to interact with others their own age.
Ss are more self-directed and have greater depth of knowledge (well prepared).	Ss lack the usual social skills.

This unit introduces the theme of cities. Students talk about what different cities have to offer visitors, using defining and non-defining relative clauses. They also learn to connect contrasting ideas to talk about what their cities or towns are like to live in.

Lesson A *Fascinating destinations*

Cities of the world

starting point   These activities introduce the topic of comparing cities around the world.

A

1 **Optional:** Books closed. Ask Ss to call out their favorite city in the world and to tell the class what they like about the place. Alternatively, bring in several photos of famous cities Ss are likely to know, and ask them what they know or like about these places.

2 Books closed. Write the names of the following cities on the board: *Seoul, New Orleans, Kyoto,* and *Salvador.* Have pairs or groups list all the information they know about these cities, including what countries they are in. Then have selected Ss tell the class what they know about these cities.

3 Books open. Explain the task and have Ss look at the photos of the four cities. Then have Ss read the sentences. Go over any new vocabulary, including the following:

> **port** harbor
> **to host** to provide space and other necessary things for a special event
> **shrine** a place for worship that is holy because of its connection with a
>   holy person or object
> **spicy** strongly flavored with spices; hot tasting
> **picturesque** pretty; attractive in appearance, especially in an old-fashioned
>   way [often used to describe landscapes and cities/towns]

4 Have Ss individually complete the task and then compare answers with a partner, before checking their answers on page 118 of the Student's Book.

Answers

1. Salvador	3. Kyoto	5. Salvador	7. Seoul
2. Seoul	4. New Orleans	6. New Orleans	8. Kyoto

B Pair work

Books open. Ask Ss to call out general questions they would ask before visiting any new city. Explain the task and have Ss work in pairs to write three specific questions they'd like to ask about the cities. Circulate to check for accuracy and to offer possible suggestions for questions.

C Group work

1 Books open. Explain the task and then combine pairs into groups of four. Ss take turns asking the questions they've written.

2 **Optional:** Have Ss stand and circulate to try and find someone who can answer their unanswered questions.

3 **Optional:** For homework, have Ss research the information they need to answer any remaining questions. Alternatively, have Ss research additional information about one or more of the cities. Have Ss present their findings in the next class.

What do you like about the city?

listening

In this activity, Ss listen to people talk about two of the cities in Exercise 1A.

1 Books closed. Explain that Ss will hear Deborah and Todd talking about two of the four cities from Exercise 1A.

2 **Optional:** Pre-teach any of the following vocabulary items that you think will be helpful for your Ss:

> **to sign off** to end a radio or TV program
> **to stand by** to wait for a turn [often used in broadcast news, e.g., *Our reporter is standing by.*]
> **metropolitan** urban; relating to a city
> **population** all the people living in a particular area
> **cosmopolitan** international; sophisticated [used to describe people and cities]
> **unique** one of a kind; different from all others
> **inhabitants** people who live in a place
> **cliff** a high area of rock with a very steep side
> **it can't be beat** it can't be topped; it's the best
> **installment** one part of a story or program

3 Play the audio program; Ss listen only. Then ask Ss to call out details they remember from what they heard. Accept any answers without correction.

4 Books open. Replay the audio program, and have Ss fill in the chart with the names of the cities and some of the features mentioned. Remind Ss to write in note form and to write only a few of the features.

5 Replay the audio program if needed before putting Ss in groups to compare their answers. Tell Ss to share information and add other features to their lists. Then go over the answers as a class. Make a list on the board of all the features Ss listed.

Answers (Note: Students should have any two of the following items.)

	City	Features
Deborah	Seoul	one of the ten largest metropolitan areas; cosmopolitan; unique spicy food; noodles, barbecued beef; very old; combination of old and new architecture; efficient subway system; discount shopping
Todd	Salvador	very old; founded by Portuguese; third largest; population of 2 million; built into a cliff; overlooks bay; on two levels; elevator between levels; beautiful beaches; African influence in music, food, and dance; can watch special kind of dancing; great nightlife; street festivals

Transcript

Listen to Deborah and Todd talking about two of the cities in Exercise A. Which city is each person talking about? What are some interesting features of each city?

Andy: Well, this is Andy Wong, and we're just about at the end of another episode of "Where in the World . . . ?" But before we sign off, I'd like to tell you a little about tomorrow's program. Tomorrow we'll have a very interesting report on two very exciting cities that I'm sure you won't want to miss. Our reporters in the field, Deborah and Todd, are standing by to fill us in on the details. Deborah! Can you hear me?

Deborah: Yes, Andy, loud and clear!

Andy: Well, where are you?

Deborah: You know I can't tell you that, Andy! You have to watch tomorrow's program to get the answer.

Andy: Oh, right, . . . that's right. Well, tell us about the place anyway.

Deborah: OK. This city is a very exciting place to visit. First of all, it is one of the ten largest metropolitan areas in the world. It is a very cosmopolitan city with a strong identity of its own. And the local food is unique. I really am enjoying the restaurants that serve barbecued beef, which is grilled right at your table. But I must warn you, much of the food is extremely spicy, so come prepared. Do you like spicy food, Andy?

Andy: Love it!

Deborah: Well, you should come on over, then! Andy, this city is very old. It was founded in the fourteenth century and is divided by the Han River. The city has a striking combination of modern and ancient architecture. In fact, most of the traditional architecture is located on the

continued

northern side of the river – where I am now. With its efficient subway system, it's very easy to get around and see the sights.

Andy: Great, Deborah. Thanks so much for . . .

Deborah: Oh, wait, Andy! One more thing I forgot to mention! The shopping – the street vendors here sell everything from shoes to electronics to furniture – all at discounted prices! Oops, have I said too much?

Andy: No, no, not at all. Sounds like you're having a fantastic time. We're looking forward to hearing your full report tomorrow, and finding out just where in the world you are right now! Before we run out of time, though, let me turn it over to Todd. Todd? Are you there?

Todd: I sure am. Hello, everyone. Well, my city is very old. It was founded in fifteen forty-nine by the Portuguese. It is now the third largest city in the country, with about two million inhabitants. It's quite fascinating. Believe it or not, it's built into a cliff, and it overlooks a beautiful bay. It's actually on two levels. To get to the upper level you can take an elevator. From there you have a wonderful view of the bay. And if you enjoy swimming, there are beautiful beaches.

Andy: Well, Todd, I guess we know where you've been the last few days! On the beach!

Todd: Well, not exactly, Andy. There's so much to see and do here. By the way, this city also has a strong African influence: you can see it in the music, food, and dance styles of the region.

Andy: Mm-hmm. What do people like to do there?

Todd: Many people enjoy watching a special kind of dance that's a mixture of dancing and fighting with an African origin. For those of you who enjoy nightlife, this city can't be beat. It has several different street festivals during the year, each one like a mini-carnival of its own.

Andy: Great! Thanks a lot, Todd. Well, that certainly has given our listeners plenty to think about, but I'm sorry to say we're out of time. That's it, folks. This is Andy Wong reminding you to tune in tomorrow for the next installment of our travel show, "Where in the World . . . ?" Good night, everybody!

Optional activity 1: *Details, details*

Time: 5–10 minutes. Ss listen for specific information about the two cities.

Books open or closed. Write the following questions on the board, and tell Ss to try to answer them.

1. *What is the name of the announcer?*
2. *When will the program with Deborah and Todd be broadcast?*
3. *Which type of food did Deborah particularly enjoy in Seoul?*
4. *Does the announcer like spicy food?*
5. *When was Seoul first established?*
6. *What kinds of things can you buy in Seoul?*
7. *Who founded Salvador?*
8. *What can be viewed from the top level of Salvador?*
9. *Which activity are the beaches good for in Salvador?*
10. *What are the street festivals in Salvador like?*

Answers

1. Andy Wong	**5.** fourteenth century	**8.** the bay
2. tomorrow	**6.** shoes, electronics, furniture	**9.** swimming
3. noodles	**7.** Portuguese	**10.** mini-carnivals
4. yes		

Optional activity 2: *Hometown features*

Time: 10 minutes. Ss compare the filled-in chart with features of their own towns or cities.

Group work Books open. Tell Ss to make a list of the features of their own hometowns or cities. Then have Ss compare their lists to the features in the chart. Put Ss in small groups to tell each other about the features their hometowns or cities share with the ones in the chart. Then select Ss to share their answers with the class.

Defining and non-defining relative clauses

grammar focus

In this activity, Ss practice using defining and non-defining relative clauses to talk about features of cities.

> **Grammar notes** Defining relative clauses function like adjectives because they describe or define the meaning of a noun or noun phrase (e.g., Customers are attracted to restaurants *that have local music.*). They must always come immediately after the nouns they describe because they give essential information about that noun or noun phrase.
>
> Non-defining clauses always present some information that can be considered nonessential to the understanding of the noun or noun phrase referred to. Their function is to comment on the noun or noun phrase, and they are set off by commas (e.g., The restaurant, *which has local music,* attracts many customers.).
>
> The terms *non-defining* and *defining* are also referred to as *non-restrictive* and *restrictive.*

1 Books closed. Write these sentences on the board :

1. New Orleans is a city that is famous for its annual Mardi Gras celebration.

2. New Orleans, which is famous for its annual Mardi Gras celebration, is located in the state of Louisiana.

Ask Ss: "In which sentence is the phrase *is famous for its annual Mardi Gras celebration* essential information? In which sentence could it be left out?"

2 Books open. Lead Ss through the information in the grammar box, and explain that a defining relative clause gives essential information about a noun (i.e., it defines or identifies the noun), whereas a non-defining relative clause gives optional information about a noun. Point out the general rule: Commas are used if the information in the clause is extra or unnecessary to the sentence and are not used if the information is essential. Tell Ss that in other books defining and non-defining relative clauses may be called restrictive and non-restrictive relative clauses.

3 Have Ss, working in pairs, come up with two similar sentences about one of the cities in Exercise 1A. Have selected Ss share their two sentences with the class, and write these on the board.

A

1 Books open. Explain the task and go over the example. Check Ss' understanding of the following vocabulary item:

> **to surround** to encircle

2 Have Ss individually underline the relative clause in each sentence and add punctuation as necessary. Also have them indicate whether the clause is defining (D) or non-defining (ND).

3 Ss compare answers with a partner before going over them as a class.

Answers

> ND **1.** Brasilia, <u>which is the capital of Brazil</u>, is less than 50 years old.
>
> D **2.** Montreal is a city <u>where both French and English are spoken</u>.
>
> ND **3.** Bangkok, <u>which is the capital of Thailand</u>, has many beautiful temples.
>
> D **4.** Bogota is a city <u>that is surrounded by mountains</u>.
>
> ND **5.** Mexico City, <u>which has a population of nearly 20,000,000</u>, is the largest urban area in the Americas.
>
> D **6.** Pusan is a busy port city <u>that is located in the southern part of Korea</u>.

B

1 Books open. Explain that Ss will join these pairs of sentences together using non-defining relative clauses. Join the first pair of sentences together with the Ss, writing on the board: *Salvador, which has excellent examples of seventeenth- and eighteenth-century colonial architecture, was founded in 1549.* Point out that in this instance the essential information was in the first sentence. Then point out that the pronoun *it* in the second sentence referred to the word *Salvador*, so when the sentences were joined, *it* was replaced with the relative pronoun *which*.

2 Check Ss' understanding of the following vocabulary items:

> **to found** to start or establish [in this case, a city or town]
> **blossoms** flowers on trees
> **steamboat** a boat that moves by steam power

> **cruise** a trip taken on a ship or boat for the purpose of pleasure
> **destination** the place a person is going to
> **antique** extremely old and often valuable
> **pottery** containers and dishes made of baked clay
> **custom-made** made for a particular person or purpose

3 Have Ss join each pair of sentences with a non-defining relative clause as you circulate to help. Then have Ss compare answers with a partner before going over them as a class.

Possible answers

1. Salvador, which has excellent examples of seventeenth- and eighteenth-century colonial architecture, was founded in 1549.
2. The carnival in Salvador, which is a popular Brazilian festival, runs for several days.
3. People often visit Kyoto in April, when they can see the beautiful cherry blossoms.
4. Kyoto, which has more than 60 museums, is a major cultural center of Japan.
5. New Orleans, which is well known for its steamboat cruises, is located on the Mississippi River.
6. New Orleans, which made an important contribution to the development of jazz in the late nineteenth century, is a favorite destination of jazz lovers.
7. Seoul is well known for its shopping areas, where everything from antique pottery to custom-made clothing can be found.
8. The month of January, which has an average daily temperature of between –9° and 0° Celsius, is very cold in Seoul.

A great place to visit

discussion   In this activity, Ss use relative clauses to explain why they would like to visit one of the cities on page 18.

A

Books open. Explain the task and have Ss individually write their sentences. Circulate to help Ss use relative clauses.

B Pair work

1 Books open. Explain the task and have Ss form pairs to take turns explaining the reasons for their choices. Encourage Ss to ask and answer follow-up questions.
2 After pairs are finished, have several Ss say which city they'd most like to visit and why.

Optional activity: *Good cities to visit*

Time: 10–15 minutes. Ss practice talking about other cities they would like
to visit.

1   *Pair work* Books open or closed. Have Ss write sentences about three cities
    in their own country they would like to visit someday (e.g., *I'd love to visit
    Pusan because it's a city that has great beaches and seafood restaurants.*).

2   Put Ss in pairs to take turns reading their sentences. Encourage them to ask
    and answer follow-up questions. Then have Ss share their sentences with the
    class. On the board, make a class list of the destinations. Are there any that
    are especially popular?

   Describing a city

vocabulary   In these activities, Ss describe individual features of a city.

A

1   Books closed. Ask the class what features are most important to them when
    choosing a city to visit. Give an example if needed, such as nightlife.

2   Books open. Explain the task and have Ss look at the photo. Ask which
    feature it illustrates (answer: architecture). Have Ss read the definition of the
    word *architecture*. Then have Ss work individually or in pairs to define the
    seven remaining words.

3   Have selected Ss share one or more of their definitions with the class. Write
    them on the board.

B

Books open. Explain the task and call Ss' attention to the examples presented,
noting the non-defining relative clause in the second sentence. Then have Ss
individually write their sentences. Remind them to use at least four of the features
from Exercise 5A. Circulate to help and check for accuracy.

C   Group work

1   Books open. Have Ss form groups of four or five to take turns describing the
    city they wrote about while their group members ask follow-up questions.

2   Have a few Ss tell the class about the city they chose to describe.

Optional activity: *The name game*

Time: 15 minutes. Ss use relative clauses to describe cities.

1   *Group work* Books open or closed. Have Ss write sentences about an
    undesirable but well-known city, using relative clauses where appropriate.
    Tell Ss not to mention the name of the city or country in their sentences.

2   Put Ss in groups of four or five and assign a secretary to record Ss scores.
    Tell Ss to read their sentences while the others guess either the country the
    city is in (worth 1 point) or the city itself (worth 2 points). Tell Ss they
    cannot ask more than ten questions. If the others in the group cannot guess,
    the S telling about his/her city receives 2 points.

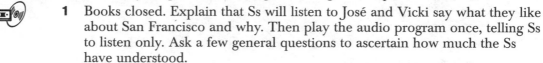
listening

In this activity, Ss practice listening both for gist and specific information.

1 Books closed. Explain that Ss will listen to José and Vicki say what they like about San Francisco and why. Then play the audio program once, telling Ss to listen only. Ask a few general questions to ascertain how much the Ss have understood.

2 Optional: Pre-teach any of the following vocabulary that you think will be helpful for your Ss:

> **on short notice** being given information or a warning right before it is going to happen
>
> **impressions** opinions, views
>
> **enthusiastic** having an energetic interest in someone or something
>
> **rolling hills** low hills grouped together
>
> **amateur** a person who does something as a hobby rather than as a job
>
> **pastries** small cakes often made with flaky dough, such as little pies
>
> **burrito** a Mexican food with beans, meat, or cheese wrapped in a thin, flat bread
>
> **Hispanic** relating to people of Latin American descent who are living in the United States

3 Books open. Tell Ss to look at the chart. Explain that Ss are to listen for what features the people like about the city and the comments they make about these features. Remind Ss to fill in the chart with notes rather than sentences. Suggest that Ss number features and corresponding comments. Then replay the audio program, and have Ss listen and fill in the chart.

4 Put Ss in groups to compare charts. Then play the audio program again while going over the answers as a class. Make a list of all the comments on the board.

Answers

	What they like	**Comments**
José	variety and quality of buildings	Victorians, skyscrapers, MoMA, Golden Gate Bridge
Vicki	beauty of the city and the bay	rolling hills, view of the bay, romantic
	exploring different neighborhoods	Italian neighborhood for pastries, Mission District for burritos
	a great place to live	can get around easily, advantages of large city

Transcript

Listen to José and Vicki talking about the same city. What do they like about it?

Interviewer: Hi, guys.

José and Vicki: Hi.

Interviewer: Thanks for agreeing to meet me here on such short notice.

José: No problem.

Interviewer: Well, listen, as I said to you on the phone, I'm doing a story for the campus newspaper. I'm interviewing foreign students to get their impressions of our city. Um, . . . this should only take about ten minutes or so. Let's see. . . . Uh, do you mind if I tape-record our interview?

Vicki: Oh no, not at all.

Interviewer: OK, then. José, why don't we start with you. What do you think of San Francisco? How do you like it here so far?

José: It's OK, I guess.

Interviewer: Oh, you don't sound very enthusiastic.

José: No, no, I like it. It's just that I've been so busy studying. I haven't had much time to explore the city.

Interviewer: Oh, that's too bad.

José: Yeah. And when I have the time, well, it's so cloudy and foggy here – especially in the summer. I never thought I'd be wearing a sweater in July!

Interviewer: Well, this is Northern California. Hey, maybe you should move south. I hear Los Angeles is warmer. Vicki?

Vicki: Oh, I love it here. I think this is a beautiful city. The rolling hills, the views of the bay – it's very romantic.

Interviewer: Yeah. So how do you guys spend your free time?

José: Well, I'm studying architecture and am somewhat of a photographer. . . .

Interviewer: Really?

José: Oh, I'm just an amateur. Anyway, I . . . I'm always taking pictures of the buildings in this city. You know, the Victorians, the modern skyscrapers downtown, MoMA, . . .

Interviewer: MoMA. You mean, the Museum of Modern Art?

José: Right. There's such a variety of buildings in this city. The architecture is really great. I also have taken pictures of other structures, like the Golden Gate Bridge – it looks totally different when the weather changes.

Interviewer: Wow! That's interesting. Ah, well, Vicki, it's your turn. What do you like to do?

Vicki: I like to explore the different neighborhoods. Yesterday I went to the Italian neighborhood, North Beach, to buy some pastries and have a cup of espresso. Today I'm going down to the Mission District to get a burrito for lunch.

Interviewer: Hey, sounds like you like to eat!

Vicki: Yes. Actually, I like the Mission a lot. It's a Hispanic neighborhood. We don't have anything like that where I come from.

Interviewer: Uh, well, that's about it. Any final comments?

José: No, not really.

> **Vicki:** I'd just like to say that this is a great place to live. It's small enough to get around easily, but big enough to offer all the advantages of a large city. I'm glad that I got a chance to study here.

Optional activity: *José's San Francisco*

Time: 5 minutes. Ss talk about San Francisco from José's perspective.

Pair work Books closed. Put Ss in pairs to discuss the following two questions.

1. Does José seem to like San Francisco more or less than Vicki?
2. Why is José so interested in taking pictures of the buildings?

Possible answers

> **1.** Less. He doesn't like the weather. / The weather is too cold, cloudy, and foggy. He has been working so hard he has not had time to explore the city.
>
> **2.** He is studying architecture, and he is an amateur photographer.

 Preferred destinations

discussion   In this activity, Ss share opinions about places they'd like to visit or live in for specific reasons.

Group work

1   Books open. Explain the task and have Ss read the questions. Ask Ss to say what features make places good for honeymoons, vacations, or long-term residence. Then have Ss form groups to discuss the questions. Encourage Ss to ask and answer follow-up questions. Select Ss to share one or more answers with the class.

2   **Optional:** Rather than having selected Ss share answers, have all Ss stand and find people who have similar answers. Or have Ss circulate in class to find the most common answers to the four questions.

 Creating topic sentences

writing   In these activities, Ss learn about and make cluster diagrams in order to generate and organize ideas, write topic sentences, and write a paragraph about a city.

A

1   Books closed. If possible, bring in a map of the United States, and call Ss' attention to the state of Florida. Ask if anyone has visited Florida or knows anyone who has done so, and what they know about Florida in general. If necessary, point out its southern location and extensive coastline to elicit that it has warm winters and lots of beaches.

2 Books open. Have Ss look at the map and the photos on page 21 and say what the pictures show about Orlando. Then have Ss look at the cluster diagram and read the information in the five circles. Point out that each piece of information represents a feature of Orlando that the writer thinks might make a possible topic sentence.

3 Explain that a cluster diagram is a graphic way to generate and organize ideas when preparing to write. Ask selected Ss to say which idea in the diagram they think would make the best topic sentence. Then have Ss read the paragraph about Orlando to decide which item the writer chose for a topic sentence.

4 **Optional:** Have Ss read the paragraph again to underline the information they think best supports the main idea.

B

1 Books open or closed. Write the name of the city where you teach on the board, and have the class call out features of the city. Make a cluster diagram by putting the information in circles around the city name. Ask selected Ss to say which of the ideas generated would make the best topic sentence.

2 Books open. Explain the task and then have Ss work alone to choose a city. Ss make their own cluster diagram with possible topic sentences about this city. Circulate to help and provide advice about effective topic sentences.

3 Either in or out of class, have Ss write a paragraph that supports their best idea as a topic sentence.

C Pair work

1 Books open. Explain the task and lead Ss through the three questions. Remind Ss of the purpose and benefits of peer feedback (see Unit 1, Lesson A, Exercise 7E). Then have partners take turns discussing their answers to the questions and making suggestions to improve each other's paragraphs.

2 **Optional:** Give Ss about 10 minutes to revise their paragraphs according to their partner's suggestions. (Alternatively, this could be done as homework.) Remind Ss that if a reader has questions, the writer should answer those questions to make the ideas clear.

3 **Optional:** Select Ss to read their paragraphs to the class.

It's my kind of city.

Contrasting lifestyles

starting point   These activities present advantages and disadvantages of cities and aspects to consider when choosing a place to live.

A

1 Books closed. Ask Ss what features they would look for in choosing a new place to live. Have Ss call out ideas, and write them on the board.

2 Books open. Explain the task and ask Ss to compare the aspects they mentioned with the ones listed. Then have Ss individually rank the five items before comparing answers with a partner.

B Pair work

1 Books open. Have Ss look at the photos of the two cities. Ask "Which do you think has a higher cost of living?" Have Ss raise their hands to indicate their answers. Then ask Ss to make predictions about the other lifestyle issues in Exercise 1A.

2 Explain the task and have Ss read the two texts to confirm their predictions.

3 Explain any new vocabulary, including the following:

> **subway** a train that runs underground
> **newcomer** a person who has recently moved to a place
> **to budget** to control the amount of money you spend on things
> **humidity** the amount of moisture in the air
> **infrequently** not often

4 Ask Ss again which city has more to offer for each category in Exercise 1A. Have selected Ss call out answers, and encourage them to give reasons.

Possible answers

> **cost of living:** city 2 has a lower cost of living
> **crime rate:** city 2 has a lower crime rate
> **jobs:** city 1 is likely to have more jobs
> **nightlife:** city 1 has a more interesting nightlife
> **weather:** city 2 has better weather

C Pair work

1 Books open. Explain the task and have Ss read the five sentences. Then have Ss complete the task in pairs, finding the best sentence for each of the gaps in the descriptions in Exercise 1B. Have Ss compare answers before going over them with the class.

Answers

1. c	**2.** e	**3.** a	**4.** d	**5.** b

2 **Optional:** Ask selected Ss if they have changed their opinion about which city has more to offer. Encourage Ss to give reasons for their answers.

 Talking about two cities

discussion **Group work**

1 Books open. Explain the task and have Ss read the three discussion questions. Then put Ss in groups of three to discuss them.

2 Combine Ss into groups of six to share ideas. Encourage Ss to give reasons for their answers. Then have one or more Ss from each group share an answer with the class.

Optional activity: *Ideal hometowns*

Time: 15 minutes. Ss further practice making cluster diagrams and freely discuss their preferred town or city.

Group work Books closed. Tell Ss to think of their ideal hometown or city. Have them make cluster diagrams for this topic. Then working in small groups, Ss use their cluster diagrams to talk about their ideal hometowns or cities.

 Order of adjectives

grammar focus In this activity Ss learn about word order for sentences in which more than one adjective modifies a noun.

> **Grammar note** Modifying phrases often begin with a preposition and are placed last in a string of adjectives.

1 Books closed. Write the following categories on the board: *age, quality, size,* and *type.* Say the name of a city everyone in class knows, and ask Ss to call out as many adjectives as they can to describe it. Have Ss call out the appropriate categories for each adjective listed while you write them in one of the categories.

2 Explain that a single noun can be modified by any combination of the four categories of adjectives. Choose one adjective from each category, and ask the class to suggest the order they think the adjectives should go in to

complete the sentence "X is a ____, ____, ____ city." Build up a sentence, and then ask Ss if they can deduce the rule for adjective order.

3   Books open. Lead Ss through the information in the grammar box. Then explain the task, and go over the example sentence.

4   Have Ss work individually to write their sentences while you circulate to offer help. Then put Ss in pairs to compare sentences and check the order of each other's adjectives.

5   **Optional:** Choose a few of the students' sentences that have only two adjectives. Write them on the board, and ask the class to think of more adjectives to add.

Optional activity 1: *Mixed bag*

Time: 5–10 minutes. Ss further practice ordering adjectives.

1   *Group work* Books open. Have Ss add to the chart two words or phrases for each category. Write them on the board. Have each student pick one adjective from each category and write it on a slip of paper.

2   Put Ss in groups of four to six, and have Ss put their slips of paper in a group bag. Then have each S pick four slips of paper. Tell Ss to try to write a sentence that makes as much sense as possible using the adjectives they have chosen.

3   Tell Ss to read their sentences to each other. Then have Ss rank them based on how logical they are (1 = most logical). Have the groups read either their silliest or most logical sentences to the class.

Optional activity 2: *A city search*

Time: 10 minutes. Ss have additional practice with descriptions of cities.

1   *Group work* Books closed. Put Ss in small groups, and pass out pictures of cities, one to each group. Have Ss work together to write a description of the city on a slip of paper. Collect the pictures and descriptions.

2   Display the pictures on the bulletin board or on a table. Give each group another group's description. Have groups search for the picture that matches the description they have received.

   ## Connecting contrasting ideas

grammar focus   In this activity, Ss use conjunctions to express contrast or concession about a stated fact.

> **Grammar notes** One says *in spite of,* but *despite* (not *despite of*). Both phrases can be followed by a noun or a verb; however, the verb must be in the *-ing* form (e.g., *In spite of working hard,* I failed my exams.).
>
> *Although* and *even though* have the same meaning. Both are always followed by the subject and a verb (e.g., *Although she was falling asleep,* she didn't want to miss the end of the show.). One cannot say *even although.*

continued

However can be used to start a second sentence that contrasts the information in the first sentence and is followed by a comma (e.g., The economy is showing signs of improvement. *However*, the unemployment rate is still too high.).

Nevertheless and *just the same* are always used to express concession and also start the second clause. They are both often followed by a comma (e.g., There are few high-paying jobs in the countryside. *Nevertheless*, many people prefer to live there because of the healthier lifestyle.).

On the other hand can express contrast. It always starts the second clause and is followed by a comma (e.g., Many people in America want an improved health-care system. *On the other hand*, they don't want to pay more taxes.).

1   Books closed. Ask Ss to come up with pairs of positive and negative statements about the city they live in (e.g. "There's a lot to do at night." or "Everything is very expensive.").

2   Have selected Ss share their pairs of statements with the class, and write them on the board. Have Ss try to link the statements together.

3   Books open. Lead Ss through the information and sentences in the grammar box, explaining meaning as necessary.

4   Ask Ss if they can use the connectors listed to connect any of the pairs of statements written on the board during the warm-up phase. Guide Ss through a few examples.

5   Explain the task. Then have Ss choose the word in the first sentence that best fits their situation and complete the second sentence with their own information.

Possible answers

1. There are many job opportunities in my town. Nevertheless, the salaries aren't very good.
    There are few job opportunities in my town. Nevertheless, they are very high-paying jobs.
2. My city has many concerts. However, they tend to be quite expensive.
    My city has few concerts. However, it has some excellent museums.
3. I'd prefer living in a city located in the mountains, even though it would get very cold in the winter.
    I'd prefer living in a city located on the seashore, even though it would get crowded with tourists in the summer.
4. My city offers many different cultural activities. On the other hand, it doesn't have many nice restaurants.
    My city doesn't offer many different cultural activities. On the other hand, it offers a lot of other kinds of entertainment.
5. I feel that the crime rate in my city is high. However, people don't seem to worry that much about it.
    I feel that the crime rate in my city is average. However, people seem

to feel it's safe to go out at night.

I feel that the crime rate in my city is low. However, people still need to be careful.

6. The winter weather in my town is very pleasant. Nevertheless, we don't get many visitors at that time of year.

The summer weather in my town is very pleasant. Nevertheless, many residents travel to other places at that time of year.

7. There is a lot of open space in my town. However, most people live fairly close together.

There isn't a lot of open space in my town. However, the beach is very close by.

8. I would really enjoy living in a big city, in spite of the noise.

I would really enjoy living in a small town, in spite of having to commute a long way to work.

 My hometown

discussion   In this activity, Ss compare their opinions of their hometowns.

Pair work

Books open. Explain the task and have Ss read the model dialog. Then put Ss in pairs to compare the sentences they wrote in Exercise 4. Encourage Ss to ask and answer follow-up questions.

6 *Life in New York City*

listening

In this activity, Ss focus on listening for specific information on quality-of-life issues.

1 Books closed. Explain to Ss that "quality-of-life" issues include things like the cost of living, job opportunities, safety and crime, and weather. Brainstorm with Ss several other quality-of-life issues, and write a list on the board.

2 Tell Ss they will hear two New Yorkers talk about quality-of-life issues in their city. Ask Ss to predict some of the issues they might discuss. Have Ss call out some possibilities.

3 **Optional:** Pre-teach any items from the following vocabulary you think will be helpful for your Ss:

> **shock** a feeling of surprise (usually unpleasant) about something unexpected
> **graffiti** illegal writing and drawing on walls of buildings and public transportation
> **sick and tired (of)** irritated and annoyed (by something)

4 Books open. Have Ss look at the chart, and remind them to fill it in using note form. Replay the audio program while Ss listen and complete the chart. Then have Ss compare their answers with a partner, replaying the audio program if necessary. Go over the answers as a class.

Possible answers

	Quality-of-life issues	How they feel about them
Lindsay	subways on-schedule	pleased
	noise from garbage trucks	unhappy; they wake her up in the morning
	nightlife: theater and restaurants	excited; wants to do everything
Eric	cleanliness and safety	thinks the city has improved in these areas
	cold weather	tired of it; ready for a change

Transcript

What quality-of-life issues are these New Yorkers talking about? How do they feel about them?

Lindsay: So, Eric, how long have you lived in New York?

Eric: All my life. I was born here. Sounds like you're new in town.

Lindsay: Two months. I just moved here from Michigan.

Eric: Wow! That's a big change. New York must be quite a shock.

Lindsay: Well, not exactly. I lived here once before, when I went to graduate school. So, I . . . I guess you could say that I'm used to life in New York, if that's possible.

Eric: When did you live here?

Lindsay: Oh, let's see, . . . it must have been about eight years ago. Boy, the city sure has changed since then.

Eric: I suppose so. I mean, they've really cleaned up Times Square. It used to be so dirty. I mean, now it's just full of tourists.

Lindsay: Yeah. And the subways seem to run more on schedule now.

Eric: Basically, I think the city is safer anywhere you go, probably because we have so many more police officers on the street.

Lindsay: Oh, that's for sure! You know, though, one thing I can't get used to is the noise – especially those garbage trucks! They come at five in the morning and are so loud. The noise wakes me up every time!

Eric: I guess I've lived here so long I don't hear it anymore. I can sleep through just about anything. You know the one thing I am tired of – the weather. I mean, I'm so sick and tired of these long, cold winters. I'm thinking about moving next year.

Lindsay: Really?

Eric: Yeah. I mean, like I said, I've lived here all my life, and I feel like I need some kind of change. You know, a new environment. It's time to get out of New York.

Lindsay: Hmm. Not me! I love the nightlife: the theater and the great restaurants. I can't wait to get out and discover all that New York is offering!

Optional activity: *Role play*

Time: 10–15 minutes. Ss talk about quality-of-life issues in New York City, followed by quality-of-life issues in their own hometowns and cities.

1 *Pair work* Books open. Make a three-column chart on the board with the following headings: *Topics, Lindsay, Eric.* List the following topics under the *Topics* heading: *Times Square, subways, safety, noise, weather, recreation,* and *culture.* Tell Ss to copy the chart onto a piece of paper.

2 Replay the audio program. Have Ss listen again to what each person says about these topics and make notes in their charts.

Answers

Topics	Lindsay	Eric
Times Square		cleaned it up, full of tourists
Subways	cleaner, less graffiti, likes riding them	
Safety		more police officers on streets, safer
Noise	garbage trucks wake her up at 5:00 A.M.	
Weather		sick of long, cold winters
Recreation	loves nightlife and restaurants	
Culture	loves the theater	

3 Put Ss in pairs to role-play the situation. Have Ss choose whether they are Lindsay or Eric (changing the gender of the names, as required). Tell Ss to use their charts to discuss their feelings about New York City. Then have Ss use the topics in the chart to talk about their own hometowns or cities with their partners.

 Quality-of-life issues

discussion In these activities, Ss learn vocabulary related to quality-of-life issues and share opinions about each issue's importance.

A

1 Books open. Explain the task and have Ss read the categories in the chart, explaining meaning as needed. Check that Ss understand the following vocabulary items:

> **intercity travel** travel between different cities
> **sanitation services** garbage removal service provided by a city or town
> **unemployment rate** the number of people looking for jobs who cannot find work

2 Have Ss work individually to categorize the issues and add four more of their own. Then put Ss in pairs to compare answers before going over them as a class.

Answers

art and culture	city services	climate/environment	cost of living
museums	hospitals	air quality	food prices
public libraries	sanitation services	humidity	taxes
radio stations	schools	sunny days	
safety and crime	**jobs**	**recreation**	**transportation**
neighborhood safety	unemployment rate	good restaurants	commuting time
		nightlife	intercity travel
		parks	

B Pair work

1 Books open. Have Ss look at the two photos and call out the quality-of-life issues pictured (answers: public transportation and pollution). Ask Ss to say which issue is more important to them personally. Explain the task and have Ss put a check (✓) beside the three most important quality-of-life issues in Exercise 7A.

2 Go over the sample language in the balloon, and then put Ss in pairs to discuss their opinions.

3 Have several Ss share their most important factors with the class. Lead a class discussion.

Optional activity: *Designing ad campaigns*

Time: 10–15 minutes. Ss talk further about important quality-of-life issues.

1 *Group work* Books open. Put Ss in groups of four or five, and tell them that they've been asked to provide information for a brochure advertising the city or town where you are. Tell Ss they have 5 minutes to agree on the five most attractive features of their city (e.g., good restaurants or low cost of living). Assign a secretary to record the group's ideas.

2 Have a spokesperson for each group share their groups' ideas with the class. List ideas on the board to use as the basis for a class discussion.

3 **Optional:** Have the entire class work together to agree on your city's five most attractive features.

reading In these activities, Ss practice reading for gist and giving opinions about ideas in a text.

Books closed. Ask Ss if they prefer to travel with a group or on their own. Have Ss indicate their choice with a show of hands. Then ask if any Ss have concerns about getting lost when they travel. Put the title of the reading, *Get Yourself Lost,* on the board, and ask Ss why a traveler might actually want to get lost. Have several Ss suggest reasons, or put Ss in pairs to brainstorm ideas.

A Pair work

1 **Optional:** Books open. Have Ss skim the text to confirm their predictions.

2 Have Ss look at the picture and say what they see. Then put Ss in pairs to read and discuss the questions.

3 Have Ss silently read the article to compare their ideas with those of the author. Tell Ss to underline new words they feel they need to know to understand the text. Go over definitions when Ss have finished reading.

B Group work

1 Books open. Have Ss read the four questions. Then put Ss in small groups to discuss them.

2 Have several Ss share answers with the class.

Optional activity: *Traveler's tales*

Time: 10–15 minutes. Ss compare the ideas of the reading to their own experiences.

1 *Group work* Books open. Have Ss think about the last time they visited a foreign or unfamiliar city. Tell them to look through the suggestions in the text and think about whether they followed any of them. If so, what were the results? If not, tell them to think about how their trip might have been different if they had, and which suggestions would have worked well for them.

2 Put Ss in groups of three to discuss their travel experiences as they apply to the suggestions in the text.

Students review ways of talking about personal likes and dislikes, making choices about education and learning, and features of city life. They also review the use of gerunds; noun clauses after *be*, *should*, and *ought to* in the active and passive; infinitives to talk about how to do things; *in order to* and *so that*; and defining and non-defining relative clauses.

1 *Gerunds*

In these activities, Ss review verbs followed by either gerunds or infinitives to talk about likes and dislikes.

A

1 Books closed. Write *doing* and *to do/doing* on the board. Ask Ss if they can remember which verbs are followed by gerunds and which are followed by either infinitives or gerunds. Have Ss call out a few verbs as you write them in the appropriate column.

2 Books open. Explain the task and have Ss read the verbs and complete the chart. Then put Ss in pairs to compare answers before going over them as a class.

Answers

> **Gerunds:** avoid, dislike, don't mind, enjoy
> **Gerunds or infinitives:** can't stand, hate, like, love

B

1 Books open. Explain the task and have Ss read the list of topics. Have the class brainstorm specific types of books, hobbies, movies, and music, and write them on the board. Give Ss a minute to think of how they feel about the topics listed.

2 Have Ss read the example, pointing out the additional sentence. Have Ss individually write sentences about topics before putting them in pairs to take turns talking about their feelings. Encourage Ss to ask follow-up questions. Then have selected Ss share their feelings with the class.

Possible answers

> I avoid reading scary books at night because I can't fall asleep.
> I enjoy playing soccer. It's great exercise and a very exciting game.
> I hate to watch action movies because they are so violent.
> I love to go to summer jazz concerts in the park. The music is excellent, and the concerts are free.

Optional activity: *I just hate . . .*

Time: 10–15 minutes. Ss prepare short quizzes using verbs followed by gerunds or infinitives.

Pair work Books open. Put Ss in pairs to make up five sentences that use the verbs in Exercise A. On a sheet of paper have pairs write their sentences with blank spaces where the verbs should be. Tell Ss to add information as needed so that it is clear which verb belongs in each blank. Provide this example: "I _____ swimming in the ocean. It's one of my favorite pastimes." Have Ss write the list of the five verbs needed below the sentences. Then have pairs exchange quizzes with another pair. After completing them, have pairs return the quizzes and check each other's work.

2   Noun clauses after be

In these activities, Ss review noun clauses after *be* and expressions used to talk about negative and positive aspects of various issues.

A

Books open. Explain the task and have Ss fill in the appropriate prepositions.

Answers

an advantage/disadvantage *of*	the best/worst thing *about*	a problem *with*

B Pair work

Books open. Explain the task and have Ss read the list of six items and the model language in the speech balloon. Tell Ss to write their sentences using the language presented in Exercise 2A. Circulate to observe problems and offer assistance. Then put Ss in pairs to compare answers. Encourage Ss to give reasons and examples, and to ask each other follow-up questions.

Possible answers

1. An advantage of being self-employed is that you don't have a boss.
2. The worst thing about being the oldest child is that you have to look after your brothers and sisters.
3. A problem with having long hair is that it takes a long time to dry.
4. The best thing about having roommates is that there is always someone to talk to.
5. A disadvantage of owning a car is that you have to spend money on gas and repairs.
6. The worst thing about owning a dog is that you have to take it for a walk every day, even when the weather is cold and rainy.

Optional activity: *Who's got the advantage?*

Time: 5–10 minutes. Ss listen to each other and determine whether they hear positive or negative evaluations.

1 *Group work* Books open. Write on the board:

In my extended family, there is always someone to help out with the chores.
So many people want to go to universities in my country that they are very difficult to get into.

Ask Ss whether advantages or disadvantages, good or bad things, or problems have been expressed. Tell Ss to write three sentences: one describing an advantage or disadvantage, one describing a good or bad thing, and one describing a problem – but without using those words. Tell Ss they can use the topics in Exercise B or any of the topics in Units 1 to 3.

2 Divide Ss into groups of four or five. Tell each group to check their members' sentences for accuracy and choose the ten best. Circulate to check the ten sentences. Help them to correct the incorrect ones.

3 Bring three or four groups together, and have them sit facing each other. Explain that one group says one of their sentences while the other groups decide if they can change it, using the correct evaluative noun, to have a noun-clause-after-*be* structure as in Exercise B. As soon as they think they can do it, they should raise their hands. If the sentence is correct, the group gets a point. If it is not, the other group gets a chance. The group with the most points wins.

Should *and* ought to *in the active and passive*

In these activities, Ss use *should* and *ought to* in the active and passive to talk about schooling.

A

Books open. Explain the task and ask Ss when the passive is used instead of the active (answer: the passive is used when the emphasis is on the action, and the active is used when the emphasis is on the person doing the action). Have Ss read the statements and rewrite them in the passive while you circulate to check Ss' progress. If necessary, do the first one with the class as an example. Then put Ss in pairs to compare answers before going over them as a class; have selected Ss or volunteers come to the board to write one of their sentences.

Answers

> **1.** Foreign languages should be taught from an early age.
> **2.** Students should be required to wear school uniforms.
> **3.** Some courses ought to be taught over the Internet in high school.
> **4.** More teachers should be recruited from other countries.
> **5.** Classes ought to be offered on the weekends.

B Pair work

1 Books open. Explain the task and give Ss a couple of minutes to think about whether they agree or disagree with each statement and why. Then put Ss in pairs to discuss their opinions. Encourage Ss to give reasons and examples to support their opinions and to ask follow-up questions.

2 **Optional:** On the board, tally the number of Ss who agree and disagree with each statement, and use this information as the basis for a class discussion.

3 Have selected Ss tell the class their reasons for agreeing or disagreeing with a particular statement.

Infinitives and gerunds to talk about how to do things

In these activities, Ss use infinitives and gerunds to talk about how to achieve goals.

A

Books open. Put Ss in pairs to look at the photograph and describe what they see, to say what these people are doing, and to speculate on why they are doing it (answer: for exercise and enjoyment). Explain the task and have Ss read the example. Then have Ss complete the sentences two ways using infinitives or gerund phrases. Don't go over the answers until after Exercise B.

B Pair work

Books open. Explain the task and put Ss in pairs to compare and discuss their answers. Encourage Ss to give reasons and examples where relevant, and to ask each other follow-up questions. Then have pairs share their best ideas with the class.

Possible answers

1. The best way to get fit is by walking 20 minutes a day.
   The best way to get fit is to join a health club and exercise regularly.
2. One way to improve your English is to make a lot of English-speaking friends.
   One way to improve your English is by reading English language newspapers in your free time.
3. The only way to give up smoking is by stopping completely and never having another cigarette.
   The only way to give up smoking is to use hypnotism or other alternative therapies.
4. A good way to have a fun vacation is to travel with a big group of friends.
   A good way to have a fun vacation is by going to the beach and forgetting about your work.

In this activity, Ss review the use of *in order to* and *so that* to introduce a reason or purpose for doing something.

A

1 Books closed. Write the following on the board: *I'm studying accounting in order to get a better job. I'm studying accounting so that I can get a better job.* Have Ss say what the differences are between the structures following the phrases *in order to* and *so that* (answer: *in order to* is followed by a verb and *so that* is followed by a pronoun + modal).

2 Books open. Explain the task and have Ss complete the sentences using either *in order to* or *so that* while you circulate to observe Ss' competence. Have Ss compare answers in pairs before going over them as a class.

Answers

> **1.** Many people buy computers *so that* they can use the Internet.
> **2.** Some people join health clubs *in order to* meet people.
> **3.** People often take night classes *so that* they can find a better job.
> **4.** People sometimes like to work overseas *in order to* learn about another culture.

B Pair work

Books open. Explain the task and have Ss rewrite the sentences so that they are true for themselves. Then put Ss in pairs to compare and discuss their sentences. Have Ss report on any particularly interesting sentences their partner has written.

Optional activity: *Chain gang drill*

Time: 5–10 minutes. Ss continue to practice using *in order to* and *so that* to express reason or purpose.

Class activity Books closed. Have Ss sit in a circle (divide large classes into two groups). Explain that one S in the circle starts by saying a sentence using either *in order to* or *so that.* The S to the right makes another sentence with either *in order to* or *so that* using the content of the second clause. For example, one person says, "I bought a new suit *in order to* wear it for job interviews." Then the next person says, "I needed a new job *so that* I could make more money." Explain that if the second clause of a S's sentence is not correct, that S is out of the game. Begin the game and after a few minutes, add the element of speed by having Ss clap rhythmically and continuously. Explain that Ss must say their next sentence before the sixth clap or they are out.

Defining and non-defining relative clauses

In these activities, Ss review the differences between defining and non-defining relative clauses.

Books closed. Write the following sentences on the board: *Florida, which is known for its warm winters, always has many tourists over the winter months. Florida is the state that is known throughout the U.S. for its warm winters.* Put Ss in pairs to discuss the differences between the structure of these two sentences. Ask Ss which sentence has a defining relative clause and which has a non-defining relative clause (answer: the second sentence and the first sentence respectively).

A

1 Books open. Explain the task and have Ss read the sentences. Check that Ss understand the following vocabulary items:

> **skyline** a pattern made against the sky, especially by buildings
> **bustling** full of busy activity
> **canal** a manmade waterway

2 Have Ss match the information in the two columns, and then read the example before making sentences with non-defining relative clauses. Point out that for most of the sentences, either clause could be made into the main clause or into the non-defining relative clause, depending on what information the speaker wants to stress. Then put Ss in pairs to compare answers before going over them as a class.

Possible answers

> 1. (c) New York, which is famous for its skyline, is home to the Empire State Building.
>   New York, which is home to the Empire State Building, is famous for its skyline.
> 2. (e) Moscow, which has artistic subway stations, is the largest city in Russia.
>   Moscow, which is the largest city in Russia, has artistic subway stations.
> 3. (a) Tokyo, which is the business center of Japan, is bustling with crowds day and night.
>   Tokyo, which is bustling with crowds day and night, is the business center of Japan.
> 4. (f) Sydney, which is well known for its Opera House, is also famous for its Harbour Bridge.
>   Sydney, which is famous for its Harbour Bridge, is also well known for its Opera House.
> 5. (d) Venice, which is built on 118 small islands, is crossed by many canals.
>   Venice, which is crossed by many canals, is built on 118 small islands.
> 6. (b) Honolulu, which has a warm climate all year round, is a favorite winter destination for tourists.
>   Honolulu, which is a favorite winter destination for tourists, has a warm climate all year round.

B

Books open. Explain the task and have Ss complete the sentences with information about places they know using defining relative clauses.

Possible answers

1. My country's capital city is an exciting place where there are many things to see and do.
2. Paris is a romantic city that is beautiful in any season.
3. Hong Kong is a cosmopolitan city where you can find people from all over the world.

7 Likes and dislikes

In this activity, Ss continue using gerunds and infinitives to talk about their personal likes and dislikes.

Pair work

Books open. Explain the task and have Ss read the sample dialog. Then have Ss read the five topics. Give Ss a couple of minutes to think of personal examples for each topic before putting them in pairs to share their responses. Encourage Ss to respond to each other's statements. Have selected Ss each share one of their personal likes or dislikes with the class.

8 This option is better for me.

In this activity, Ss practice using noun clauses after *be* to talk about the advantages and disadvantages of different learning styles.

Pair work

Books open. Explain the task and have Ss read the model language in the speech balloon. Put Ss in pairs to discuss the advantages and disadvantages of the situations listed. Tell them to make notes of the ones they prefer and why. Then have selected pairs share their preferences and their reasons with the class.

9 Hidden benefits

In this activity, Ss practice using the grammar and vocabulary of the lesson to discuss the benefits of studying a variety of subjects.

Pair work

1 Books open. Put Ss in pairs to look at the two photographs and say what each person is doing (answer: computer programming and public speaking). Explain the task and have Ss read the list of study areas. Then have Ss read

the model language in the box and in the speech balloons. Tell Ss to have a short discussion with their partner about the value of studying any of these topics. Circulate to observe Ss' progress and to encourage the use of the language in the box.

2   Have selected Ss or volunteers share their thoughts on one topic with the class. Lead a brief class discussion about each topic.

Optional activity: *Different needs*

Time: 5–10 minutes. Ss continue discussing the value of studying these topics from different career perspectives.

1   *Group work* Books open. Put Ss in groups of three or four, and tell them to discuss what kind of people might need or want to study each of the areas listed in Exercise 9 (e.g., a person training to work in the travel business might want to learn foreign languages in order to be more effective in his or her job). Circulate to help Ss with vocabulary and to encourage them to explain their choices.

2   Have selected groups share answers with the class.

10   The People's Action Committee

In this activity, Ss make recommendations for improving their city.

A Pair work

1   Books closed. Ask Ss where they would go to make recommendations for improving their city (answer: the city council). Then ask Ss what kinds of tasks and issues city council members work on. Have Ss call out their answers while you write them on the board.

2   Books open. Explain the task and point out the picture of a main street in a typical small town in the United States. Then have Ss read the model language in the box and in the speech balloon.

3   Put Ss in pairs to make a list of improvements they think their own city needs. Then have Ss practice presenting the items on their list to each other with reasons and background information. Suggest that they use *should* and *ought to*.

B Group work

Books open. Explain the task and then combine pairs to form groups of four to present their recommendations to each other. Encourage group members to ask follow-up questions. Each group chooses the four most interesting recommendations to present to the class. Write these recommendations on the board, and lead a class discussion about the best ones.

Optional activity: *City council members*

Time: 15–20 minutes. Ss prioritize the recommendations for their city.

Group work Books closed. Explain that Ss are members of a city council and that the council, which has limited funds for city improvements, must choose the two most important projects. Set an appropriate monetary limit, and put Ss in groups of six or seven, and have them decide which two projects will get their money and why. Tell them to write down the amount of money they think these projects will require. When they are ready, have them present their proposals to the class. Write the recommendations and costs on the board for the purpose of comparison. Then, when all the groups are finished, lead a class discussion about the projects that were chosen, and whether or not the costs were realistic.

1 *Welcome to my city.*

In this activity, Ss use the vocabulary and grammar structures reviewed to talk about favorite places to visit in their city.

Group work

Books open. Have Ss look at the photograph and the model language in the speech balloon. Ask Ss, "If you were visiting this city, would you want to visit this church?" Explain the task and put Ss in groups of four or five to choose the three most interesting places to visit in their city and why. Have groups present their places and reasons to the class.

This unit introduces the themes of personal energy levels, sleep, and dreams. Students talk about ways to avoid tiredness and stress, using adverbs of time. They also use adverb clauses of reason and condition to talk about sleeping habits and dreams.

Lesson A *Your energy profile*

What's your best time of day?

starting point   These activities introduce Ss to the topic of personal energy levels and corresponding personality types.

A

1 Books closed. Ask the class questions such as: "Do you have more energy in the morning or the afternoon? Do you ever take naps in the afternoon? Do you find you do your best work late at night?" Have Ss answer each question with a show of hands.

2 On the board, write the words *early bird, night owl,* and *catnapper.* Ask Ss to guess the meaning of these phrases, and have selected Ss share their ideas with the class (answers: An early bird is someone who gets up early in the day and feels best before noon. A night owl stays up late and has lots of energy when most other people are in bed. A catnapper often sneaks short daytime naps into his/her schedule.)

3 Books open. Explain the task and have Ss scan the texts to see who is an early bird (Cecilia), a night owl (Yuri), and a catnapper (Jennifer). Then put Ss in pairs to come up with a term to describe Tetsuo.

4 Have Ss silently reread the four texts to determine which of the four people they are most similar to. Check that Ss understand the following vocabulary items:

> **to sneak** to do something secretly [often used as *sneak around, sneak up on, sneak out of*]
>
> **spurt** a sudden burst of something
>
> **to concentrate** to focus attention on a particular activity, subject, or problem

5 Ss discuss their answers with a partner. Encourage them to give reasons for their choices. Then have several Ss share their answers with the class.

B Pair work

1 Books closed. Ask the class, "What's the best time of day for you to study for an exam?" Have selected Ss answer.

2 Books open. Explain the task and go over the information in the chart, making sure Ss understand the following vocabulary items:

> **creative** imaginative, artistic
> **vigorous** energetic, very active

3 Ss work alone to fill in the chart and then read the sample dialog. Put Ss in pairs to share answers and discuss their best times of day for doing the activities. Ask a few Ss to share their answers with the class.

Optional activity: *More on birds, owls, and cats*

Time: 5–10 minutes. Ss further explore the three different personality types within the framework of personal energy profiles.

1 *Group work* Books open or closed. Take a survey to find out how many early birds, night owls, and catnappers there are in the class, writing the numbers on the board.

2 Put Ss in groups of like types to discuss coping strategies. For example, ask early birds what they do when they have to work late, night owls how they cope with having to work or study in the early morning, and catnappers how they manage to sneak their naps.

3 A spokesperson from each group reports back to the class.

 The time is right.

discussion   In this discussion activity, Ss compare their answers in Exercise 1B with additional information on the topic.

Pair Work

1 **Optional:** Have Ss number the activities in Exercise 1B from 1 to 5. Then have Ss quickly scan the text and write the number of the activity from 1B next to the appropriate advice. Go over the answers with the class.

2 Books open. Explain the task. Check that Ss understand the following vocabulary items:

> **alert** wide awake and ready to act
> **to dip** to go down; to decrease

3 Have Ss silently read the information and underline any advice they agree with. Then put Ss in pairs to discuss their opinions about the advice they read, and whether the information in the text makes them think differently about any of their answers in Exercise 1B.

4 Have several Ss share one or more answers with the class. Encourage Ss to give reasons for their answers. Lead a class discussion.

Time relationships

grammar focus This grammar focus presents adverbs of time, which show the chronological relationship between two clauses or parts or a sentence.

> **Grammar notes** Although adverbs of time are presented in the grammar focus as occurring at the beginning of a sentence, this is not always the case. An adverb of time can come either at the beginning of a sentence (*As soon as* I get up, I get dressed and race off to work.) or at the beginning of the second clause of a sentence (I get dressed and race off to work *as soon as* I get up.) without any change in meaning. When the adverb of time begins the second clause, no comma is needed.
>
> The subject can be omitted with *while, after,* and *before,* in which case the verb takes the gerund form (e.g., *while working, after finishing work, before going to bed*).

1 Books closed. Write the first clause of each of the sentences in the grammar box on the board. Then ask Ss to complete each sentence with information that is true for them, and write this on the board (e.g., *As soon as I wake up, I brush my teeth.*). Remind Ss that adverbs of time show a chronological relationship between two actions in a sentence, answering the question "When?"

2 Books open. Go over the sentences in the grammar box, explaining meaning and providing additional explanations as necessary. Check that Ss understand the following vocabulary item:

> **exhausted** extremely tired

Pair work

1 Books open. Explain the task and ask Ss to look at the photographs. Have selected Ss make sentences about the photographs using the adverbs of time in the grammar box.

2 Have Ss read the eight items. Point out that the first four sentences have the adverb clause in the initial position, and that the second four sentences have the adverb clause as the beginning of the second clause. Ask Ss to deduce the rule about the comma (answer: no comma is needed when the adverb clause starts the second clause).

3 Ss individually complete each sentence with information that is true for them, as you circulate to help and check for accuracy. Have Ss read the sample dialog, pointing out the follow-up questions. In pairs, have Ss take turns reading their sentences to each other. Encourage them to ask and answer follow-up questions.

4 Either have selected Ss share an answer with the class or have selected Ss tell the class the most interesting thing they learned about their partner.

Possible answers

1. As soon as I wake up in the morning, I make a pot of coffee.
2. Whenever I have trouble concentrating on something, I stand up and stretch.
3. While working on a very difficult task, I never answer the phone.
4. After I've stayed out too late in the evening, I can't get up the next day.
5. I become really exhausted whenever I have too much to do.
6. I can never concentrate after not getting enough sleep.
7. I don't feel awake in the morning until I take a shower.
8. I think it's a good idea to take a short nap whenever you feel sleepy.

Optional activity: *Substitution*

Time: 5 minutes. Ss further manipulate and practice adverbs in time clauses.

1 *Pair work* Books open. Write the first sentence in the grammar box on the board. Then ask Ss to change it so that the time clause is in the second clause rather than in the initial position. Write it on the board.

2 Have Ss, working in pairs, change the remaining sentences in the grammar box. Go over them as a class. Then tell Ss to change the positions of the clauses in the eight sentences they wrote in the pair work exercise.

More or less energy?

discussion Ss are presented with vocabulary for activities that raise or lower energy levels. Ss share ideas about what they do when they need to increase or decrease their energy.

A

1 Books closed. On the board write *Activities that raise energy levels* and *Activities that lower energy levels*. Ask the class to call out activities for either category. Write all suggested ideas in the appropriate category on the board.

2 Books open. Explain the task and have Ss read the list of activities. Explain any new vocabulary as needed, including the following:

> **an argument** an angry disagreement
> **brisk** fast and energetic

3 Have Ss individually complete the chart and add ideas of their own. Tell Ss that certain activities are open to interpretation, so if they disagree with one another, they should be ready to give reasons for their opinions. Then have Ss call out their answers. Write these on the board, and discuss any differences of opinion.

Suggested answers (Note: Ss answers may vary.)

Activities that raise energy levels	Activities that lower energy levels
doing vigorous exercise	eating a large meal
drinking strong coffee	playing video games
eating a chocolate bar	sleeping late in the morning
having an argument	taking a hot bath
taking an afternoon nap	watching television
taking a brisk walk	
taking a cold shower	

B Group work

1 Books open. Explain the task and have Ss read the questions and sample language. Then put Ss in groups of four or five to share and discuss their ideas.

2 Each group shares their best suggestions with the class.

3 **Optional:** Write the suggestions on the board to create a class list. Then have Ss vote on the best suggestion for each question.

5 *Managing stress*

listening

In these activities, Ss think about ways to reduce stress and listen for specific information about the causes of stress and stress-reducing methods.

A Class activity

1 Books closed. Ask the Ss if they know what *stress* is, and have them call out their ideas. If Ss know the meaning of the word, ask them to call out some causes of stress and the methods they use to reduce stress. Write them on the board.

2 Books open. Read the first sentence, which expresses the relationship between stress and fatigue and a lack of energy, and explain the task.

3 **Optional:** Pre-teach any of the following vocabulary items that might be of help to your Ss:

> **herbal tea** tea made from herbs and spices
>
> **massage** the action of pressing and rubbing a person's body to relieve pain and/or stress
>
> **to meditate** to focus attention on one thing and not think of anything else (may be done for religious training or relaxation)
>
> **to vent your feelings** to express your feelings to others

4 Have Ss check (✓) the things they do to reduce stress and add other suggestions to the list. Then ask several Ss to share their suggestions with the class. Lead a class discussion.

B

1 Books open. Explain that Ss will listen to three people talk about the causes of stress and the methods they use to reduce stress. Play the audio program once, and have Ss listen only. Put Ss in pairs to discuss what they heard.

2 **Optional:** Go over any items from the following vocabulary list that you think will help your Ss:

> **freelance writer** a self-employed writer who does work for various companies
> **office politics** the interactions between a group of people who work together, resulting in some people having more power than others
> **disciplined** hardworking and self-controlled
> **self-motivated** not relying on other people to make you do things
> **tremendous** extremely large
> **under pressure** pushed to finish something quickly, which causes a feeling of stress
> **to cope with** to deal with, to handle [often used to talk about stressful situations]
> **to be addicted (to something)** to be unable to stop doing or using (something) [often used to discuss negative or self-destructive habits]
> **to do wonders for someone** to make someone feel better, refreshed

3 Replay the audio program, and have Ss individually complete the chart. Remind them to fill in the chart in note form. Then have Ss compare answers with a partner.

Answers

	Frequent cause of stress	Method of lowering stress
Lisa	job is hard; has to be organized, disciplined, and self-motivated	takes a hot bath, watches TV, drinks tea
Sean	traffic, rude drivers	listens to music in car, watches funny movie, goes to friend's house
Victor	demanding doctors, pressured people	goes to gym, goes for a drive in the country

Transcript

> **Listen to the methods Lisa, Sean, and Victor use to lower stress. Complete the chart and then compare with a partner. Which of these methods would work best for you?**
>
> **Lisa:** Uh, well, I'm a freelance writer, and that means that I work at home. And a lot of people think my job is easier because I don't have to go to the office every day. And I don't have to deal with office politics. But, you know, the truth is, my job is very hard. I have to be very organized and very disciplined. And pretty self-motivated. And when I have a problem, there is no one around to help me – I have to solve it myself. And sometimes I worry about money.

So when I get stressed, I take a hot bath to relax, and then I curl up in front of the TV with a cup of hot tea. And that usually does the trick at the end of a long and very hard day.

Sean: Traffic stresses me out. I do a lot of driving to school and to my part-time job. Drivers can be so rude, especially during rush hour. I try to ignore them by listening to my favorite music in the car. Then, when I get home, I try to do something fun to relax. I'll watch a funny movie or go to a friend's house – something like that. Anything to take my mind off school and work.

Victor: I work in the hospital emergency room. You can imagine how stressful that is! Everyone is in a hurry and under tremendous pressure. The doctors are demanding, and there's always too much to do. I cope with all this stress by going to the gym at least four times a week. My friend got me started weight lifting, and now I'm addicted. When I feel especially frustrated, it feels good to go to the gym and throw those weights around.

The other thing I do is get out of the city. Every month or so, I go for a drive in the country. The fresh air and the quiet do wonders for me.

Optional activity: *Details, details*

Time: 5 minutes. Ss listen intensively for details.

Books open. Ss listen again – this time for the specific factors causing each person's stress – and write the factors on a sheet of paper. Replay the audio program while Ss take notes. Then go over the answers as a class.

Answers

Lisa: having to be organized, disciplined, and self-motivated; having to solve all problems on her own; worrying about money

Sean: rude drivers, rush hour traffic

Victor: hospital emergency room work, everyone in a hurry, demanding doctors, pressure, too much to do

C Pair work

1 Books open. Explain the task and then put Ss in pairs to take turns telling their partner about the most stressful and relaxing things in their life. Partners offer suggestions for lowering stress.

2 After 5 to 10 minutes, ask several pairs to share their best ideas for lowering stress with the class.

3 **Optional:** Tell Ss to compare their causes of stress to those of Lisa, Sean, and Victor. Put them back in pairs to use their charts to discuss how they would cope with the problems they heard on the audio program.

6   *I need some advice.*

role play   In this activity, Ss describe problems and offer advice.

Pair work

1   Books closed. Ask Ss if they ever listen to radio call-in programs, where people call in to talk about their problems and the radio host offers advice. If Ss have listened to shows like this, ask what kinds of call-in shows they've listened to and what the shows are usually like. Explain that Ss will take turns playing the roles of host and caller on a radio call-in program about stress and energy levels.

2   Books open. Explain the task and have Ss silently read the four problems and the sample dialog. Put Ss in pairs to take turns playing the role of radio host and caller. Remind Ss playing the roles of host to suggest advice they might give the caller for each of the problems.

3   Have selected pairs act out a call for the class.

4   **Optional:** Have Ss share their best ideas for each problem with the class.

7   *Choosing the best topic sentence*

writing   In these activities, Ss practice writing effective and interesting topic sentences that express the main idea of a paragraph without being too general or specific.

1   Books closed. Conduct a quick review of what Ss already know about topic sentences and main ideas. Have Ss call out anything they remember, and list this information on the board.

2   Books open. Lead Ss through the information in the box about topic sentences, and provide additional explanation and examples as needed. Explain that a good topic sentence contains an interesting idea that can be supported by the sentences following it.

A

1   Books open. Explain the task and have Ss read the topic sentences and the two questions following the reading. Then have Ss read the paragraph and choose the best topic sentence.

2   Check that Ss understand the following vocabulary item:

> **to drag (yourself through something)**   to move slowly and with difficulty (through something)

3   Put Ss in pairs to compare and discuss answers before going over the answers with the class.

Answer

> The best topic sentence for this paragraph is *The world is divided into two types of people: "morning people" and "night people."* The first choice, *There are many different kinds of people in the world,* is too general. The third choice, *A 24-hour day is not long enough for some people,* does not relate to the other sentences in the paragraph. The fourth choice, *Almost everyone knows someone who's a "morning person,"* is too specific because it does not cover the part of the paragraph that discusses "night people."

B

1 Books closed. Ask Ss if they know what aromatherapy is. Give Ss this definition: *Aromatherapy is a form of therapy in which pleasant smelling oils are rubbed into the skin, or the vapors they produce are breathed in, to increase feelings of relaxation and reduce stress.*

2 **Optional:** Another way of warming up is to list on the board words and phrases such as *pleasant smell, peppermint candle, soak in the bath, bath oils, smell your way to a more relaxed state,* and have Ss use these cues to come up with a definition for aromatherapy.

3 Books open. Explain the task and then have Ss silently read the paragraph about aromatherapy. Have Ss write an effective and interesting topic sentence that supports the main idea. Circulate to provide guidance and check for accuracy.

4 Check that Ss understand the following vocabulary items:

> **aromatherapy** the use of pleasant scents as a treatment for stress
> **scents** odors
> **tranquility** peacefulness
> **peppermint** a plant with sweet, spicy leaves used for tea and flavoring in candies, tea, and ice cream
> **chamomile** a plant with flowers that are used to make herbal tea that relaxes people
> **tensions** worries

5 Have Ss write their topic sentences (anonymously) on a piece of paper. Mix them up and then choose a few sentences to write on the board. Ask other Ss to comment on whether or not the topic sentences are effective and interesting.

Possible answers

> Aromatherapy is a safe and healthy way to relieve stress and smell your way to relaxation.
> Aromatherapy provides a soothing way to relax.

C

Books open. Explain the task and have Ss read the three suggested topics. Either in class or as homework, have Ss choose a topic and then work alone to write an effective topic sentence and a short paragraph that supports the main idea.

D Group work

1 Books open. Explain the task and put Ss in groups of four or five. Have Ss take turns reading their paragraphs *without* the topic sentence while others in the group try to guess what the topic sentence is.

2 Encourage Ss to suggest ways to make each other's topic sentences more effective and interesting, or ways to support their topic sentences better.

Sweet dreams

Sleep statistics

starting point These activities present statistics regarding sleep patterns in the United States and Canada and have Ss compare their own sleep patterns with the ones presented.

A

1 Books closed. Ask questions such as the following: "How many of you sleep more than 9 hours a night? Who sleeps less than 6 hours a night? Do you ever have problems falling asleep at night? Are you a light sleeper or a heavy sleeper? Do you dream every night?"

2 "Do you remember your dreams?" Use Ss' responses as the basis for a quick class discussion about sleep and dreams.

3 **Alternate presentation:** Tell Ss that the focus of this lesson is sleep and dreams. Put Ss into small groups to write five interesting questions they'd like to ask their classmates about these topics. Then either have groups exchange and answer each other's questions, or have Ss stand and mingle, asking their questions to as many classmates as they can in 5 minutes. Have selected Ss share their most interesting question and answer with the class.

4 Books open. Explain the task and check that Ss understand the following vocabulary items:

> **insomnia** a condition in which you have difficulty sleeping over a period of time
> **insomniacs** people who suffer from insomnia
> **caffeine** the chemical in some foods and drinks, such as chocolate and coffee, that keeps many people awake and active
> **jet lag** the feeling of tiredness after changing time zones as a result of an airplane trip
> **to prescribe drugs** to issue medicines to a patient (by a doctor)

5 Ss silently read through the information in the box and check (✓) the facts that are true for them. Put Ss in pairs to compare answers. Circulate to encourage Ss to ask and answer follow-up questions.

6 Have several Ss tell the class what information in the box is true for them.

B Pair Work

1 Books open. Ask Ss to describe what they see in the photograph. Explain the task and have Ss read the six statements and check (✓) the appropriate boxes.

2 Put Ss in pairs to compare and discuss their answers. Encourage Ss to ask and answer follow-up questions to each statement.

3 After 5 to 10 minutes, have selected Ss share an answer with the class. Lead a class discussion, as appropriate.

Talking about sleep and dreams

vocabulary In these activities, Ss work with collocations associated with sleep and dreams.

A

1 Books closed. Explain that a collocation is a common phrase formed from two or more words that are often used together, in this case, adjectives and nouns. Ask students to fill in the blanks of these sentences or phrases with common collocations:

What a beautiful _____. (day)   *Sweet _____. (dreams)*
Have a nice _____. (day)

2 Books open. Explain the task and have Ss read the list of adjectives and nouns associated with sleep and dreams. Check that Ss understand the following vocabulary items:

> **chronic** continuing for a long time (often used to describe severe or unpleasant situations)
> **vivid** very clear
> **nightmare** a frightening, bad dream
> **snoring** loud breathing noises made while sleeping

3 Have Ss work alone to form as many collocations as they can from the adjectives and nouns listed. Point out that some of the adjectives can be paired with more than one of the nouns.

4 **Optional:** Give Ss a time limit of 5 minutes, and make the activity a contest, with the winner being the S who comes up with the most collocations within the specified time.

5 Have Ss compare answers with a partner. Go over the answers either by having Ss call out possible collocations while others check to see if they've listed them, or by having Ss write one or more of their collocations on the board.

Answers

chronic insomnia
funny dream
heavy sleeper, heavy snoring
horrible dream, horrible insomnia, horrible nightmare
light nap, light sleeper, light snoring
loud snoring
short dream, short nap
vivid dream, vivid nightmare

B Pair work

1 Books open. Explain the task and have Ss read the sample dialog. Ask Ss to explain the humor. Then pairs take turns asking and answering questions using the collocations they came up with in Exercise 2A.

2 Have selected Ss share their most interesting question and answer with the class.

Optional activity: *Seeking help*

Time: 10 minutes. Ss use the collocations from Exercise 2A and the facts about sleep from Exercise 1 to take turns role playing a patient seeking help from his or her doctor.

1 *Pair work* Books open. Tell Ss to review the facts about sleep in Exercise 1A and the collocations in Exercise 2A to use in a role play between a doctor and a patient with sleep problems. Put Ss in pairs to take turns role playing the doctor/patient situation.

2 Have selected pairs perform the role play for the class.

Clauses stating reasons and conditions

grammar focus

This grammar focus presents adverb clauses used to give reasons or state conditions.

> **Grammar notes** These conjunctive adverbs connect a main clause and an adverb (or subordinate) clause in a sentence. They show an adverbial relationship of reason or condition between two ideas (e.g., We decided to take the bus *because* our car wouldn't start.).
>
> The adverb clause can appear in either the first clause or the second clause of a sentence, without changing the meaning of the sentence (e.g., *Because our car wouldn't start*, we decided to take the bus.).

1 Books closed. Write the first clause of each sentence in the grammar box on the board. Then ask Ss for information to complete each idea. Reword the suggestion, if necessary, to complete the sentence. Write the completions on the board. Underline the adverb in each sentence. Then

ask Ss the following questions: Which word shows the consequences of something happening? (answer: *unless*) Which adverb shows that one situation depends on another? (answer: *provided that*) Which words show the reason why something happened? (answer: *because* and *since*) Which adverb shows that one thing did not influence another? (answer: *even if*)

2 Books open. Go over the information in the grammar box, providing explanations and further examples as needed. Make sure Ss understand that the purpose of these adverb clauses is to show the relationship between the two clauses in a sentence.

A

Books open. Explain the task and do the first one with the class as an example. Then have Ss individually match the clauses to make logical sentences. Have Ss compare answers with a partner before going over the answers with the class, either by calling on selected Ss to share an answer or by having selected Ss write an answer on the board. Alternatively, read out the first clause, and have selected Ss supply a logical second clause.

Answers

1. c	**2.** d	**3.** f	**4.** e	**5.** b	**6.** a

Optional activity: *Making connections*

Time: 10–15 minutes. Ss practice using adverb clauses of reason and condition.

1 *Pair work* Books open. Have Ss work in pairs to come up with a logical second clause of their own for each of the six sentences in the exercise. Circulate to help and check for accuracy.

2 Have pairs share their best sentence with the class. Write these on the board, and ask others in the class to revise any errors that may have been made.

B

1 Books open. Explain the task. Then have Ss individually complete each sentence with their own information while you circulate to help and check for accuracy.

2 Have Ss compare answers with a partner before going over the answers as a class, either by reading out the first clause of a sentence and having selected Ss provide an appropriate second clause, or by having selected Ss write an answer on the board.

Possible answers

1. I can usually sleep pretty well, provided that I haven't had too much coffee.
2. Unless I have enough sleep at night, I can lose my temper easily.
3. Even if I have a case of insomnia, I never have trouble getting up in the morning.
4. Sometimes I don't set my alarm clock because I wake up early anyway.
5. Since sleep is extremely important for my health, I always try to get eight hours a night.

A good night's sleep

discussion   In this activity, Ss share their own ideas about sleep and dreams.

Group work

1   Books open. Explain the task and have selected Ss say what they see in the picture. Then have Ss read the questions. Explain any vocabulary that may be new to the Ss, including the following:

> **to prevent** to keep from happening
>
> **shades** window coverings that block out sunlight

2   Have Ss read the sample dialog, drawing Ss' attention to the follow-up questions of B and C.

3   **Optional:** Have Ss individually write two interesting questions about sleep and dreams to add to the list.

4   Ss form small groups of three or four to discuss each of the ten questions. Encourage Ss to ask and answer follow-up questions. Then have a spokesperson share each group's most interesting question and answer with the class.

 I had the wildest dream.

listening   In this activity, Ss listen for both gist and specific information.

A

1   Books closed. Ask Ss how many of them remember their dreams each night. Then ask who thinks dreams have meaning. Have Ss respond with a show of hands.

2   Ask Ss what a "wild" dream might be (answer: in this informal use of the word *wild*, it means "a bit unusual"). Ask for volunteers to briefly tell the class about a recent unusual dream, or tell the class about one that you had. Then ask Ss what they think it might mean. Accept all answers as viable.

3   Books open. Explain the task and draw Ss' attention to the chart, pointing out the kind of information they need to listen for. Remind Ss to fill in the chart in note form.

4   **Optional:** Go over any of the items from the following vocabulary list that you think your Ss might need:

> **recurring** happening over and over again
>
> **to wind up (somewhere)** to find yourself somewhere without having planned to go there
>
> **(to feel) overwhelmed** (to feel) helpless, unable to change a situation
>
> **terrifying** very frightening

5 Play the audio program once, and have Ss fill in the chart as they listen. If you wish, have Ss fill in only the column for *dreams* the first time they listen and then the column for *meanings* the second time they listen.

6 Replay the audio program to give Ss an additional opportunity to complete the chart. Then have Ss compare answers with a partner. Replay the audio program as needed before going over the answers as a class.

Answers

	Dreams	Meanings
Lucia	back in high school; lost her class schedule; can't find the main office; late for class; doesn't know what homework she must do; missed an important test	she's worried or overwhelmed about something in her life
Rick	in danger but unable to move or scream; in his own bed and senses something coming closer; needs to alert someone, but can't move	not in control of something (once had a dream when one of his children was sick)

Transcript

Listen to Lucia and Rick describing a dream they each had. What did each person dream about? What do they think the dreams mean?

Lucia: I have this recurring dream. I'm back in high school, and in my dream, the school looks mostly the same as it did, but much bigger. The weird thing is . . . that although I'm now twenty years old, I had to go back to high school and study with all these fifteen-year-olds. It's very embarrassing. No one seems to notice that I'm much older and shouldn't be there in the first place. But still, it's very uncomfortable. I keep thinking, "What am I doing here?"

Well, I think it must be a couple of weeks into school, and I've lost my class schedule. I start walking through the halls trying to find the main office. I can't find it. No matter how far, how many hallways, I just can't find it. I know I'm late for class, and this really worries me. Finally, I wind up in my math class, but it's almost over – so I've missed most of it, and I don't know what the homework is, and I think I've missed an important test, or something.

Basically, that's the dream. I think I have that dream when I'm worried or overwhelmed about something that is happening in my life at the time.

Rick: My name is Rick, and I sometimes have this dream, this bad dream. Really it's a nightmare. I'm in danger, but I'm not sure from what, and I can't move or scream or anything. I can feel something coming closer and closer to me, and, you know, it's really strange because usually in the dream I am exactly where I am in real life – like in my own bed in my bedroom – and everything is very realistic. The only part that is dreamlike is that I can't move. Sometimes I can't even open my eyes, or I can only open one eye. Usually I have to alert

continued

someone, or possibly save someone, although the person often changes. Anyway, I can't do anything because I can't move. It's really terrifying.

You know, I think the dream means that I'm feeling there's something in my life that I can't control, although I should be able to. Once I had the dream when one of my children was very sick, and I just felt completely helpless. I hate feeling that way.

B Pair work

Books open. Explain the task and then put Ss in pairs to discuss what they think the two dreams mean and whether or not they've had similar dreams. After 5 to 10 minutes, ask how many Ss have had similar dreams, and have selected Ss recount them for the class.

Optional activity: *Details, details*

Time: 5 minutes. Ss listen for more specific details.

1   Books open. Write the following questions on the board:

   1. Why is Lucia embarrassed?

   2. Why doesn't Lucia know where she is supposed to be?

   3. Why does she want to find the main office?

   4. What does Rick feel is happening?

   5. Where is he in the dream?

   6. What does he need to do?

   7. What was happening to one of his children when he had this dream once?

2   Replay the audio program while Ss listen for the answers to the questions. Then put Ss in pairs to compare answers before going over the answers as a class.

   Possible answers

   1. She's 20 and has been sent back to high school with the younger students.
   2. She has lost her class schedule.
   3. So she can find out where she is supposed to be.
   4. Someone or something is coming closer to him with the intention of harming him.
   5. In his bedroom.
   6. Warn or save someone.
   7. One of his children was very sick.

discussion In these activities, Ss match common dreams with their meanings and then discuss and interpret the meanings of some unusual dreams.

A Pair work

1 Books open. Explain the task and have Ss read the dreams and the meanings. Answer questions about vocabulary as they arise, including:

> **a sensation** a feeling
> **to approach** to come near
> **to feel superior to (someone)** to feel that you are better than (someone)
> **to threaten** to suggest that something unpleasant will happen unless a
> particular instruction is followed
> **to feel insecure** to have very little self-confidence

2 Have Ss work in pairs to match each common dream with its meaning. Then combine pairs into groups of four to compare and discuss their answers before going over the answers with the class.

Answers

Falling 5	Being chased 6	Failing 7	Being ashamed 4
Flying 3	Being embraced 1	Winning 2	

B Pair work

1 Books open. Explain the task and have Ss read the four dreams and the sample language. Check that Ss understand the following vocabulary items:

> **a stage** a raised platform where performances are held
> **a balloon** a rubber bag that is filled with air
> **a hot-air balloon** a large balloon that can carry passengers in a basket underneath
> **amazed** very surprised
> **a corridor** a hallway
> **to stand for** to represent something else
> **a symbol** an object that is used to represent something else
> **to symbolize** to represent
> **an interpretation** an explanation containing a point of view

2 Put Ss in pairs to discuss their interpretation of each of the four dreams. Then have selected pairs share their interpretations with the class.

C Group work

1 Books open. Explain the task and put Ss in small groups. Ss take turns adding a sentence to each of the four dreams.

2 Have each group share their most interesting dream with the class.

3 **Optional:** Have the class vote on which group came up with the most interesting and unusual dream. If time permits, have the class reinterpret the newly completed dreams.

Optional activity: *Recurring dreams*

Time: 10 minutes. Ss use adverb clauses stating reason and conditions to discuss dreams.

1 *Group work* Books open or closed. Ask Ss to raise their hands if they have ever had a recurring dream. Take a class survey to find out if the recurring dreams are more often bad or good dreams. Ask Ss to make statements based on the results of the survey.

2 Put Ss in groups with at least one S who claims to have had a recurring dream. Ask Ss to tell the group their recurring dream and why they think they have it. Encourage group members to ask follow-up questions.

Avoiding insomnia

reading In these activities, Ss discuss methods for getting a good night's sleep.

Books open. Write the title of the article on the board. Ask Ss about the kind of information they think will be included in the article. Have selected Ss or volunteers answer.

A Pair Work

1 Books open. Explain the task and put Ss in pairs to list four things they do when they have trouble getting to sleep. Then Ss silently read the article on their own to compare their ideas with the ideas presented in the text.

2 **Optional:** Ss underline up to five words they don't know but feel are essential for understanding the text. When they've finished reading, have Ss compare their underlined words with a partner. Then ask them to call out their underlined words, and go over meanings as time permits.

B Group work

1 Books open. Explain the task and have Ss read the two questions. Then put Ss in groups of four or five to discuss their answers.

2 Have selected Ss share an answer with the class, or have a spokesperson from each group share the group's most interesting answer with the class.

Optional activity: *Studying upside down*

Time: 10–15 minutes. Ss prepare silly suggestions on how to stay awake at night.

1 *Group work* Books open. Tell Ss that they've been asked to prepare a list of five suggestions for someone who has a big exam coming up, needs to study, but has trouble staying awake to do so. Put Ss in groups of four or five to prepare the suggestions. Tell Ss that the sillier their suggestions, the better.

2 Have a spokesperson from each group read their five suggestions to the class. Then have the class vote on which group came up with the best and the silliest ideas.

This unit focuses on the theme of typical people in the United States and their lifestyles, beliefs, and concerns, and how these compare with other societies. Students describe how they are similar to or different from other people using connecting words, clauses of contrast and exception, quantifiers, and conditional sentences.

Lesson A   *What's typical?*

The average American

starting point   This activity introduces the theme of characteristics of the average American and previews the grammar.

1   Books closed. Have Ss work with a partner to write a definition of the word *average* (e.g., the standard considered to be typical or usual). When most Ss are finished, have several pairs share their definition with the class. Provide feedback and correction as needed. Explain that the unit will present information on the average American.

2   Write the topics listed in *The Average American* (age, sex, education, employment, etc.) on the board, and go over the meaning of any new words with the class. Then have Ss work in pairs to predict the answers. Ask selected Ss to call out their predictions while you write them on the board.

3   Books open. Explain the task and check Ss' understanding of the following vocabulary items:

> **manufacturing company**   a company that produces goods in large numbers, especially a factory using machines
>
> **a clerical worker**   a person who does general office work
>
> **a mortgage**   the money borrowed from a bank to buy a house, apartment, or land that is repaid over time
>
> **spectator sports**   popular sports activities that are watched by large crowds, such as baseball, football, and soccer
>
> **to eat out**   to have a meal in a restaurant
>
> **environment**   the natural world (air, water, plants, and animals) outside towns and cities
>
> **environmentalist**   a person who tries to protect the environment from being damaged by human activities

4   Have Ss check their predictions against the information in the box. Ask them to make a note of any information they find surprising. Then ask selected Ss to share with the class one thing that surprised them.

5   Have Ss individually fill in the blanks in the four sentences below the box. Then have them compare answers with a partner or around the class before having selected Ss or volunteers share one or more answers with the class. Lead a class discussion.

Possible answers

1. use credit cards	**3.** don't own two TVs
2. eat out	**4.** eat steak and potatoes/eat fish and rice

Optional activity: *What's average?*

Time: 15–20 minutes. Ss describe the average person in their own country.

1 *Pair work* Books open. Have Ss look again at the information and categories listed in the box in Exercise 1. Then, if possible, have pairs of Ss from the same country write information for each category that is true for the average person in their own country. Explain that Ss will need to guess at some of the answers.

2 Combine pairs to form groups of six to compare and discuss their answers. Ask groups to discuss the differences between their averages.

What questions would you ask?

discussion In this activity, Ss think of questions an interviewer would ask to find out about the average student in their country.

A Pair work

1 Books open. Explain the activity and, if necessary, provide one or two example questions, such as: "How many hours a day do you study? What's your favorite class?"

2 Put Ss in pairs to write their questions while you circulate to help and check for accuracy.

3 Combine pairs to form groups of four to compare questions before having selected pairs share their most interesting questions with the class.

B Pair work

1 Books open. Explain the task and have Ss form new pairs to take turns interviewing each other. Ss try to find two things they have in common with the average American and two things that are different. Encourage Ss to ask and answer follow-up questions.

2 Several Ss tell the class about their partner's similarities and differences.

C Group work

1 Books open. Explain the task and go over the model language. Then have Ss work with a partner to discuss the ways they are and are not an average person in their countries.

2 **Optional:** Have Ss write their answers on a slip of paper either before or after discussing with a partner. Collect the papers, redistribute them around class, and have Ss try to find the person who wrote the paper they received.

3 Circulate to help Ss. Bring the class back together, and have selected Ss or volunteers share one or more answers. Lead a class discussion as appropriate.

 ## Showing contrast and exception

grammar focus This grammar focus presents the use of conjunctions to talk about differences between cultures.

> **Grammar notes** The conjunctions *while* and *unlike* show contrast between the information in two clauses of a sentence, and the conjunctions *except that* and *except for* show an exception. (*In contrast to* shows contrast between a noun phrase and a clause.)
>
> When the conjunctions presented in this grammar focus come at the beginning of a sentence, the two clauses are separated by a comma.

1 Books closed. Write these clauses on the board:

    1. While most Americans live on their own before marriage, . . .

    2. Unlike the average American student, . . .

    3. In contrast to most Americans, . . .

        a. students in Brazil are in school for five hours a day.

        b. people here don't usually have more than one TV.

        c. people here usually live with their parents until they get married.

2 Have Ss match the clauses to make sentences. Go over the answers (1c, 2a, 3b). Point out the conjunctions and how the information in the second clause contrasts with the information in the first clause. Then have Ss work in pairs to write a new second clause for the three numbered items. Circulate to help and check for accuracy. Have several Ss share answers with the class while you write them on the board, correcting as necessary.

3 Next write these sentences on the board:

    People in my country don't use credit cards <u>except for</u> big purchases.

    I'm very similar to the average student here <u>except that</u> I study Spanish.

Point out that the information in the second part of the sentence provides an exception to the information in the first part. Also note the lack of a comma between clauses. Finally, point out that *except for* is followed by an adjective or noun, whereas *except that* is followed by a subject or a subject pronoun.

4 Have Ss work in pairs to suggest a second clause for each of the two sentences. Then ask several Ss to share answers with the class while you write them on the board, correcting as necessary.

5 Books open. Lead Ss through the information in the grammar box, and go over the model sentences.

A

1 Books open. Explain the task and go over the example. Check that Ss understand the following vocabulary items:

> **to split the bill** to share the cost of the bill by paying equal amounts (often done in restaurants)
>
> **to behave** to act in a particular way
>
> **to misbehave** to behave badly

2 Have Ss individually rewrite the sentences. Put Ss in pairs to compare answers. Then ask several Ss to share an answer with the class.

3 **Optional:** Ask students at random to call out their answers. Write them on the board. Then have the class work together to correct any errors in these sentences.

Possible answers

1. While Americans often study Spanish, if people in my country study a foreign language, it's usually English. **or**
   Unlike Americans, who often study Spanish, people in my country prefer to learn French and German as a foreign language.
2. People in my country don't usually shake hands except in business situations. **or**
   Unlike Americans, people in my country don't usually shake hands when they meet each other.
3. While the bride's parents pay for most of the wedding in America, in my country both families split the cost equally. **or**
   In contrast to Americans, it is the groom's family who pays most of the costs of the wedding in my country.
4. Unlike the average American, friends in my country usually take turns treating each other when they go out to eat together. **or**
   In my country friends usually split the bill at a restaurant, except for special occasions.
5. In contrast to American children, in my country children are not usually sent to their rooms when they misbehave. They have some of their privileges taken away. **or**
   While American children are often sent to their rooms when they misbehave, in my country parents often punish children by giving them more housework to do.
6. People in my country are similar to Americans about calling before visiting friends except that young people living on their own sometimes don't have a phone. **or**
   Unlike Americans, people in my country often drop in for a visit without calling first.

B

Books open. Explain the task and lead students through the four items. Then have Ss individually complete each sentence with information of their own. Put Ss in pairs to compare answers. Then ask several Ss to either call out an answer or to write it on the board.

Possible answers

1. Unlike most men in my country, I don't smoke.
2. In contrast to the majority of my friends, I like listening to classical music.
3. While quite a few of the people in my class have part-time jobs, I don't.
4. Unlike most people who are my age, I don't go to movies much.

Optional activity: *Logical sentences?*

Time: 10–15 minutes. Ss have additional practice with the grammar.

1 *Class activity* Books open. On a slip of paper, have Ss individually write the first clause of a sentence, similar to the ones in Exercise 3B. Ask Ss to pass their sentence to the S sitting to their right. The next S keeps the sentence facing down so that he or she can't see it.

2 Tell Ss that when you say "go," they must turn over their papers and complete their sentences. When you say "stop," Ss are to put down their pens. Give Ss 30 seconds to complete their sentences. Ask a few Ss to call out their answers while others say whether or not the sentences are correct and logical.

  Typical or not?

discussion In these activities, Ss examine their ideas about the typical American and further practice using conjunctions.

A Pair work

1 **Optional:** Books closed. Write these words on the board: *eating out, exercise, protecting the environment, watching TV*. Have pairs choose one of the topics and then write a sentence or two to say what the typical American behavior or belief about the topic might be. As an example for *eating out*, say, "The typical American doesn't enjoy cooking and probably eats out quite often." Have several pairs read their sentences to the class.

2 Books open. Put Ss in pairs to talk about the people pictured. Tell them to guess their ages. Then explain the task, and have Ss silently read the four statements to decide how typical each person is. Check Ss' comprehension of the following vocabulary item:

> **to tolerate** to be able to bear something unpleasant or annoying

3 Have several Ss report back to the class about their ideas and their reasons. Lead a class discussion if there are differences of opinion.

B Pair work

1 Books open. Explain the task and have Ss read the model language. Then put Ss in pairs to discuss who they are most similar to and most different from. Encourage Ss to ask and answer follow-up questions.

2 **Optional:** After they finish their discussion, have Ss write out their answers using the conjunctions from the grammar focus.

Optional activity: *Typical people in my country*

Time: 10–15 minutes. Ss practice using the grammar of the lesson to talk about people in their own countries.

Group work Books open. Put Ss in groups of four or five to write four statements about typical people in their country, similar to those in Exercise A. Each group reads their statements to the class.

In what ways are you unique?

discussion In these activities, Ss consider and discuss the things that make them unique.

A

1 Books open. Explain the task and clarify the meaning of *unique*. Have Ss silently read through the ten items, checking that they understand the following vocabulary item:

> **to irritate** to annoy

2 Have Ss individually answer the questions about themselves and for most of their friends.

B Group work

1 Books open. Explain the task and put Ss in groups to take turns asking and answering the questions from Exercise A, making notes of the answers they receive.

2 Have Ss look through the model language in the box and the speech balloon. Then ask one or two Ss to use one of the expressions to give an additional example. Write the example on the board.

3 Have Ss work in the same group to prepare a class report, using the expressions and language in the box. Give each group a chance to share one or more of their answers with the class.

How are they different?

listening

In these activities, Ss listen to people talking about how they are similar to or different from others in their peer group, and organize the information into lists of similarities and differences.

A

1 Books open. Explain the task and have Ss look over the chart, making sure they know what information they need to complete it. Ask Ss where they think each speaker is from.

2 **Optional:** Pre-teach any of the following vocabulary items that you think will be helpful for your Ss:

> **tough** difficult
> **to head (in a direction)** to move (in a direction)
> **to head off to (school)** here, to leave home to go to (college)
> **midday** around 12:00 in the afternoon
> **to hang out** to spend a lot of time in a place [informal]
> **peer pressure** the strong influence of a group on members of that group to behave as everyone else does [often used when describing the behavior of teenagers]
> **to do one's own thing** to do what you want to do (without concern for others' approval)
> **to think for oneself** to make your own decisions
> **to get along with (someone)** to enjoy someone's company
> **decent** good, acceptable
> **core** basic or most important

3 Play the audio program once all the way through, and have Ss just listen. Then ask Ss to fill in as much of the chart as they can at this point. Remind Ss to write in note form. Tell Ss to fill in only a couple of things for the similarities column. Then replay the audio program, and have Ss complete the chart as they listen. If needed, pause the audio program briefly after each speaker to give Ss time to write their answers.

4 Put Ss in pairs to compare answers and to compile a list for the similarities column. Then ask if anyone needs to listen again. Replay the audio program as needed before going over the answers as a class. Ask volunteers to call out their answers.

Answers

	Similar	Different
Yoshiko	goes to a public high school, wears a uniform, goes to school five and a half days a week, similar interests to friends, plays video games, fan of American movies, likes Brad Pitt	lived outside Japan for six years, learned to speak English while living overseas
Renato	goes to school from seven until midday, after school studies or plays soccer, on weekends hangs out with friends in shopping centers	does his own thing, doesn't always hang out with group, thinks for himself
Suzanne	worries about grades and getting along with parents, goes to classes, attends club meetings, does homework, sleeps late on weekends	goes to special school for arts where she studies core subjects and music, dance, and art

Transcript

How are Yoshiko, Renato, and Suzanne similar to people their own age? How are they different? Listen and complete the chart.

Yoshiko: In some ways, I'm a typical Japanese teenager. I go to a public high school and wear a uniform, just like everyone else. I go to school five and a half days a week – I get Sundays off. I have interests similar to most of my friends: I like to play video games and am a big fan of American movies. Brad Pitt is one of my favorite actors.

There's one big way I'm different, though. I spent almost six years living outside Japan. My father's company transferred him overseas, and of course we went with him. Living in a foreign culture was really tough at first, but I guess I'm lucky in a way. I learned to speak English, and I made a lot of new friends. So you can see that I'm really quite a bit different from my classmates!

Renato: My life is pretty typical, I think. I head off to school at seven in the morning, and school finishes at midday. After school, I usually study or play soccer. On weekends, I like to get together with my friends. We usually hang out in one of the shopping centers. Everyone just shows up there on Saturdays and Sundays. It's a lot of fun . . . most of the time.

I think one way I'm different is that I like to do my own thing sometimes. I don't always want to hang out with the group. There's a lot of peer pressure to spend time with my friends, but I don't listen to what they say. I guess you could say that I think for myself. Sometimes it makes my friends angry, but that's just the way I am.

Suzanne: I guess I worry about the same things other kids my age do . . . you know, grades, getting along with my parents. . . . I'm doing OK in school, but I have to study really hard. I want to make sure that my grades are good enough so I can get into a decent university. I'm pretty typical: I go to classes, attend club meetings after school, and do homework at night. Weekends are great because I get to sleep late. Oh yeah, I'm also a member of the orchestra at school. I play the violin.

My school is different from a typical school in the United States. We study all the core subjects – like most other students – in the morning: science, math, English, history – the usual stuff. In the afternoon, though, we study things like music, dance, and art. You see, I go to a special school for the arts. A lot of us have dreams of becoming dancers or singers someday. That's why we spend so much time learning about the arts.

B Pair work

Put Ss in pairs to discuss the questions. After five minutes, have selected Ss describe to the class who their partner is most similar to/different from.

discussion   In these activities, Ss interview each other about their habits and daily routines.

A Pair work

1   **Optional:** Books closed. Write the following mixed-up questions on the board, and have Ss work alone or in pairs to match items to form logical questions. Then have Ss open their books and check their questions against the ones given there.

1. Can you cross . . .	. . . a diary?
2. Do you make . . .	. . . in a particular order?
3. Do you eat your foods . . .	. . . rubber bands?
4. Do you always replace . . .	. . . your eyes?
5. Do you collect . . .	. . . the last helping of food?
6. Do you ask before taking . . .	. . . your bed every day?
7. Do you give up . . .	. . . an alarm clock?
8. Do you use . . .	. . . the cap on a toothpaste tube when finished?
9. Do you keep . . .	. . . your seat on a bus or train for someone needier?

2   Books open. Explain the task and have Ss read the nine questions. Clarify the meaning of any new vocabulary, including the following:

to cross your eyes to position your eyes so they look at each other

to make your bed to straighten your bedcovers after you have slept in them

a helping of food a single serving or portion

to give up (something) to stop doing or having (something)

to give up your seat to offer your seat to another person [often used to describe behavior on buses or trains]

needier more in need of something than you are [often refers to a person who is poorer or weaker than average]

3   Put Ss in pairs to take turns asking and answering the nine questions. Encourage Ss to take notes and to ask and answer follow-up questions. Then have selected Ss share one or more answers with the class.

B Group work

1   Books open. Explain the task and then put Ss in groups of four or five to compare their answers with the ones on page 118 of the Student's Book and to discuss which of them is the most "normal."

2   **Optional:** Tally the results of Ss' answers on the board, and have Ss speculate on what they think normal behavior is.

writing In these activities, Ss identify topic sentences and main ideas in a paragraph. They also learn how supporting statements develop the main idea by adding specific facts, or by giving reasons or examples.

A

1 Books open. Go over the information in the box, and make sure students understand the meaning of the terms *main idea, supporting statements,* and *specific facts.*

2 Put Ss in pairs to talk about the picture. Tell them to say who they think these people are and what they are doing. Then explain the task, and have Ss read the paragraph silently and underline the information that develops the main idea.

Answer

> The reason for this is cultural. In my country, the family unit is very strong, and parents worry a lot.

3 Ask selected Ss to read aloud sentences they underlined, and go over the answer with the class.

4 Have Ss silently read the paragraph again and then answer the three questions below it. Then have Ss compare answers with a partner or in a small group before going over the answers with the class.

Answers

> 1. As a rule, young people in my town don't really start dating until they're about 16.
> 2. Fact: Before this age, people go out in groups rather than as a couple. A family member often comes along as a chaperone.
>   Reason: In my country, the family unit is very strong, and parents worry a lot.
>   Example: For example, when I was 15, my parents never let me go out with my girlfriend unless my brother or her sister came along with us.
> 3. Answers will vary.

B

1 Books open. Explain the task and have Ss read the three sentence stems. Have Ss individually complete the three sentences.

2 Put Ss in groups of four or five to compare answers. Ask Ss to take turns reading their sentences to each other and discussing why they would or wouldn't make good topic sentences. Encourage Ss to give reasons for their answers.

Possible answers

> **1.** As a rule, most teenagers in my country don't start dating until age 15.
>
> **2.** In general, people from the city have more opportunities to go out with their friends.
>
> **3.** If young couples in my country want to get married, they need to ask permission from their parents.

Optional activity: *Funny topic sentences*

Time: 10–15 minutes. Ss practice writing topic sentences and supporting statements.

1 Give each S a number starting from 1. Ask Ss with even numbers to finish the sentences in Exercise B in a funny but true way, and Ss with odd numbers to finish them in a serious, informative, but completely false way.

2 Have Ss form pairs composed of one S with an even number and one S with an odd number. Have pairs take turns reading their topic sentences to each other.

3 Have Ss choose one of their partner's topic sentences and add at least two supporting statements written in the same style.

4 Have several Ss read the topic sentence and their supporting statements to the class. Have other Ss say whether the information is true or false.

C

Books open. Explain the task and have Ss individually choose one of their topic sentences from Exercise B and add at least four supporting statements to make a complete paragraph. Circulate to offer help to Ss whose supporting sentences do not support their main idea.

D Pair work

1 Books open. Explain the task and ask Ss to read the three questions. Then Ss exchange papers with a partner, read their partner's paragraph, and answer the questions. Remind Ss of the purpose and value of peer feedback, if necessary.

2 Have pairs take turns explaining their answers.

3 **Optional:** Have Ss revise their paragraph, in class or for homework, based on their partner's answers.

 Lesson **B** *Topics of concern*

 1   *The American mind-set*

starting point   In these activities, Ss talk about typical concerns and worries of Americans and compare them to the concerns and worries of people in their own countries.

A

1 Books closed. Write *What Americans worry about* on the board, and ask Ss to call out any ideas they might have. Add these ideas to the ones Ss call out: *drug use, the economy, safety from crime, immigration, politics,* **and** *challenges for women having to work.* Then ask Ss to silently rank these concerns from what they think Americans worry about the least to the most. Have several Ss call out their answers. Lead a class discussion.

2 Books open. Put Ss in pairs to look at the three pictures. Tell Ss to describe what they see and tell each other what concern each picture depicts (answers: People protesting cuts in health-care services. A man being arrested. Working women going to/leaving the office.). Then have Ss skim the information in the box to check their predictions.

3 Explain the task and have Ss silently read the information in the box and check (✓) the things that they and the people in their countries worry about. Ask volunteers to call out their answers.

B Pair work

1 Books open. Explain the task and ask one or two Ss to call out an issue they think people in their country worry about. Then have Ss individually list three additional issues that people in their country are concerned about.

2 Have Ss either call out their answers or come up to the front of the class to write them on the board. Lead a class discussion. Encourage Ss to say why people in their country are concerned about the issues they listed and how common this concern is.

Optional activity: *Different viewpoints*

Time: 10–15 minutes. Ss talk about concerns from the viewpoint of different demographic groups.

1 Write the following demographic groups on the board: *children, young people, parents,* and *senior citizens.* Put Ss in small groups to write concerns that they think would be specific to each group.

2 Have the groups write the concerns in lists without headings, and then exchange lists with another group. Tell Ss to decide which demographic group goes with each list of concerns. Then have groups return their papers to each other and discuss their answers.

---

2 *How do you feel about it?*

vocabulary In these activities, Ss use adjectives to express their opinions about the issues mentioned in Exercise 1, and give reasons for their opinions.

A

1 Books open. Explain the task and lead Ss through the list of twelve adjectives, clarifying meaning as necessary.

> **alarming** worrying
> **appalling** shocking
> **fascinating** very interesting
> **fortunate** lucky
> **heartening** encouraging
> **mind-boggling** hard to imagine
> **reassuring** comforting

2 Have Ss individually complete the task. Then put Ss in pairs to compare answers before going over the answers with the class.

Answers

– alarming	+ fortunate	N mind-boggling	– sickening
– appalling	+ heartening	+ reassuring	N surprising
+ fascinating	+ interesting	– shocking	– unfortunate

Optional activity: *Quizzing one another*

Time: 10–15 minutes. Ss write sentences that illustrate the differences in meaning between the adjectives in Exercise 2A.

1 Books open. Put Ss in pairs to write sentences for six of the words from Exercise A, putting blanks in place of the words. Circulate to help and check for accuracy.

2 Have pairs exchange papers and fill in the blanks of each other's quizzes. Then have pairs return each other's papers to see how well they did.

B Pair work

1 Books open. Explain the task and have Ss read the model language in the speech balloons. Then put Ss in pairs to do the exercise. Encourage Ss to use adjectives from Exercise A.

2 Combine two pairs together to form groups of four. Have groups compare their points of view. Then have selected Ss or volunteers share one of their opinions with the class.

Optional activity: *International concerns*

Time: 5–10 minutes. Ss share ideas about concerns that people might have in different countries.

1 *Pair work* Books closed. Write the names of a few countries on the board, and ask pairs to choose a country they know about. Ss list at least two issues they think people in that country might worry about.

2 Have pairs join to form groups of four to compare ideas. Then ask each group to share an answer with the class. Lead a class discussion if time permits.

Quantifiers

grammar focus This grammar focus presents quantifiers that are used to show approximate quantity, without mentioning a specific number.

> **Grammar notes** The preposition *of* is required in the quantifier *the majority of,* but it is optional in the quantifiers *quite a few (of), about half (of),* and *hardly any (of).*
>
> Quantifiers are usually followed by *of* and *the,* but sometimes these can be omitted (e.g., with *most, quite, a few,* and *hardly any).* The quantifier *almost no one* never takes *of the,* but it can be followed by either a prepositional phrase such as *in my class,* a relative clause (*almost no one who lives near me . . .*), or a simple subject.

1 Books closed. Write the quantifiers in the exercise on the board; put them out of order. Then have Ss put them in order of quantity or degree. If necessary, start them off with *The majority of . . . .*

2 Books open. Have Ss look through the information in the grammar box to check their answers. Then lead Ss through the sample sentences, adding explanations and examples, as needed.

3 **Optional:** Put Ss in pairs to complete each sentence in the grammar box in a different way. Circulate to help and check understanding.

4 Explain the task and lead Ss through the nine issues listed. Check Ss' understanding of the following vocabulary items:

> **economic performance** the state of the economy; how well or badly it is doing
> **reform** change
> **population control** limiting the growth of the number of people

5 Go over the model sentence, and then have Ss individually write a sentence about each issue. Remind Ss to give reasons for their answers. Circulate to offer assistance when requested.

6 Put Ss in pairs to compare and discuss their sentences. Have selected Ss or volunteers share sentences with the class. Write them on the board to form the basis of correction work or class discussion.

Possible answers

> The majority of my friends are worried about crime because the economy isn't good and street gangs are getting stronger.
> Most of my friends are concerned about the economic performance of the country because we will be looking for jobs in a few months, after we graduate.
> Quite a few of my friends are worried about tougher graduation requirements from educational reform. They worry that they might cause them to have to delay their graduation.
> Hardly any of the people I know are concerned about immigration controls because immigration is not a big problem in my country.

continued

Quite a few of the people I spoke to are worried about political reform because they feel the government needs to do a better job.

The majority of people I know are concerned about pollution and what it is doing to the air and water.

About half of the people I've talked to are aware of the need for population control. The rest don't consider it a problem that concerns them.

Most of the people I know are interested in tax reform because they hope it will lower taxes for them.

Almost no one I've talked to disapproves of providing child care for working women, as this is becoming a popular idea these days.

Conditional sentences

grammar focus This grammar focus reviews the use of conditional clauses for expressing unreal or imaginary situations.

Grammar notes When using the conditional clause to talk about imaginary or unreal situations, the simple past tense is used in the *if* clause, and *would* + verb is used in the main clause. Imaginary or unreal situations are those that can only come true if the conditions described in the *if* clause are realized. The two clauses may appear in either position, but a comma must separate them when the *if* clause starts the sentence. *Might* and *could* can be used in place of *would*, but they both show slightly less certainty.

1 Books open. Review the information in the grammar box and the sample sentence. Have Ss point out the two clauses, and check Ss' comprehension of a *hypothetical* situation by giving them other situations (e.g., "If it rained today, we wouldn't need to water the flowers."). Ask selected Ss to make up similar sentences. Provide additional explanations and examples, as necessary. Explain the task and go over the model answer.

2 Alternatively, explain the task and go over the model answer. Have Ss individually write sentences that offer solutions to the issues they wrote about in Exercise 3. Circulate to offer help where needed. Have Ss compare their sentences in small groups before sharing one of their sentences with the class.

3 **Optional:** Have the class vote on the best solution to each of the problems expressed in Ss' sentences.

Possible answers

If there were more jobs for people without much education, then people would have an alternative to joining gangs and becoming criminals.

> If the government encouraged more foreign investment, it would help improve the performance of the economy.
>
> If schools were better informed about the changes involved in educational reform, they would help their students to do well.
>
> If more companies provided child-care facilities at work, they would really help mothers who have to work.

Optional activity: *Mixed-up sentences*

Time: 10–15 minutes. Ss continue using conditional sentences.

1 *Class activity* Books closed. Split the class into two groups, Group A and Group B. On slips of paper, have Ss in Group A write the *if* clause of an unreal or imaginary conditional sentence with *people* as the subject (e.g., *If people walked more . . .*) Ss in Group B write the main clause of an unreal or imaginary conditional sentence with *they* as the subject (e.g., *. . . they would worry less about things.*)

2 Make sure Ss don't look at each other's papers. Circulate to help and check for accuracy.

3 Bring the class back together and have a S from Group A read his or her clause aloud. Then a S from Group B reads his or her clause aloud while the others say whether or not the resulting sentence makes sense.

4 Continue until all Ss have had a chance to read their clauses aloud. Then have the class vote on the most logical and the silliest or funniest sentences.

5 Alternatively, after Ss have written their clauses, collect them, mix them up, and spread them out on desks in the front of the room. Then have Ss stand and try to find and combine as many clauses as they can to make logical sentences. When there are no more possible (logical) sentences to be made, have Ss sit down and then read out their sentences to the class. Others vote on whether or not each sentence is logical.

 The next generation

discussion In this activity, Ss talk about their own concerns and the concerns of their peer group, and practice using quantifiers and conditional sentences.

Class activity

1 Books open. Explain the task and have Ss cover the results of the survey. Have Ss read the survey question in the box, and put Ss in groups of four or five to discuss the survey question. Then have the groups uncover the results and compare their thoughts with the results in the box.

2 Conduct a class survey and note the number of Ss who answered each way on the board. Then, in their groups, have Ss list the main concerns of their classmates and possible solutions. Tell groups to write one sentence about these concerns using a quantifier and one conditional sentence to describe the possible solution.

3 Ask groups to share their sentences with the class. Lead a class discussion.

Optional activity: *Telling the future*

Time: 15–20 minutes. Ss continue using quantifiers and conditional clauses.

1 Photocopy or write the following four sets of survey statements on a piece of paper. Prepare them so that there is one set per page. Divide the class into Groups A, B, C, and D, and distribute one set to each group.

2 Explain that Ss will conduct their own survey about how the next generation will solve their problems. Have Ss stand and mingle, asking their questions to as many people as they can in about 5 minutes.

3 When the allotted time is up, have Ss return to their groups to compare results. Then ask groups to write four sentences about their survey results, using quantifiers and conditional sentences. Then have one S from each group tell the class what their statements were, and have another S from the same group read aloud the sentences the group wrote about the results.

Group A

I think the future generation will protect the environment by ...	Yes	Probably not	No
finding new ways to avoid cutting down so many trees.	_____	_____	_____
dealing with the problem the same way it is dealt with today.	_____	_____	_____
developing recyclable products.	_____	_____	_____
other: _____	_____	_____	_____

Group B

I think the next generation will deal with violent crime by ...	Yes	Probably not	No
increasing use of the death penalty.	_____	_____	_____
punishing criminals more severely.	_____	_____	_____
offering more appropriate rehabilitation programs for criminals.	_____	_____	_____
other: _____	_____	_____	_____

Group C

I think the future generation will control pollution by ...	Yes	Probably not	No
making people more aware of the causes.	_____	_____	_____
giving severe punishments to all those who contribute to it.	_____	_____	_____
coming up with new technological advances for cars, industries, etc.	_____	_____	_____
other: _____	_____	_____	_____

Group D

I think the future generation will reform government by . . .	Yes	Probably not	No
reducing the number of government workers.	____	____	____
considerably decreasing politicians' salaries.	____	____	____
demanding higher moral standards from politicians.	____	____	____
other: _____	____	____	____

6 Personal concerns

discussion   In these activities, Ss discuss personal concerns and ways to address them.

A

1   Books open. Explain the task and have Ss read the list of concerns. Have Ss individually add at least two of their own personal concerns to the list, and then discuss with a partner which worries are a personal concern to them and why.

2   **Optional:** Write the following model language on the board.

    A: Do you worry about going to a party with strangers?

    B: No, not really. How about you?

    A: Yes, it worries me a lot because I'm very shy, and . . .

3   Have selected Ss or volunteers tell the class one thing that worries them and why.

B Pair work

1   Books open. Explain the task. Have Ss describe what they see in the picture. Ask Ss what they think the man's problem is and what he should do about it.

2   Go over the sample language, checking that Ss understand the meaning of the following:

> **resume** a written summary of a person's educational and professional experience, used when seeking a job

3   Have Ss form new pairs to discuss what they plan to do about the things that concern them.

4   **Optional:** Have two or three pairs join together to compare answers and solutions. Groups can then brainstorm other possible solutions to each other's problems.

The different approaches to problem solving

listening

In these activities, Ss listen for specific information while people talk about their personal concerns and how they address them, allowing Ss to practice listening for specific information.

A Pair work

1 Books closed. Write three different problems on the board, and ask Ss to think about how they would solve these problems. For example:

You're having a problem with a good friend who has become too attached to you.

Your computer is broken and you have no idea how to fix it.

You can't seem to manage your time effectively.

2 Put Ss in pairs or small groups to talk about how they would solve each problem. Then, after a few minutes, ask several Ss to share an answer with the class. Lead a class discussion.

3 Books open. Ask Ss to read about the three kinds of problem solvers. Then put Ss in pairs to discuss what kind of problem solver they are. Encourage Ss to give examples to support their answer.

4 Have selected Ss or volunteers share their answer with the class.

B

1 Books open. Explain the task and make sure Ss know what kind of information they are listening for. Remind Ss to fill in the chart in note form.

2 **Optional:** Pre-teach any items from the following vocabulary list that you think will be helpful for your Ss:

> **to get stuck (with something you don't want)** to buy something and then find out it isn't what you want
>
> **consumer** a person who buys goods or services
>
> **knowledgeable** knowing a lot about something
>
> **fanatic** a person whose strong admiration for something is considered extreme
>
> **to mull over** to think about
>
> **input** opinions and ideas about a specific matter
>
> **to analyze** to study something carefully in order to understand it
>
> **to pose a question** to ask a question

3 Play the audio program through once, and have Ss listen only. Then have Ss fill in whatever information they can on the chart.

4 Replay the audio program, pausing briefly after each speaker to give Ss time to complete the chart. Then have Ss compare answers with a partner. Go over the answers with the class.

Answers

	Concerns	Type of problem solver
Dominique	making expensive purchases; making a mistake and getting stuck with it	meditative (reads consumer magazines for car ratings, speaks to knowledgeable people in the field, then test-drives the car)
Carla	hiring the right person	assertive (doesn't like to waste time making decisions, prefers to go with her instincts and act quickly)
Wayne	where to spend Christmas holidays	cooperative (talks to a lot of people to get their input, analyzes the problem from different people's perspective)

Transcript

Listen to Dominique, Carla, and Wayne talking about their personal concerns. How do they solve them? What type of problem solver is each person?

Dominique: You see, I find making an expensive purchase quite difficult. Probably because I don't want to make a mistake and get stuck, especially for something that costs a lot of money, like a car. You see, when I bought my car, I knew I just couldn't go into a showroom and choose a car! No impulse purchases for me! I needed a lot of time to think it over and consider the options. So, I read consumer magazines to see how they rated their cars. I wanted to know the average prices and safety records of different cars. I mean, you never know. . . . I also talked to people in the field who are knowledgeable. You know, the guy down the street who works in the garage, oh, and, uh, also, my brother-in-law – he's a car fanatic. And once I decided which one I liked, I finally went to the showroom to test-drive the car. I suppose you could say that my approach takes a lot of time, but I feel secure in my decisions.

Carla: I'm in charge of hiring new staff for my department at work. I mean, several of us do the interviews, but I'm the person who gives the final approval. If I say "no," then the person isn't hired. It's a lot of pressure! Sometimes I get stressed out about it.

I have to admit that I hate to waste time making decisions. It's funny, my boss does it completely differently. She just likes to sit and think, you know, mull over the information and let the decision "come to her." We have completely different styles!

I think I've learned a lot from my previous mistakes: You just have to go with your instincts – that is, do what you think is best and then just hope that it works out. I mean, we all get strong feelings about things, and usually those feelings are right. The important thing is to act quickly! Up until now I've been pretty lucky. The people I've hired have all worked out – no major problems so far.

continued

Wayne: When I have to make an important decision, I find I need to talk to a lot of people, get their input. If I have to do it myself, I get confused. It's like the more I think about something and consider all the options, the more frustrated I get. I could sit and analyze something forever. My friends say that I can always see both sides of everything, which makes it hard to decide on anything! You can imagine how irritated my friends must get.

When I was deciding where to spend my long Christmas holidays last year, I asked everyone for help. Basically what I did was pose this question: "Where would you go in December if you had three weeks?" I listened to all the answers and then made my decision. You might think I'm strange, but it worked. Based on everyone's advice, I went to Miami. I had an amazing vacation!

C Pair work

Books open. Explain the task and then put Ss in pairs to discuss the question. Encourage Ss to explain their answers and to ask and answer follow-up questions. After 5 minutes or so, have several selected Ss or volunteers share their answer with the class.

Optional activity: *Applying different problem-solving techniques*

Time: 10 minutes. This activity practices talking about ways to solve problems.

1 Books open. Put Ss in groups of three to decide how an assertive problem solver would solve Dominique's problem, how a meditative problem solver would solve Wayne's problem, and how a cooperative problem solver would solve Carla's problem.

2 Have two or three groups join to compare ideas. Ask Ss to discuss how much the nature of the problem itself determines the best way to solve it.

8 *An American profile*

reading This reading presents statistics about the average American.
Ss predict the information that will be in the reading and then follow-up with a discussion of how their perceptions of Americans may have changed.

A Pair work

1 Books open. Have Ss read the title of the article, and ask the class to predict what kind of information the article is likely to contain.

2 Explain the task and ask Ss to read the questions, clarifying meaning as needed. Then have Ss individually answer the questions. Put Ss in small groups to compare and discuss their answers.

3 Ask Ss to read the article and confirm their predictions. Tell Ss to underline up to five words they don't know but feel are essential for understanding the text. After they have finished reading, clarify the meaning of any unknown words. Then go over the answers with the class.

Answers

1. white non-Hispanics	5. Over 80% of Americans say that they believe in God.
2. nearly 20 million	
3. 2.63	6. Over half of all Americans believe that there should be a complete ban on smoking in public places.
4. almost two-thirds	

Optional activity: *Scanning to win*

Time: 5 minutes. Ss practice scanning skills.

1 Photocopy or reproduce the following quiz. Distribute facedown, one for each student.

2 Books open. Tell Ss that when you say "go" they should look over the questions on the quiz and then scan the article to find the answers. Explain that the objective is to find the answers and complete the quiz as quickly as possible; the first three people to finish are the winners. Tell Ss to raise their hand as soon as they're done.

3 Shout "go" and have Ss turn their papers over and begin. Try to maintain a gamelike atmosphere as students complete the quiz. Go over the answers with the class.

Quiz

1. Which ethnic group constitutes 32.5 million of the American population?
2. What percentage of Americans are Asian or Pacific Islanders?
3. How many ethnic groups are mentioned in the article?
4. How many Americans speak a language other than English at home?
5. What percentage of Americans are high school graduates?
6. What is an average salary for a person without a high school diploma?
7. What is the average annual earnings of a person with a doctorate degree?
8. What portion of Americans think UFOs probably exist?
9. What percentage of Americans support the death penalty?

Answers

1. African Americans	4. more than 31 million	7. $54,982
2. 3.5%	5. more than 80.2%	8. over two-thirds
3. five	6. $14,391	9. 47%

B Group work

1 Books open. Explain the task and have Ss read the two questions. Put Ss in groups to discuss them. Encourage Ss to ask and answer follow-up questions and to give reasons for their answers.

2 Have one or more Ss from each group share an answer with the class. Lead a class discussion.

This unit introduces the theme of interpersonal communication, focusing on conversational styles, politeness, and making small talk. Students use infinitive phrases, gerund phrases, and reported speech to discuss these topics.

Lesson A *Making conversation*

Conversational styles

starting point

These activities introduce the theme of polite and impolite conversational styles.

A

1 Books closed. Ask Ss if they think they are good conversationalists, explaining the term, if necessary. Then write these two questions on the board:

What are the qualities of a good conversationalist?

What makes a conversation interesting or boring?

2 Put Ss in pairs or small groups to discuss the questions for a few minutes. Have selected Ss or volunteers share their ideas with the class. Write Ss' answers on the board, and lead a class discussion.

3 **Optional:** On the board, write the names given to the six kinds of conversationalists presented in the box. Go over the meaning of words that may be new to Ss. Then have Ss work in pairs to predict how each type might act in a conversation. Have two pairs join to compare answers before reading the information in the box.

4 Books open. Explain the task and have Ss skim the six descriptions. Ask about any words that may be new, including the following:

> **accomplishments** difficult things that somebody has completed successfully
> **to ignore** to pay no attention to somebody or something
> **wandering eye** a person who avoids making eye contact with the person speaking
> **customary** normal, usual
> **appropriate** correct in a specific situation

5 Have Ss silently read the six descriptions and match each to one of the illustrations. Then put Ss in pairs to compare answers before going over them as a class.

Answers

1. interrupter	**3.** wandering eye	**5.** complimenter
2. conversation starter	**4.** bragger	**6.** bore

B Pair work

1 Books open. Explain the task and put Ss in pairs to decide which of the people described in Exercise A have good conversational styles (answers: complimenter and conversation starter). Encourage Ss to give reasons to support their answers and to ask and answer follow-up questions.

2 Have several Ss share their answer with the class. Lead a class discussion.

Optional activity: *Role play*

Time: 15 minutes. Ss try out the different conversational types described in Exercise A.

Group work Books open. Put Ss in groups of three to role-play one of the situations pictured in Exercise A. Have the class decide which conversational type is being demonstrated.

Poor conversationalists

discussion   This activity extends the theme of the lesson and previews gerund phrases.

Pair work

1 Books open. Explain the task and have Ss read the four examples of poor conversationalists.

2 Put Ss in pairs to discuss and share stories of similar people they've met. (Note: If Ss can't think of similar people, they could talk about what they would do if they met such people.) Encourage Ss to ask and answer follow-up questions.

3 Have several Ss share a story with the class.

Infinitive and gerund phrases

grammar   This grammar focus presents the structures *it* + *be* + adjective + infinitive phrase
focus   and gerund phrases.

> **Grammar note** In the structure *it* + *be* + adjective + infinitive phrase, the subject is *it*. This type of sentence can be changed to start with either a gerund (e.g., *Asking about other people's personal business* is impolite.) or an infinitive phrase (e.g., *To ask about other people's personal business* is impolite.). Beginning a sentence with a gerund is more common and less formal than starting with an infinitive phrase.

1 Books closed. On the board write the sentence *It's not polite to talk about yourself too much.* Then ask, "What else is it not polite to do in a conversation?" Have Ss call out their answers, and write them on the board in sentences that follow the pattern: *it* + *be* + adjective + infinitive phrase.

2 Next, on the board write:

Asking other people about their family is _____.

a) polite   b) impolite   c) customary

Ask volunteers to complete the sentence appropriately (answer: *a* or *c*). Then ask a few selected Ss to substitute the word *family* in the sentence with something else, such as *personal business*. Write the new sentences on the board, and have Ss, using the same three choices, answer each with a show of hands.

3 Books open. Lead Ss through the information and sample sentences in the grammar box, starting with *it + be +* adjective + infinitive phrase and then showing how gerund phrases can be used to say the same thing.

A

1 Explain the task and go over the example. Have Ss individually complete each sentence with one of the six adjectives to show what would be typical or appropriate behavior in their own cultures. Remind Ss that *not* is needed in some of the sentences. Circulate to help. Then have Ss compare answers with a partner and discuss the sentences they have answered differently.

2 Ask several Ss or volunteers to share an answer with the class, and lead a class discussion. Then go over the sample answers with the class. Answers may vary depending on culture or individual opinion.

Possible answers (These answers are culturally dependent.)

1. not polite	**3.** customary	**5.** polite	**7.** not polite
2. not appropriate	**4.** unusual	**6.** acceptable	**8.** important

Optional activity: *Blind clauses*

Time: 5–10 minutes. Ss have additional practice with the grammar.

1 *Group work* Books open. Write sentence stems like the ones in Exercise A, such as *It's not polite . . .* , and *_____ing too much is . . .* , on pieces of paper (one to a paper). Divide the class into small groups and give each group a piece of paper, facedown.

2 Have groups turn their paper over, and give them 1 minute to complete their sentence in as many ways as they can. The group with the most (correct and logical) sentences is the winner. Continue as time allows.

B

1 Explain the task and go over the example. Have Ss individually write sentences about their culture, using the eight cues. Remind Ss they can use any adjective they wish and either sentence pattern in the grammar box.

2 Ss compare answers with a partner. If answers differ, encourage pairs to discuss and give reasons for why they answered as they did.

3 Ask a few Ss to share answers with the class. Write them on the board, and lead a class discussion.

What should you do?

discussion   In this activity, Ss practice giving advice about speaking appropriately and consolidate their understanding of the lesson's grammar.

Group work

1   Books open. Explain the task and have Ss read the four situations in the box. Then model the example dialog. Put Ss into groups of four or five to discuss what they would do in the four situations. Encourage Ss to supply reasons and explanations. Ask Ss which situation would be the hardest for them to handle.

2   Have one or two Ss from each group share an answer with the class. Lead a class discussion.

Making small talk

discussion   In these activities, Ss consider appropriate small-talk topics, and then practice making small talk and opening and closing a conversation.

A Pair work

1   Books open. Explain the task, and check Ss' comprehension of the term *small talk*. Explain that it is the type of conversation you might have with an acquaintance you run into at the mall or at a party.

2   Have Ss read the list of topics. Check that they understand the following terms:

> **current affairs** major events in the world that are reported in the news
> **marital status** the state of being either married, single, divorced, or widowed

3   Put Ss in pairs to discuss which of the eight topics listed are most suitable for small talk. Have pairs check their answers. Then have Ss call out the topics they've checked.

Possible answers

> **Topics suitable for small talk:**
> current affairs   entertainment   hobbies   the weather   work

Optional activity: *Uncomfortable small talk*

Time: 5–10 minutes. Ss discuss why some topics are not suitable for small talk.

Group work Books open. Put Ss in small groups to discuss which topics are unsuitable for casual conversations in their cultures. Tell Ss to discuss how these topics might make people feel, and what unique features of their cultures contribute to making these subjects unsuitable for small talk.

B Pair work

1 Books open. Explain the task and lead Ss through the eight expressions above the chart. Model the expressions and lead the class in choral and/or individual repetition.

2 Have Ss form pairs to complete the chart. Then have two or more pairs join together to compare and discuss their answers, before going over the answers with the class.

Answers

Starting a conversation	Introducing a topic	Closing a conversation
Hi. How's life been treating you?	Can you believe this weather we're having?	Catch up with you later.
It's been a long time!	How's everything at school?	Sorry, I've got to run.
How have you been?	How's the job going?	Talk to you later.
		Well, it's been nice talking to you.

3 Put Ss in pairs to think of any other small-talk expressions they know. Then have Ss call them out while you write them on the board. Add common ones of your own to the list such as: *What's new? How's it going? What's happening? What have you been up to lately? How's the family? Have you seen _____* (mutual friend) *lately? See you later. Got to go. Give me a call sometime.*

C Class activity

1 Books open. Tell Ss to look at the photograph and describe the scene. Explain the task and have Ss read the sample conversation.

2 Tell Ss to imagine they are at a party and that they need to talk to five people in five minutes. Have Ss stand up and begin a conversation. At the end of 1 minute, say "change," and Ss move on to make small talk with the next person. Repeat this procedure three more times. Then have Ss sit down, and ask a few to tell the class about one of the conversations they had.

---

6   *What are they talking about?*

listening

In these activities, Ss listen to other people's conversations and evaluate them according to what they know about good and poor conversational styles.

A

1 Books open. Explain the task and make sure Ss understand what information they need to listen for to complete the chart. Tell Ss to complete the *topic* column in note form and to try to write the exact words used in the *closing phrase(s)* column. Explain that you will play the audio program as many times as needed.

2 **Optional:** Pre-teach any items from the following vocabulary list that you think will be helpful for your Ss:

> **to sample** to taste a small amount
> **lively** energetic, fast-paced
> **challenge** a dare; an invitation to compete in a game or argument
> **to have (a party) catered** to have a party with food prepared by an outside company
> **to sign up** to register
> **to convince** to persuade

3 Play the audio program, and have Ss listen only. Then give Ss a moment to write down any answers they can at this point.

4 Replay the audio program, pausing briefly after each conversation. Have Ss complete the chart as they listen. Put Ss in pairs to compare answers. Replay the audio program as necessary, before going over the answers with the class.

Possible answers

	Topic	Closing phrases
First conversation	the party, after graduation plans, job plans	**Pete:** Excuse me, Mrs. Morton, I've got to talk to him before he goes. **Liz:** Certainly. It was nice meeting you, Pete. Good luck with your job search.
Second conversation	the music, dancing	**Man 1:** Excuse me. It's been real nice talking to you, but I've got to go.
Third conversation	the food, husbands and cooking	**Woman 2:** I think I'll go mention it to him. Talk to you soon. **Woman 1:** OK. Bye.

Transcript

> **Listen to people at a party making small talk. What topic is introduced in each conversation? What closing phrase is used to end the conversation?**
>
> **First conversation**
> **Liz:** Hi, . . . Pete?
> **Pete:** Yes. Hello.
> **Liz:** I'm Liz, Donna's mother. Donna has told me all about you.
> **Pete:** Nice to meet you, Mrs. Morton.
> **Liz:** It's nice to meet you, too. So, are you enjoying the party?
> **Pete:** Yeah, it's great. This might be the last time I see some of these people for a long time, so I've been pretty busy. I haven't had much time to sample the food.
> **Liz:** I know what you mean. I can't believe that all you kids are finally graduating. Donna has

continued

grown up so fast! Do you have any plans after graduation?

Pete: Well, I've applied for a teaching job overseas. I guess I'll probably find out if I got the job or not next week.

Liz: You're more adventurous than Donna. She's going to take a job right here in town, at least for the summer. After that, who knows?

Pete: Well, you might be seeing me around here for a while longer, too. Oh, . . . wait a minute. I'm sorry. I think Dan is leaving the party. Excuse me, Mrs. Morton, I've got to talk to him before he goes.

Liz: Certainly. It was nice meeting you, Pete.

Pete: Same here.

Liz: Oh, and good luck with your job search.

Pete: Thanks. Thanks a lot.

Second conversation

Man 1:   You know, I . . . uh . . . I kind of like this music.

Man 2:   Well, it is lively. I'll say that for it.

Man 1:   Great music for dancing.

Man 2:   Dancing? Yeah. I guess. For young people, anyway.

Man 1:   What? What, you think we're too old?

Man 2:   Oh, no. You're not thinking . . .

Man 1:   And why not? It looks like fun! Why should we sit here while everyone else is having a great time?

Man 2:   If you start dancing to this music, you're going to make a fool out of yourself.

Man 1:   Hmm. That's what you think.

Man 2:   Anyway, who would you dance with?

Man 1:   Oh? Is that a challenge?

Man 2:   Oh, no.

Woman: Hey, there. Want to dance?

Man 1:   Uh, . . . why, . . . why, yes, I would, young lady. *(turns to Man 2)* Uh, excuse me. It's been real nice talking to you, but, uh, I've got to go.

Third conversation

Woman 1:   Mmmm, . . . this is delicious. I love stuffed grape leaves.

Woman 2:   Ummm. Me, too. It all tastes delicious. Do you think they made all this themselves? Or did they have it catered?

Woman 1:   Oh, no. George is a great cook. Why would they cater it?

Woman 2:   Really?

Woman 1:   Oh, yeah.

Woman 2:   George cooks?

Woman 1:   You didn't know that? Lynn's always saying that's half the reason she married him!

Woman 2:   Well, that is a good reason. She is really lucky. I wish my husband liked to cook. He completely avoids anything that has to do with the kitchen.

Woman 1:   You know, my husband's talking about signing up for an Italian cooking class on Saturdays. Oh, I hope he does it.

Woman 2:   Oh. I wonder if I could convince my husband to do that. I'd sure love being the taste tester for his recipes.

Woman 1:	Exactly what I was thinking. Well, I'll let you know when the class starts.
Woman 2:	Great! Please do. In the meantime, I think I'll go mention it to him. Talk to you soon.
Woman 1:	OK. Bye.

Optional activity: *Inferencing, evaluating, and intensive listening*

Time: 5 minutes. Ss listen more intensively, make inferences, and evaluate the conversations.

1 Books closed. Write the following on the board:

First conversation: *1. How does Liz open the conversation?*
2. Which type of conversationalist is Liz?
(Look back at Exercise 1, page 46.)

Second conversation: *1. How old do you think the men are?*
2. Is the woman a friend of either of the men?
3. How old do you think the woman is?

Third conversation: *1. Who do the women think provided the food?*
2. What kind of course is one husband thinking of taking?

2 Replay the audio program while Ss write their answers on a piece of paper. Go over the answers with the class.

Possible answers

First conversation

1. Liz opens the conversation by saying: "I'm Liz, Donna's mother. Donna has told me all about you."
2. She is a conversation starter.

Second conversation

1. over 60   2. no   3. early 20s

Third conversation

1. George, the host   2. an Italian cooking class

B Pair work

1 Books open. Explain the task and replay the audio program, if necessary, while Ss take notes to use during their discussion. Put Ss in pairs to discuss the questions. Encourage Ss to give reasons for their answers and to suggest ways the speakers could have been more effective conversationalists.

2 Have several Ss tell the class their opinion about one of the conversationalists. Lead a class discussion.

Possible answers

> **First conversation** Both are good conversationalists because Liz asks Pete questions to keep the conversation going, and both speakers offer more information than required when responding to each other.
> **Second conversation** Possibly not because both men immediately react to and reject what the other has said, rather than listen first and then respond. They seem critical of each other, but good friends sometimes joke with each other in this way.
> **Third conversation** Both are good conversationalists. They ask each other questions and show that they have listened to the answer in the way they respond.

Keeping a journal

writing   These activities have Ss examine the same narrative from three different perspectives and then write about a personal piece of news they've received recently.

A

1 Books closed. Ask Ss to say what a journal or diary is. Then ask them to raise their hands if they keep a journal now or have in the past.

2 Books open. Explain the task and have Ss silently read the three paragraphs to decide who wrote each one: Soo Mi's sister, Soo Mi's mother, or Soo Mi's friend.

3 Have Ss compare answers with a partner. Encourage Ss to discuss how they decided upon their answers, giving reasons and examples from the paragraphs. Then have selected Ss or volunteers share their answers and the reasons for them with the class.

Answers

> **1.** B   **2.** C   **3.** A

B

Books open. Explain the task and, either in class or for homework, have Ss write a paragraph about a piece of news they have received recently. Remind Ss that they should include their reaction to the news. If the writing is done in class, circulate to help with vocabulary and grammar.

C Pair work

1 Books open. Explain the task and ask Ss to exchange paragraphs, reminding Ss of the purpose of peer editing. Tell Ss to read what their partner has written and answer the two questions in the book. Then have pairs take turns talking about their partner's paragraph and telling each other how they answered the two questions.

2 **Optional:** Have Ss revise their paragraph based on their partner's suggestions.

Optional activity: *Reporting the news*

Time: 15–20 minutes. Ss continue practicing with perspective in writing.

1 Have Ss rewrite their paragraph, in class or for homework, from the perspective of another person who is affected by the news.

2 Have Ss exchange papers with a partner and give their partner their original paragraph as well. Pairs read each other's papers and decide whose perspective is given in the new paragraph. To make this easier, ask Ss to supply their partner with three possible choices.

 Lesson B *Personal secrets*

 Sharing personal information

starting point In these activities, Ss examine who people in the United States share personal news with and make comparisons with their own experience.

A

1 Books closed. On the board, write the categories of news listed in the chart: *good news, bad/tragic news, gossip about others,* and *a secret about yourself.* Check Ss' comprehension of the following:

> **tragic** very sad, usually because it involves death or suffering
> **gossip** news about a person's private life

2 Put Ss in pairs, and ask them to come up with an example of each kind of news. Then elicit examples from Ss, and write them on the board.

3 Ask the class to think about whether they would normally share good news first with a parent, close friend, or sister or brother. Then ask Ss to think about whether they would share very bad or tragic news first with the same person or a different person? Have Ss answer with a show of hands. Then ask some of those who indicated they'd ask a different person who they would share this news with.

4 Books open. Explain the task and have Ss scan the information in the box to compare their answers with the data in the chart. Then put Ss in pairs to discuss the chart.

5 Have several Ss share an answer with the class.

B Pair work

1 Books open. Explain the task and have Ss read the sample language. Then put Ss in pairs to discuss the reasons why they would tell secrets to one person and not another. Encourage Ss to give examples to support their answer. Have pairs also ask and answer follow-up questions.

2 Have several Ss share an answer. Lead a class discussion.

Optional activity: *He talks, she talks*

Time: 5–10 minutes. In this activity, Ss explore the different secrets kept by men and women.

Books open or closed. Ask Ss if they think women and men tend to keep different types of personal secrets. Then put Ss in single-gender groups or pairs, if possible, to discuss the different types of personal secrets that they keep (e.g., about their love lives, their jobs, their health, etc.). Tell Ss to make a list of these different types. Then have Ss compare lists to see what kinds of differences there are.

News about other people

discussion This activity expands the topic of personal news and previews reported speech.

Pair work

1 Books closed. Ask pairs to think of examples of personal news that should never be shared with others. Have several pairs share one of their ideas, and lead a brief class discussion.

2 Books open. Explain the task and have Ss silently read the three texts. Put Ss in pairs to discuss the two questions. Have selected Ss or volunteers share answers with the class.

Reported speech

grammar focus This grammar focus presents rules for changing direct speech into reported speech.

> **Grammar notes** When one changes a statement in direct speech into reported speech, the tense in the reported clause often changes to a tense one step in the past. This process is called tense harmony, and it helps show the time relationship between the reporting clause (e.g., *he said*) and the reported clause (e.g., *that they had gotten engaged*).
>
> Usually the tense in the reported clause changes from present to simple past (e.g., He said that they *got* engaged.), and from simple past and present perfect to past perfect (e.g., He said that they *had gotten* engaged.). (See the table in item 5.)
>
> However, there are many exceptions to this rule, especially in informal speech. There is no tense change in commands, general truths, and immediately reported statements. Commands are changed to reported speech by changing the commanding verb to an infinitive (e.g., He told me *to pick up* the tickets.). In negative commands, the *not* comes before the infinitive.
>
> Yes/no and *Wh*-questions are changed by introducing the question with *whether* or *if* followed by the statement word order rather than the inverted word order (e.g., I asked him *if the date had been set yet.*).

1 Books closed. Explain that Ss are going to work with reported speech (i.e., language used to tell others what someone else said), and ask Ss to read the three texts in Exercise 2 on page 50. As they read, Ss should underline examples of reported speech.

2   Books open. Lead Ss through the information in the grammar focus, pointing out and explaining verb tense and language changes in reported speech. Also call Ss' attention to these things: use of the verb *said* to report a statement, the expression *X wants to know/would like to know* for reporting questions, and the verb *told* + object pronoun + *to/not to* to report commands.

3   **Optional:** Give Ss the following chart, which illustrates general tense changes between direct speech and reported speech.

	Direct speech	Reported speech
Tense	simple present	simple past
	simple past	past perfect
	present continuous	past perfect continuous
	present perfect	past perfect
	past perfect	past perfect (no change)
Modals	may	might
	can	could
	shall	should
	will	would
	must	had to

4   On the board write these sentences and questions:

They got married. The sun sets in the west. Has the plan been made? Stand up!

As a class, work together to change the first one into reported speech (He/She said [that] they had gotten married.) Point out that *that* in a reported statement is optional. Then put Ss in pairs or small groups to change the other three sentences into reported speech. Elicit answers from a few students, then write them on the board. Work with the class to revise and correct them.

Answers

He/She said [that] they had gotten married.	He/She said [that] the sun sets in the west.
I asked him/her if the plan had been made.	He/She told me to stand up.

5   **Optional:** Have Ss say which sentence on the board is a command, a yes/no question, a statement, and a general truth. As a class, try to deduce the rules for changing these types of sentences into reported speech.

A

Books open. Explain the task and read the example. Have Ss call out the type of sentence each item is (a yes/no question, statement, etc.). Remind Ss to use the examples in the grammar box as a reference. Then have Ss individually change each item into reported speech. Circulate to offer assistance. Have Ss compare answers with a partner, before going over them with the class.

Answers

1. She told me [that] she wasn't feeling well.
2. He asked me if I had heard the shocking news.
3. They asked me when my friends were arriving.
4. She asked me why I wasn't going to the party.
5. He told me to try it again.
6. She told me [that] she was getting married next year/the following year.
7. The teacher said [that] water boils at 100°C.
8. They told me [that] we would be leaving at 7:00.
9. The children asked me if the movie had been scary.
10. The teacher just said [that] our essays are due next week.

B Pair work

1 Books open. Explain the task and have Ss read the conversation between Ryan and Emily. Model language in the speech balloon. Then put Ss in pairs to take turns changing each line of the conversation into reported speech.

2 **Optional:** Have Ss write out the dialog in reported speech.

3 Ask selected pairs to act out or read their conversation in reported speech for the class. Correct any errors made.

Answers

Ryan told Emily [that] he had a secret to tell her. He asked Emily if she knew Don and Sally at work.
Emily told him [that] she had heard their names but that she had never met them.
Ryan told her [that] they were getting married.
Emily asked him how he had found out.
Ryan told her [that] Don's sister had told him.
Emily asked Ryan when the wedding was going to be.
Ryan told her [that] he didn't know.

Secrets

discussion In this activity, Ss play a game of reporting secrets to one another.

Group work

1 Books open. Explain the task and put Ss in groups of six or seven. Have Ss sit in a circle. The first S in each group whispers a secret to the S to the right. That S then uses reported speech to tell the next S the secret and so on, until the last S in the group hears it. The last S reports the secret back to the group. The first S then says whether the secret was accurately reported or not. Explain that Ss are to whisper the secret only once and at their normal speaking speed.

2 Have groups share any funny or unusual things they heard.

 Responding to news

vocabulary These activities present adjectives that describe negative or positive emotional responses.

A

1 Books open. Explain the task and lead Ss through the list of twelve adjectives. Clarify the meaning of the following:

> **delighted** very happy
> **depressed** unhappy; without hope
> **flattered** pleased with yourself because someone has given you a compliment
> **offended** hurt or angry because someone has been rude or disrespectful
> **relieved** happy because something you were worried about didn't happen

2 Have Ss individually complete the chart and then compare answers with a partner.

Possible answers

> **Positive** delighted, excited, flattered, pleased, proud, relieved
> **Negative** annoyed, appalled, depressed, embarrassed, irritated, offended

B Group work

1 Books open. Explain the task and have Ss read the sample language in the speech balloon. Then put Ss in groups of four or five to take turns telling each other about two pieces of personal news they received and how they reacted to this news. Remind Ss to tell where and how they heard the news. Encourage Ss to elaborate and to give reasons for reacting the way they did. Have Ss ask and answer follow-up questions.

2 Have one S from each group use reported speech to tell the class about the most interesting story they heard.

3 **Optional:** Ask one S from each group to visit a different group to find out their most interesting story. Then have Ss return to their original group to report what they heard.

6 *Tell me all about it!*

In these activities, Ss listen to people talking about and responding to each other's news, and then discuss how they would have reacted.

A

1 Books open. Explain the task and make sure Ss know what kind of information they need to listen for to complete the chart.

2 **Optional:** Pre-teach any items from the following vocabulary list that you think will be helpful for your Ss:

> **to see someone** to date someone [informal]
> **to propose** to ask someone to marry you
> **bridesmaid** female friend or relative of the bride who participates in the wedding
> **to have a long face** to look unhappy or serious
> **to lay (someone) off** to stop employing a worker, often because there isn't
> enough work to do
> **indefinitely** without a clear time limit
> **to pick up** to increase, to improve
> **seniority** status; the position a person has in relation to others
> **outcome** result
> **preserved** maintained

3 Play the audio program through once without pausing, and have Ss listen only. Then have Ss individually fill in the chart with any information they can at this point. Replay the audio program, and have Ss continue completing the chart as they listen, pausing briefly after each speaker to give Ss time to write.

4 Have Ss compare answers with a partner. Replay the audio program as necessary while going over the answers with the class.

Possible answers

	What was the news	What happened exactly
Nicole	Her sister is getting married.	Sister proposed to her boyfriend.
Tony	He lost his job.	He's been laid off as of April 30th.
Darren	His parents are moving.	His parents decided to move to Mexico.

Transcript

Listen to Nicole, Tony, and Darren telling different pieces of news. What was the news? What happened exactly?

Nicole: I got some incredible news over the weekend!

Man: Yeah? What happened?

Nicole: Well, my sister is finally getting married.

Man: Really? Well, that is exciting! How long have they been seeing each other?

Nicole: Oh, I mean, it's been over four years. We all knew that they would get married someday, but no one expected it to happen now. And you know what? The funny part is how it happened.

Man: Yeah?

Nicole: Yeah. OK, listen. They were on a cruise, and one night while they were sitting on the deck of the ship, looking at the stars . . .

Man: Ah, . . . let me guess. He pulled out a ring and asked her to marry him.

Nicole: No, smarty. The other way around. She asked him! She got right down on one knee and proposed.

Man: Yeah?

Nicole: Yeah! And he was pretty surprised, I think, but of course he immediately said "yes." Listen, they're planning a wedding for the fall.

Man: Well, that is great news. Yeah, . . . and I'm sure they'll be very happy together.

Nicole: Yeah. Now I have to start thinking about the wedding. I'm going to be a bridesmaid in the wedding, so, you know, I have to buy a dress and then . . .

Woman: Why the long face, Tony?

Tony: Oh, I just got some bad news today.

Woman: What happened?

Tony: Well, you know my job at the design studio?

Woman: Yes.

Tony: Well, . . .

Woman: Oh, no!

Tony: Oh, yes. Today the boss called me into his office and told me they had to lay me off indefinitely. That means as of April thirtieth, I'm out of work.

Woman: Oh!

Tony: No more job.

Woman: Tony, I am so sorry. You really liked working there.

Tony: Yeah, well, it's not all bad news. There's still a small chance that the company will call me back in the summer if the work picks up. You never know what'll happen. They may still need me then.

Woman: Oh, this is so sudden, isn't it?

Tony: Well, sort of. Two other employees lost their jobs last month, and I had a feeling I might be the next one in line. You know, I've only been working there ten months, so I don't have any seniority. If they're going to lay someone off, it's always going to be the newer employees first.

Woman: What are you going to do?

Tony: Like I said, I've still got a job until the end of the month. Starting in May, I plan to send out resumes and go on some interviews. Depending on the outcome of the interviews, . . .

continued

Darren: I just found out that my parents are moving.

Woman: Mmmm. Are you surprised?

Darren: Well, not really. They've been trying to sell their house for, gosh, six months to a year now.

Woman: Oh, well, I thought they liked it where they were.

Darren: They do. They love it. But they're getting older. Dad wants to live in a smaller town. And Mom says she's sick and tired of the fast pace and taking care of the house, you know.

Woman: Hmmm. So where are they going to move?

Darren: You're not going to believe this!

Woman: What? What?

Darren: They're going to Mexico. Can you believe it?

Woman: Oh, my gosh. You're kidding.

Darren: Nope. They're going to San Miguel de Allende. It's this gorgeous little town in the mountains.

Woman: Wow! I've never heard of it.

Darren: Ah, . . . it's about a hundred and fifty miles northwest of Mexico City.

Woman: Wow. Do your parents speak Spanish?

Darren: No, but they're going to learn.

Woman: Wow. That is a big change! Why don't they stay in the U.S.?

Darren: Well, they have always wanted to live abroad. Now that they're retired, they finally get to do it. And my Dad, he adores Mexico. He's been there six or seven times at least.

Woman: Wow. Sounds like this is going to be quite an adventure.

Darren: It should be. And San Miguel – it is stunning. The government has made sure that there's no new buildings ever built there, so the traditional feeling of the town . . . well, it's been preserved. Oh, and they make pottery there, which is perfect for my mother because she collects the stuff.

Woman: Oh, that's great for her. So, . . . I guess now you're going to have a place to stay in Mexico.

Darren: Yeah, . . .

Woman: And a place for your friends to come and visit in Mexico.

Darren: Well, if my friends are nice to me, I suppose something could be arranged. Did you have anybody in particular in mind?

Woman: Oh, very funny. So, when exactly are they moving?

Darren: Oh, in a couple of months. They have to pack up and take care of all the business here. I'm going to help them with the move. I may even try to stay a couple of months if I can swing the time . . . .

Optional activity: *Story telling*

Time: 5–10 minutes. Ss have additional practice with reported speech.

1 *Group work* Books open. Put Ss in groups of three, and assign each the task of reporting Nicole, Tony, or Darren's story. Replay the audio program if necessary to refresh Ss' memories. Have Ss take turns reporting their assigned story.

2 **Optional:** Ask students to think of follow-up questions they would like to ask Nicole, Tony, or Darren, and add these to their report.

B Pair work

1 Books open. Explain the task and put Ss in pairs to take turns describing how they would have reacted to the three pieces of news in Exercise A. Encourage Ss to use vocabulary from Exercise 5A and to give reasons to support their answers.

2 Have selected Ss or volunteers share answers with the class. Lead a class discussion.

Did you hear that…?

discussion   In these activities, Ss share and report personal news.

A

Books open. Explain the task and have Ss read the two samples of personal news. Ask Ss to use these as models as they prepare their own note. Then have Ss silently (and secretly) write at least five sentences about a piece of personal news on a sheet of paper. Remind Ss to write their names on the papers. Circulate to help and check for accuracy.

B Group work

1 Books open. Put Ss in groups of six or seven. Explain the task and have Ss read the sample dialog. Collect each S's paper within a group. Shuffle the papers and randomly redistribute them so that each S in the group has someone else's personal news. Tell Ss to read the personal news on the paper they received and think about how they would report the news to others.

2 Ss take turns reporting to their group.

3 Select a S at random from each group to use reported speech to tell the class about the most interesting or unusual piece of news they heard from someone else in their group.

4 **Optional:** Have Ss talk with the person who wrote the personal news they received in order to find out more information that they could report on in writing.

Improving your conversational style

reading   The reading text presents information about the traits of boring conversationalists, and the activities allow Ss to practice prediction and inferencing skills.

A

1 Books closed. Tell the class they are going to read an article titled "Don't be a bore!" Ask Ss to predict what kind of information might be in the text. Have Ss call out their answers, and accept any reasonable predictions.

2 Brainstorm with the class about what makes someone boring, and have Ss call out their answers. Simply acknowledge Ss' answers without comment.

3 Books open. Explain the task and have Ss individually list three traits that make someone a boring person. Have Ss compare and discuss answers with a partner.

4 Have Ss silently read the text to compare their ideas with those of the author. Tell Ss to underline up to five unfamiliar words they feel they need to know to understand the text.

5 Ask Ss to write a check (✓) next to their answers in Exercise A if they found information about them in the text. Ask Ss how accurate their predictions were and what other information they found in the text they thought was interesting. Go over the words Ss underlined.

B Pair work

1 Books open. Explain the task and then have Ss individually match each of the four people described with the appropriate adjective from the article. Have Ss write a sentence offering advice to each person about how they could be less boring or a better conversationalist.

2 Have Ss compare answers with a partner or in small groups, before going over the answers with the class. For the four people described, have several Ss tell the class the advice they have for each. Lead a class discussion.

Answers

Appropriate adjectives	Sample advice
1. self-preoccupied	He should ask others about their interests.
2. ingratiating	She should be more self-confident and not worry about having to impress others.
3. negative	She should stop complaining so much and be more positive.
4. tedious	He should keep the conversation flowing more smoothly.

3 **Optional:** Take a class survey to find out which of the nine traits described in the article Ss find the most boring. Have Ss respond with a show of hands, and tally Ss' answers on the board. Lead a class discussion, and encourage Ss to explain why they find each trait so boring.

C Group work

1 Books open. Explain the task and have Ss read the two discussion questions with the class. Then put Ss in groups to discuss. Encourage groups to give reasons to support their answers and to ask and answer follow-up questions.

2 Have several Ss share answers with the class. Lead a class discussion.

3 **Optional:** After explaining the task, have Ss use the information in the text as the basis for two discussion questions of their own. Have Ss silently write their questions either to discuss with their partner or to pass on to another pair to discuss.

Optional activity: *The secrets of being an interesting person*

Time: 20 minutes. Ss extend the topic of the reading to talk about what makes a person interesting.

1 *Group work* Books open. Brainstorm with Ss some of the traits of an interesting conversationalist, and write them on the board without comment as Ss call them out.

2 Put Ss in groups, and ask them to prepare a list of nine traits that make a person interesting, along with a brief description of each one. Have Ss use the descriptions in the reading as a model. Circulate to help and check for accuracy. Have one S from each group report their answers to the class.

3 If time permits, lead a class discussion, and try to get all Ss in class to agree on a class list of the nine traits of an interesting person.

Students review the use of adverb clauses, quantifiers, conditional sentences, infinitive and gerund phrases, and reported speech to talk about the daily routines and the habits/beliefs and personal secrets of typical people.

1 *Time relationships*

In these activities, Ss practice using adverbs in time clauses to talk about effective strategies for learning a language.

A

1 Books closed. Ask Ss if they remember any time phrases, such as *whenever, as soon as,* etc. Have Ss call out as many as they can while you write them on the board. Then have Ss make sentences with the ones you have listed. Remind Ss that they can use gerunds after *while, after,* and *before.*

2 Books open. Explain the task and have Ss individually complete the sentences. Then put Ss in pairs to compare answers before going over them as a class.

Possible answers

1. As soon as I come across a new word in a book or a magazine, I stop and try to figure out what it means.
2. Before I start writing a composition, I brainstorm all the ideas I can think of and write them down.
3. I don't like to say a new word aloud until I feel I can pronounce a new word correctly.
4. Whenever I don't understand somebody, I politely ask them to repeat what they said.
5. While I'm listening to native speakers of English, I try not to translate into my own language.
6. After I have read something in English, I write down my impressions of it.

B Pair work

Books open. Explain the task and then put Ss in pairs to add more learning strategies to the list in Exercise A. Have Ss individually rate the strategies for effectiveness before talking with each other about their ratings. Then have pairs report to the class about the strategies they feel work the best.

Optional activity: *It doesn't work!*

Time: 5–10 minutes. Ss continue using time phrases to talk about learning strategies that are not effective.

Group work Books open. Put Ss in groups of three or four to talk about bad learning habits, such as always translating before they write or being too shy to talk to native speakers. Have Ss make a list of these bad habits to present to the class.

2 Clauses stating reasons and conditions

In this activity, Ss practice using adverb clauses stating reasons and conditions to give advice on sleep habits.

1 Books closed. On the board, write: *because/since, provided that, even if, unless.* Remind Ss that these words and phrases are used to state reasons and conditions. Put Ss in pairs to make sentences using each word or phrase while you circulate to observe progress.

2 Books open. Have Ss look at the picture and say what is happening. Explain the task and have Ss individually complete the sentences. Then put Ss in pairs to compare answers before having selected Ss share their answers with the class.

Possible answers

1. Sleepwalking is not dangerous, provided that you don't leave your room.
2. Since people always get sleepy in the afternoon, they should try and complete their most important work in the morning.
3. Taking a nap is OK, provided that it isn't too long.
4. Try to sleep eight hours a night even if you have a very busy schedule.
5. Unless you set your alarm clock, you won't be able to wake up on time.
6. You shouldn't exercise in the evening because it might keep you awake at night.
7. You won't be able to wake up early tomorrow morning unless you go to bed early tonight.
8. Try to avoid taking sleeping pills even if you have difficulty sleeping.

3 Quantifiers

In this activity, Ss use quantifiers to talk about typical beliefs, concerns, and interests among people they know.

1 Books open. Have Ss look at the photograph, and ask what the people are doing. Then ask if Ss play ice hockey or know anyone who does. Elicit a sentence using a quantifier, and write it on the board. Then have Ss read the example.

2 Explain the task. Have Ss individually complete the statements about people they know while you circulate to check their progress. Then put Ss in groups of four or five to compare and discuss answers. Encourage Ss to talk about possible reasons to explain their statements. Have groups share one statement with the class, and ask the class to say whether in their experience they agree or disagree with the generalization made.

Possible answers

> 1. The majority of my friends enjoy playing hockey.
> 2. Hardly anyone I know believes in the possibility of life on other planets.
> 3. Quite a few of my friends are worried about getting good jobs.
> 4. Most of the people I go out with are interested in what is going on in the world today.
> 5. Almost no one I know has ever cheated on an exam.
> 6. The majority of people who are my age feel that women and men should have equal rights.

Optional activity: *Find the errors*

Time: 5 minutes. Ss correct sentences and check that they know how to use quantifiers correctly.

1 Books closed. Explain that Ss will see ten sentences with quantifiers, some of which will have errors. Ss have to find the errors and note the corrections on a slip of paper all within a time limit of 3 minutes (or another time limit appropriate for your Ss).

2 Write these sentences on the board, or photocopy them to hand out to Ss.

> 1. Quite a few the mothers in the U.S. work.
> 2. Almost any one I know gets enough sleep every night.
> 3. About half people in my class are under twenty-one.
> 4. The majority of people I know commute to work by car.
> 5. Hardly none of my friends smoke cigarettes.
> 6. Quite few of the people I know speak at least a little English.
> 7. About half of my friends say they sleep only six hours a night.
> 8. Most of teachers at our school come from the U.S.
> 9. Hardly a few students at this school live nearby.
> 10. Almost no one I know speaks German.

3 Tell Ss to start. Have Ss raise their hands as soon as they are finished; collect their papers in the order in which they finish. Make Ss stop when the time limit is up, and collect the remaining papers. Redistribute the papers in the order you collected them for Ss to mark. Go over the answers. The first S to have finished with the most accurate corrections wins.

Answers

1. Quite a few *of* the mothers in the U.S. work.
2. Almost ~~any~~ *no* one I know gets enough sleep every night.
3. About half (*of*) *the* people in my class are under twenty-one.
4. The majority of people I know commute to work by car. (no corrections needed)
5. Hardly ~~none~~ *any* of my friends smoke cigarettes.
6. Quite *a* few of the people I know speak at least a little English.
7. About half of my friends say they sleep only six hours a night. (no corrections needed)
8. Most ~~of~~ (*of the*) teachers at our school come from the U.S.
9. ~~Hardly~~ *Quite* a few (Hardly ~~a few~~ *any*) students at this school live nearby.
10. Almost no one I know speaks German. (no corrections needed)

Conditional sentences

In these activities, Ss talk about topics of concern and make suggestions for solving problems using conditional sentences.

A

1   Books closed. Write the following on the board: *People waste too much water. There is a serious water shortage in our city.* Ask Ss to combine the sentences in order to suggest a solution to this problem. If Ss don't produce the following sentence, write it on the board: *If people didn't waste so much water, there wouldn't be such a serious water shortage in our city.* Review the relevant grammar.

2   Books open. Have Ss look at the photographs and say what problems are being depicted. Explain the task and have Ss read the example. Then have Ss write conditional sentences to suggest solutions to the problems. Put Ss in pairs to compare and discuss answers before going over them as a class.

Possible answers

1. If people had to pay high fines for littering, they wouldn't throw out their trash along the highway.
2. If politicians made stricter laws, factories wouldn't discharge waste products into rivers.
3. If public transportation were safe and dependable, many people would use it.
4. If students got better advice about future careers, college graduates would be able to find jobs when they graduate.
5. If the government gave out more student loans, students could attend good universities.

B

1 Books open. Explain the task and have Ss circle the sentence number of the most serious problem in their country. Then have Ss write three more sentences that give solutions to that problem.

2 Put Ss in pairs to compare and discuss their problems and solutions. Circulate to check the accuracy of Ss' sentences. Have selected Ss share their solutions with the class while others indicate with a show of hands whether or not they think that this is a problem in their country. Lead a class discussion about these problems. Encourage Ss to give reasons and examples where relevant, and to ask follow-up questions.

5 Infinitive and gerund phrases

In these activities, Ss review the use of *it* + *be* + adjective + infinitive and gerund phrases to practice giving advice about appropriate behavior.

A

1 Books closed. Write the following on the board: *appropriate, important, inappropriate, nice, polite*. Have Ss write sentences with each, showing what the words mean.

2 Books open. Explain the task and go over the examples. Have Ss read the situations and decide which adjective fits each best. Then have Ss write two sentences about each situation using the appropriate adjective. Have Ss compare answers in pairs before going over them as a class.

Possible answers

1. It's inappropriate to ask too many personal questions when you meet a foreign visitor for the first time.
   Asking too many personal questions is inappropriate when you meet a foreign visitor for the first time.

2. It's polite to offer to help with the dishes when you stay as a guest in someone's house.
   Offering to help with the dishes when you stay as a guest in someone's house is polite.

3. It's nice to go up and introduce yourself when you notice someone at a party who doesn't seem to know anyone.
   Going up and introducing yourself when you notice someone at a party who doesn't seem to know anyone is nice.

4. It's important to try to help when you notice that one of your friends seems worried or depressed.
   Trying to help when you notice that one of your friends seems worried or depressed is important.

5. It's inappropriate to correct someone when you hear them speaking English and making lots of serious grammar mistakes.
   Correcting someone when you hear them speaking English and making lots of serious grammar mistakes is inappropriate.

B Pair work

Books open. Explain the task and put Ss in pairs to determine the best piece of advice. Then have each pair share one piece of advice with the class.

6 Reported speech

In this writing activity Ss review the use of reported speech.

1   Books open. Explain the task and have Ss read the sample dialog and the example. Check that Ss understand the following vocabulary:

> **to treat** to buy or pay for something for someone else

2   Put Ss in pairs to take turns telling each other what Ed and Sue said. Then have Ss individually rewrite the conversation using reported speech. Go over answers as a class.

Answers

> Ed asked Sue why she was an hour late. Sue told him that she'd been very busy at work and that she'd forgotten about their appointment. Then she asked Ed if he had been waiting a long time. Ed told Sue that he hadn't been waiting long. He said that he'd almost gone home but had decided to wait. Sue told Ed that she was glad he was really patient. She said that since she was so late, she'd treat him to dinner. Ed told her not to worry about it because he had been more than half an hour late himself.

7 Sensible solutions for "pesky" problems

In these activities, Ss practice using adverbs in time clauses to talk about effective strategies for solving common personal problems.

A

1   Books open. Explain the task and have Ss read the model language in the speech balloon. Ask Ss to call out possible time phrases they could use in their solutions.

2   Give Ss a few moments to think of sensible solutions to their problems.

Possible answers

> 1. Whenever I feel depressed, I call up a friend and talk for a while. That usually makes me feel better.
> 2. I get up and watch TV. As soon as I get sleepy, I go back to bed.
> 3. Before I finish studying, I like to take a break. I often relax and have a cup of coffee.
> 4. I go to the gym and exercise until I'm too exhausted to feel angry anymore.

B Pair work

Books open. Explain the task and put Ss in pairs to compare answers and decide which ideas are the best. Have each pair share its best ideas with the class.

8 What's average for parents and teenagers?

In these activities, Ss practice using expressions of contrast to talk about typical parents and teenagers.

A

1   Books open. Explain the task and have Ss read the questions in the chart. Check that Ss understand the meaning of the following:

> **a valued possession** something that is very important to its owner
> **a view** an opinion

2   Have Ss complete the chart.

B Pair work

Books open. Explain the task and have Ss read the model language. Ask Ss to call out expressions of contrast, eliciting *while*, *unlike*, and *in contrast to*. Put Ss in pairs to write at least four sentences contrasting typical parents with typical teenagers. Tell Ss to use the information in their charts and the expressions of contrast. Have pairs share their best statements with the class.

Possible answers

> While the average parents are concerned about their children, the average teenager is concerned about friends.
> In contrast to the average parents, the average teenager's most valued possession is his or her stereo system.
> Unlike the average parents' hobbies of reading books and dining out, the average teenager enjoys watching music videos and skateboarding.
> They might have similar political views, except that the average teenager's views would be less conservative./While their political views might be similar, the average teenager's would be less conservative.
> In contrast to the average parents, who like to play golf and relax on their vacation, the average teenager likes to go surfing and swimming.

In this activity, Ss use the grammar and vocabulary they've been reviewing to discuss their own and other people's senses of style.

A Pair work

1 Books open. Put Ss in pairs to look at the photograph and describe what they see. Tell them to say how the person in the middle is different from the others. Explain the task and have Ss read the list of questions. Check that Ss understand the following:

> **prominent** most noticeable

2 Have pairs use the questions to decide whether they are similar or different. Ask pairs to tell you if they are similar to or different from one another.

B Group work

Books open. Explain the task and then combine pairs to form groups of four to discuss their answers and to decide who in the group has the most interesting answer to each question. Have groups share their most interesting answers with the class.

Optional activity: *Similarities and differences*

Time: 10 minutes. Ss continue discussing their personal senses of style.

Class activity Books open. Tell Ss to stand up and find other people in the room who are very similar to them by asking the questions again. Ss who answered most of the questions in a similar way should group together while they continue searching for other students similar to themselves. After about 5 minutes, tell groups of Ss to go to different corners of the room and see which group has the most Ss. Have groups tell the class how they are similar, and have the individuals who are left standing alone tell the class how they are different.

10   *That's surprising!*

In these activities, Ss review adjectives of feeling to describe negative or positive emotional responses to a piece of news.

A Pair work

1   Books open. Have Ss read the headline about the mother. Ask Ss how it makes them feel. Then have Ss read the four topics and underline the "feeling" adjectives (answer: heartening, interesting, appalling, surprising). Have Ss say which adjectives are positive, negative, and neutral.

2   Explain the task. Put Ss in pairs to discuss the topics. Circulate to encourage Ss to ask and answer follow-up questions.

B Group work

Books open. Explain the task and then combine pairs to form groups of four to share their answers for each topic. Encourage group members to ask each other follow-up questions. Then have groups present the four most interesting answers to the class.

11   *We're really close.*

In these activities, Ss talk about why they share personal information with some people and not others.

A

Books open. Explain the task and have Ss read the list of people. Brainstorm with the class a list of topics they like to talk about, and write these on the board. Then give Ss a few minutes to consider what they usually talk about and avoid talking about with each of the people.

B Pair work

Books open. Explain the task and have Ss read the model language in the speech balloons. Then put Ss in pairs to discuss their ideas from Exercise A. Have selected pairs share some of their ideas with the class.

Let me tell you something.

In these activities, Ss listen to people talking about their recent news and take notes about the gist of what happened.

A

1 Books open. Explain the task and have Ss look at the chart to make sure they know what information they need to complete it. Explain that the first time they listen they will fill in the first line of the chart.

2 **Optional:** Pre-teach any items from the following vocabulary that you think will help your Ss:

> **suspicious** causing people to feel that something is wrong
> **awkward** uncomfortable and clumsy
> **off-limits** forbidden
> **to go for (something)** to try to achieve or obtain (something)

3 Play the audio program. As they listen, Ss should complete the first item in the chart by writing in note form the things that Stephanie and Lee are talking about.

B

1 Books open. Explain the task and then replay the audio program. Have Ss complete the second item in the chart.

2 Have Ss compare answers with a partner. Replay the audio program as necessary. Then have selected Ss or volunteers share answers before going over them with the class.

Possible answers

	Stephanie	**Lee**
What they're taking about	the Neighborhood Watch program; Stephanie was asked to join it	a new job opening at work; Lee applied for the same job as his friend Bill
How each situation has changed	Minor problems on the block have been solved. Everyone knows neighborhood is "off-limits" for troublemakers. Group won a special award from the mayor's office.	Lee got the job. It was awkward at first and Bill was upset, but now they are friends again.

Transcript

Listen to Stephanie and Lee talking about something. What news are they reporting?

Stephanie: Last night I was asked if I wanted to join the Neighborhood Watch program in my neighborhood. I didn't understand what it was, so I asked my next-door neighbor. She said that this new program was starting up. It's a new way of keeping our streets safe. Every two months we meet with a police officer to get tips on how to stay safe. We also are trained to watch for anything that happens. You see, everyone is given a telephone number and told to report anything suspicious. We also learn what to do in case of an emergency. Our neighborhood is already pretty safe. But you can never be too careful.

Lee: There's a new job opening up at work. It's in a different department, and I think the work is more interesting than what I'm doing now. I'm tired of this job. . . . Anyway, my friend and co-worker, Bill, told me that he's applying for the job. I didn't know what to say. So I told him that I was going to apply for the job as well. It's a little bit awkward, but I guess it's better that he knows. I mean, even though we're both competing for the same job, we should still be honest with each other. I have to say that I hope I get the position. We'll just have to wait and see!

Listen again. How has each situation changed?

Stephanie: Well, the Neighborhood Watch program has been running for more than five months and has been incredibly successful. We used to have a lot of minor problems on our block, but now it's very quiet. Everyone knows that our neighborhood is "off-limits" for troublemakers. Just last week we won a special award from the mayor's office. All of us were invited to a big awards ceremony – we had dinner, heard some guest speakers, and then accepted our award for outstanding community service. We all felt so proud. And it feels great to be living in this neighborhood.

Lee: To make a long story very short, um, . . . well, . . . I got the job. There were five of us who went for it, and I was chosen. At first it was very awkward because I know that Bill really wanted it. He was very upset. But now that a few weeks have gone by, he's calmed down a bit. I've gotten used to my new position, and my friendship with Bill is better than ever. You could say that I'm very relieved. And I love my new job!

This unit helps Ss expand their ability to talk about news events and tell personal stories, using adverbs of time and different forms of the past tense (simple past, past perfect, and past continuous tenses).

Storytelling

That's some story!

starting point These activities introduce the theme of storytelling and give examples of how to order events in a logical sequence, using adverbs of time and verbs in the simple past and past perfect tenses.

A Pair work

1 Books closed. Tell the class the very beginning and the very end of a frightening or embarrassing experience you've had. For example: "My friends told me not to go diving alone. . . . Afterwards, I realized how dangerous it had been." Ask Ss to guess what happened to you. Have Ss call out their answers. Then tell Ss the entire story.

2 **Optional:** Ask one or two Ss to tell the beginning and ending of a frightening, funny, or embarrassing story the same way you just did while others try to guess what happened. Then the Ss who introduced the stories tell the class what really happened.

3 Books open. Have Ss look at the pictures in the activity but not the texts (have Ss cover the text under each picture with a slip of paper). Put Ss in pairs and tell them to first describe what they see and then guess what might have happened in each picture. Have Ss call out their answers, and accept any that are reasonable.

4 Explain the task and have Ss silently read the six texts. Check Ss' comprehension of the following:

> **to pick up** to increase; to get stronger
> **to assure** to remove someone's doubt about something

5 Point out that different pictures need different parts of their stories filled in (see answers that follow). Then have Ss work in pairs to fill in the gaps. Have Ss make notes or write out the stories on a piece of paper. Circulate to help with ideas, grammar, or vocabulary. Have a few Ss share answers with the class.

Possible answers

1. I entered a contest and won free skydiving lessons. Normally, I would never do anything like skydiving, but I decided to give it a try since the lessons were free. At first, I just watched. Then it looked like lots of fun, so I listened to the instructions. The next thing I knew, I was being pushed out of the plane. It was fun, but I won't do it again. Afterwards my knees were shaking for several hours.

2. My friend lent me her watch because mine had broken. She told me to be very careful with it. I put it in my pocket because it was too small for my wrist. I must have used it several times that day. But when I got back to my friend's house and checked my pocket, I couldn't believe it. The watch was gone. Up until then, I had never lost anything important. I didn't know what to do. I decided to retrace my steps, and you know where I found it? On the floor of my car. I was so relieved.

3. My friend couldn't go windsurfing that day, so I decided to go alone. I had never gone windsurfing alone, but I thought it wouldn't be a big deal. When I started windsurfing the day looked great, and the wind was blowing softly. As soon as I was some distance from the shore, the wind really picked up. I started being blown out to sea, and I panicked and started shouting for help. Luckily some people in a motorboat heard me and came to my rescue. They lifted me and my board onto their boat, and we rode back to the beach in no time. Boy, that really taught me a lesson about sailing alone!

4. I left my home to go to work at the normal time. But it was raining really hard, and there was a terrible accident on the road. Also, the bus I was on was stopped on a huge highway in the middle of nowhere, so I had no way of getting to a phone to call my office. I was stuck there for about an hour. Finally the bus started up again and I arrived at work, very late. As soon as I arrived at work, my boss asked to speak to me. I knew he would never believe why I was late.

5. I assured my wife that I knew the way to the airport. It was only when I turned onto the main road, though, that I noticed I had made a mistake, and I didn't know how to get back on the road to the airport. I got hopelessly lost and had to ask directions several times. Luckily, our plane was delayed. Later, we laughed about it, but it wasn't funny at the time!

6. I flew to South America last summer. Before that, I'd never been on a plane. I had a cousin who was living in South America and had invited me to visit. I was really excited about the vacation, and I didn't really think about the plane trip until I got on the plane. I hated it. My ears felt strange, and every time I looked out the window, I thought I was going to be sick. The moment the plane landed, I felt relieved.

B Group work

1 Books open. Explain the task and then put Ss into groups of four or five. Have Ss take turns sharing the stories they created and then telling each other about similar experiences they've had. Encourage Ss to ask and answer follow-up questions about their similar experiences.

2 Have selected Ss or volunteers share either the story they created or a similar experience with the class.

How did it all end?

listening

In this activity, Ss practice listening for the main ideas.

1   Books open. Explain the task and make sure Ss know what information they need to listen for to complete the chart. Remind Ss to write in note form and summarize the story into one or two sentences/phrases only.

2   **Optional:** Play the audio program through once, and have Ss match each story to the correct picture from Exercise 1A (answers: story 1 and picture 2; story 2 and picture 4).

3   **Optional:** Pre-teach items from the following vocabulary list that you think will be helpful for your Ss:

> **an errand** a chore involving a short journey (e.g., going to the post office to mail letters)
>
> **a receipt** a slip of paper that shows you have paid for something you bought
>
> **panic** a feeling of uncontrolled fear
>
> **to be stuck (in something)** to be fixed tightly (in a position) and unable to break free

4   Play the audio program, and have Ss complete the chart as they listen. Then Ss compare answers with a partner.

5   Ask selected Ss or volunteers to share answers with the class. Then go over the answers with the class.

Possible answers

> **Story 1:** Took mother's ring to be repaired and left it at jeweler's by mistake. Jeweler called.
>
> **Story 2:** Was late for work because got skirt stuck in subway door and had to go several stops out of her way before she could get off.

Transcript

> **Listen to two entire stories from Exercise A. What happened in each situation?**
>
> **Man:** You see, my mother had this ring. It was kind of old. It had been given to her by *her* mother, my grandmother. It had been in our family for years. Anyway, my mother asked me to take it to the jeweler's to get it repaired. She told me to be very careful with it.
>
> Later that day, I dropped the ring off at the jeweler's and ran off to do the rest of my errands. It was a busy day, and I was feeling really crazy. I had to get back to the jeweler's before they closed at five P.M. and pick up the ring.
>
> I got to the jeweler's at about a quarter to five, paid for the ring, and raced home. It was getting pretty late. But when I went to give my mother the ring, the worst thing happened. I couldn't find it. I checked all my pockets, but all I found was the receipt. The ring wasn't there. I looked everywhere! You can imagine how panicked I felt. Up until then, I had never lost anything important. I didn't know what to do.

Just then, the phone rang. It was the jeweler's. They were calling to say I had run out of the store in such a hurry that I'd forgotten to take the ring! They still had the ring at their store. So, the ring wasn't lost after all. What a relief!

Woman: I had this big meeting at work that day. Really important.

I left my home to go to work at the normal time. I always take the subway to work. On this morning, the train was especially crowded, and I could barely squeeze onto it. I got on just as the doors closed.

Well, after a couple of minutes, I realized that my skirt had been caught in the subway doors. I couldn't pull it out! A man standing next to me tried to help me, but we still couldn't get it. By this time, I was so embarrassed. Other people were staring at me. And my skirt was really stuck.

Well, wouldn't you know it, the doors to the subway opened on the other side for the next six or seven stations. I had to miss my stop. I just stood there, with my skirt stuck in the door, unable to move. Finally, the doors opened on my side. I was able to leave the train. Now I was really late.

As soon as I arrived at work, my boss asked to speak to me. I knew he would never believe why I was late. I felt so stupid! Of course, later we all laughed about it.

Optional activity: *Details, details*

Time: 5–10 minutes. Ss listen for specific details about the stories.

1 Books open. Explain that you will be replaying the audio program and that Ss are to listen for the answers to the following questions. Write these questions on the board:

Story 1

1. Why was the ring so special?

2. What time did the jeweler's close?

3. What time did he get to the jeweler's?

4. What did he find when he was looking for the ring?

Story 2

1. Why was it especially important to be on time that morning?

2. Why did she get her skirt stuck in the door?

3. Who tried to help her?

4. Why couldn't she get her skirt unstuck at the next stop?

Possible answers

> **Story 1: 1.** because it was old and had been his grandmother's (it had been in the family for years)
> **2.** 5:00
> **3.** 4:45 *or* a quarter to five
> **4.** only the receipt
> **Story 2: 1.** because she had an important meeting

continued

> **2.** She got on the train just as the doors were closing, and they closed on her skirt.
>
> **3.** a man standing next to her
>
> **4.** because the doors were opening on the other side

2 Ss first attempt to answer the questions from memory. Then replay the audio program while Ss check their answers and complete the remaining ones. Go over the answers as a class.

3 **Optional:** Ask Ss to say how they would have felt and what they would have done in similar situations.

Adverbs with the past and past perfect

grammar focus This grammar focus presents the use of adverbs with the past and past perfect tenses to logically connect a chain of events in the past.

> **Grammar notes** These are adverbials of time that describe when in the past an action or event happened.
>
> The past perfect is used with the first set of adverbs when talking about a past action completed before another action in the past (e.g., Before that, I *had* never *lost* anything important.).
>
> The simple past is often used with the second set of adverbs to describe events happening simultaneously in the past (e.g., The moment it happened, I *screamed.*).
>
> The simple past is also used with the third set of adverbs to describe an event that happened later in the past (e.g., The next day, I *felt* tired.).
>
> When the past perfect is used in sentences with two clauses, it usually appears in the dependent clause, introduced by an adverbial of time (e.g., Just after I *had started* working, my boss arrived.).

1 Books open. Lead Ss through the information and examples in the grammar box. Have them look back at the texts in Exercise 1A on page 58 to find and underline additional examples of adverbs with the simple past and past perfect tenses. If necessary, review the use of the simple past and the past perfect tenses.

2 Explain the task and go over the example with the class. Have Ss work alone to write two sentences for each of the remaining situations. Remind them to use the adverbs from the grammar box. Point out that their sentences should form a story.

3 Have Ss compare answers in small groups of three to five. Have groups choose their group's most interesting sentences to share with the class.

Possible answers

1. Up until then, I had never had anything stolen before. The moment it happened, I screamed, "Pickpocket!"

2. The moment I started talking, my legs started shaking. Before that, I had never made a speech to such a large group of people.

3. As soon as I got the results, I began jumping up and down. Later, I felt this huge sense of relief.

4. When I arrived, I discovered my suitcase was missing. Before that, I'd never experienced any problems on a trip, but this trip was a disaster.

5. Before that, I had never been late for anything. The moment I saw the traffic jam, I realized there was no way out of it.

6. Until that time, I'd always thought I'd never get married. The next day, I had trouble believing it.

Optional activity: *Passing it on*

Time: 10–15 minutes. Ss use the adverbs and verb tenses presented in the grammar focus.

1 *Group work* Books closed. Write the adverbs from the grammar box on the board. Then have Ss form groups of six to eight and sit in a row or circle. Tell Ss you are going to write the beginning of a story on the board and their job is to finish it, with each S adding one sentence. Tell Ss they can continue the story any way they like, as long as they use one of the adverbs on the board and complete the story as quickly as possible.

2 Write the beginning of a story on the board (e.g., *The police came to my house last night.*). Then have groups complete the story as just described.

3 As soon as a group is finished, tell them to raise their hands. Go over to check the group's work. If there are any grammatical errors, tell them to work together to find the errors and that you'll come back to check again when they've corrected them. Alternatively, circle the errors but have the group try to correct them on their own.

4 The first group to complete the story with no errors in their sentences is the winner.

Uncomfortable situations

discussion   These activities consolidate and expand the grammar of the lesson.

A

1 Books open. Have Ss look at the three pictures. Ask selected Ss or volunteers to say what they think has happened or is happening in each. Have Ss call out their answers.

2 Explain the task and go over the example. Put Ss in pairs to complete the task by matching each sentence to the appropriate picture. Then have Ss compare answers with another pair before going over the answers as a class.

Answers

1. C	3. A	5. C	7. A	9. B
2. B	4. B	6. A	8. C	

B Pair work

Books open. Explain the task and go over the model language in the balloon. Then put Ss in pairs to take turns telling one of the stories. Explain that Ss will need to add details to the story. Remind Ss to use the adverbs presented in the lesson. When most pairs have finished, bring the class back together and choose some Ss at random to tell one of their stories to the class.

C Pair work

1   Books open. Explain the task and tell Ss what you would have done in the first situation and why. Ask one or two Ss if they would have done the same thing. If they say no, ask them to tell the class what they would have done and why.

2   Put Ss in pairs to discuss what they would have done in each situation. Encourage Ss to give reasons for their answers and to ask and answer follow-up questions.

Unexpected experiences

discussion   In these activities, Ss tell their own stories and practice using past tenses and adverbs to put events in a logical sequence.

A Pair work

1   Books open. Explain the task and have Ss look at the picture. Ss describe what is happening and what the boy is probably feeling. Then have Ss read the sentences in the box and the example in the speech balloon.

2   Put Ss in pairs, and have them take turns telling each other their stories. Encourage them to use the adverbs from the grammar focus to describe the order of events, and to ask and answer follow-up questions. Circulate to provide help as needed.

B Group work

1   Books open. Explain the task and combine pairs into groups of four. Ss should take turns sharing their stories. Encourage Ss to monitor each other's use of adverbs, making sure that the stories are logical and the teller provides enough information and detail.

2   **Optional:** Each group votes on the best story. Then the "winner" in each group shares his or her story with the class. If you wish, have the class vote on the best story of all.

Optional activity: *True or false?*

Time: 10–15 minutes. Ss continue to relate experiences using the adverbs from the grammar focus.

1 *Group work* Books open. Have Ss form groups of four, and send one S from each group out of the room. Tell the remaining Ss that two of them should prepare false stories and one should prepare a true story about an experience similar to one they talked about in Exercise 5B. Remind Ss to use adverbs to order the events in their stories. Give groups 3 minutes to prepare their stories. Circulate to provide help as needed.

2 When the time is up, invite the fourth S to return to the group. Have the others take turns telling their stories. The fourth S guesses which story is true and explains why he or she thinks so. The other Ss confirm or correct this S's answer. If time permits, repeat the activity with students swapping roles in their group.

6 | ## My most embarrassing moments

listening

In these activities, Ss first practice listening for gist and details.

A Pair work

1 Books closed. Ask if any Ss are easily embarrassed and what kinds of things embarrass them. Have a few volunteers share an answer with the class.

2 Books open. Explain the task and put Ss in pairs to take turns telling each other some embarrassing things that have happened to them.

B

1 Books open. Explain the task, making sure Ss know what kind of information they need to listen for in order to complete the chart. Point out that Ss need to write only a few words to sum up each speaker's most embarrassing moment. Play the audio program once without stopping, and ask Ss not to worry about details at this point; rather, they should try to get the general idea of each situation as they listen.

2 **Optional:** Pre-teach items from the following vocabulary list that you think will be helpful for your Ss:

> **to struggle** to make a great effort and experience difficulty doing something
> **on the spot** immediately
> **war stories** here, used figuratively to mean stories about dangerous or
>   difficult personal experiences
> **desperate** willing to take risks to change a bad situation

3 Have Ss write whatever answers they can. Then replay the audio program, this time pausing occasionally to give Ss time to write their answers. Put Ss in pairs to compare answers with a partner before going over the answers with the class.

Answers

> Getting fired from her job at the department store because she was napping under the hat racks.
>
> Working as a painter and having an allergic reaction to the paint. Also, being too sore after her first day on the job to go back to work the next day.
>
> Losing her job as a taxi driver after she crashed into a pole.
>
> *Note:* These situations are embarrassing because Stella couldn't do anything right until she became a famous actress!

Transcript

> **Listen to actress Stella Hamptons talking about her life. What are some of her most embarrassing moments?**
>
> **Host:** Hello, everyone. We're talking to Stella Hamptons, famous Hollywood actress. Before the break, we were talking about your life, Stella, before you became a big star.
>
> **Stella:** Yes, . . . Oh, but do we have to?
>
> **Host:** Well, I think it's interesting. And I think our listeners will find it interesting, too. I mean, you didn't become a big star overnight. You struggled for many years.
>
> **Stella:** You can say that again.
>
> **Host:** Tell us a little about it.
>
> **Stella:** Oh, yes. I think I must have worked twenty or thirty different jobs.
>
> **Host:** Really?
>
> **Stella:** Sure! I couldn't find work as an actress for many years, so I had to do something. You have to eat, right?
>
> **Host:** What kinds of jobs did you have?
>
> **Stella:** A little bit of everything: I worked as a waitress, in a department store, painting houses. . . . I think I got fired from most of those jobs.
>
> **Host:** Oh, yeah? C'mon, tell us a few stories.
>
> **Stella:** This is so embarrassing. . . . Well, I remember I worked for a big department store in the hats department. It was so boring. We never had any customers during the day, and that's when I worked. When I got sleepy, I used to lie down under the hat racks and take an occasional nap.
>
> **Host:** What happened?
>
> **Stella:** Well, one day I got caught – by my boss. And I got fired on the spot. Then there was the time I decided to paint houses. It turned out that I was allergic to the paint. And my body was so sore after working the first day, I could hardly get out of bed the next day. I couldn't take the physical work. I got fired again.
>
> **Host:** Any other war stories?
>
> **Stella:** Well, . . . you're not going to believe this, but I actually drove a taxi for a few days. I got hired as a cab driver.
>
> **Host:** No! You?

Stella: Yes. I was desperate and thought I could make good tips. I needed the money at the time. Unfortunately, it didn't last.

Host: Fired?

Stella: Yep. How did you guess? On my third day, I hit a pole. No one was hurt in the accident – my passenger was fine – but it scared me to death. That was the end of my career as a driver.

Host: Well, Stella, thanks for sharing those details with us. It's a good thing you made it as an actress! After the commercial break, we'll talk more with Stella about her new movie that's being released in September.

 Creating a chain story

discussion In this activity, the whole class works together to create fun stories while practicing the grammar learned in this lesson.

Class activity

1 Books open. Explain the activity and have Ss read the opening sentences in the box and the model language below it. Check Ss' comprehension of the following vocabulary items:

> **exotic** unusual, exciting and far away
> **shortcut** a quicker way to get somewhere than the usual route

2 Have the class choose one of the six sentences to begin the story. Then have each S add a sentence. Remind Ss to use the adverbs presented in the grammar focus. Also encourage them to come up with creative and interesting sentences to continue the story. After each S has had a chance to add one or two sentences, choose one S to bring an end to the story.

 Putting events in order

writing These writing activities focus on ordering a story chronologically and combining sentences into paragraphs.

A

1 Books closed. Ask Ss to call out what a narrative is (answer: another word for a story). Then ask Ss to call out what chronological order is. Explain that chronological order refers to the time sequence of events, and that writers often use chronological order to organize narratives when they want to describe a sequence of events. Point out that Ss were using chronological order in the storytelling activities on page 60 of the Student's Book.

2 Books open. Have Ss look at the three pictures, and ask the class if they can guess what the story is about. Have Ss call out their answers, but don't comment on them at this point.

3 Explain the task and have Ss read the thirteen sentences, pointing out that the first three sentences introduce the story. Then have Ss work individually to put the sentences in chronological order. Have Ss compare answers with a partner. Then go over the answers with the class.

Answers

> (from beginning to end: 4, 9, 8, 6, 10, 12, 1, 2, 11, 3, 13, 7, 5)
> I was taking a walk on the beach and stopped to look at the waves.
> I thought I saw something struggling in the water.
> It looked like a man who was having trouble swimming.
> I reached for my glasses, and then remembered I'd left them at home. I couldn't see the object clearly.
> A big wave came, and the man was gone.
> I ran as fast as I could to get the lifeguard.
> We arrived back at the spot where I had seen the man.
> The lifeguard looked through his binoculars.
> He said he didn't see a thing.
> I bought a newspaper. There was an article about dolphins swimming near the shore.
> I read the article. I realized that I had seen a dolphin in the water – not a man!
> I was pretty embarrassed.
> I never went anywhere without my glasses again.

B

Books open. Explain the task. Point out that there is more than one way to combine the sentences. Have Ss work individually to combine the sentences from Exercise A using the adverbs listed. Circulate to help. Have Ss compare answers with a partner. Then have a few Ss share their paragraphs with the class before going over the following sample paragraph. Remind Ss again that more than one solution to the exercise is possible.

Sample paragraph

> *One day* I was taking a walk on the beach and stopped to look at the waves. *Suddenly,* I thought I saw something struggling in the water. It looked like a man who was having trouble swimming. *At that moment,* I reached for my glasses, and then remembered I'd left them at home. I couldn't see the object clearly. *Just then,* a big wave came, and the man was gone. I ran as fast as I could to get the lifeguard. *After that* we arrived back at the spot where I had seen the man. *When* the lifeguard looked through his binoculars, he said he didn't see a thing. *The next day* I bought a newspaper. There was an article about dolphins

swimming near the shore. *As soon as* I read the article, I realized that I had seen a dolphin in the water – not a man! I was pretty embarrassed. *After that* I never went anywhere without my glasses again.

C

1 Books open. Explain the task and tell Ss they can write their paragraph either about one of the stories they told in Exercise 5 on page 60 or about a new story. Also point out that they can make up a story about an imagined experience. Remind Ss that they should organize their paragraph in chronological order, using adverbs with past tenses.

2 **Optional:** Have Ss make a list, in chronological order, of the events in the story they plan to tell before they write.

3 Either in class or for homework, have Ss individually write their paragraph.

D Group work

1 **Optional:** Books closed. First collect all the Ss' stories. Read four or five aloud, and ask Ss to guess who wrote each. Then return the papers.

2 Books open. Explain the task and put Ss in groups of four or five. Have Ss take turns reading their paragraphs aloud. When each S finishes reading, have the other group members ask follow-up questions.

3 Have each group vote on the most interesting story. Then have the S with the most interesting story in each group read his or her paragraph to the class.

 What's in the news?

 News events

starting These activities introduce the theme of news events and news stories and
point preview the grammar of the lesson.

A

1 Books closed. Ask the class a few questions about newspapers, such as: "Do you read the newspaper every day? What newspaper do you usually read? What kind of news stories do you enjoy reading most?" Then write the six headlines in the book on the board. Have Ss work in pairs to guess what each headline is about. Then ask selected Ss or volunteers to share one or more of their predictions with the class. Accept all reasonable answers.

2 Books open. Have Ss quickly skim the six articles to check their predictions. Then explain the task, and have Ss read the questions below the box. Then tell Ss to read the articles, pointing out that it is not necessary to understand the meaning of every word because their purpose is to understand what each article is about. Ss read the articles and answer the questions.

3 Ask a few selected Ss which article they'd most like to read and which article interests them least.

B Pair work

1 Books open. Explain the task and have Ss read the model language in the balloon. Put Ss in pairs to compare answers. Encourage them to give reasons for their answers and to ask and answer follow-up questions. Then have selected Ss or volunteers share answers with the class. Lead a class discussion, as appropriate.

2 **Optional:** Tally Ss' answers to the second question on the board. Lead a class discussion, as appropriate.

C Group work

1 Books open. Explain the task and have Ss individually or in pairs write an ending for one of the articles in Exercise A. Put Ss in groups of six or seven to read their endings to each other.

2 **Optional:** Have the Ss read their article endings to the rest of their group without telling them which article it belongs with. Group members guess the title of the correct article.

Optional activity: *Beginnings and endings*

Time: 15–20 minutes. Ss practice writing short news stories.

1 Books closed. Divide the class into two groups. Give Ss a news headline, such as "1000 Dancers Are Not Enough." Have one group of Ss individually write the beginning of the story and the other group write the end of the story.

2 Have the two groups stand and circulate, reading to each other their parts of the story to try to find the beginning or ending that best matches what they've written. When Ss find a suitable partner or partners, have them work together to fill in the gaps in the story. Then have several Ss share their story with the class.

 What section is it?

discussion In this activity, Ss classify newspaper articles according to the sections of the newspaper where they fit best.

Pair work

1 Books closed. Bring a few English language newspapers to class and point out the various sections to the class. Then distribute the different sections of the newspapers to groups of Ss to share. (Alternatively, ask Ss ahead of time to bring a newspaper of their own to class.) Ask Ss to say in which sections they would find specific news items, such as the movie schedule and the weather. Have Ss call out their answers.

2 Books open. Explain the task and lead Ss through the sections of the newspaper listed. Check that Ss understand the following vocabulary items:

> **editor** a person who is in charge of a newspaper or magazine
> **editorials** newspaper articles that express the editor's opinion on a current topic or news item
> **feature stories** special articles in a newspaper about topics rather than news stories

3 Direct Ss' attention back to the articles in Exercise 1A. Ask in what sections they would find the first article. Have Ss call out their answer (answer: feature stories *or* international news).

4 Put Ss in pairs to match the remaining articles in Exercise 1A to the appropriate sections of the newspaper. Then have Ss discuss the questions, encouraging them to give reasons for their answers.

5 Have selected Ss or volunteers share one or more answers with the class.

Possible answers

> Woman Pilot Completes Journey: feature stories or international news
> New Show Succeeds in Multiple Markets: entertainment news or business news
> New Film Has Brightest Stars: entertainment news
> Nowhere to Run: local news or weather news
> Local Man Sets Doughnut Record: local news or feature stories
> Music Craze Continues: entertainment news

Present perfect vs. past

grammar focus This grammar focus reviews and contrasts the use of the present perfect tense and the past tense.

> **Grammar notes** The present perfect is used to express a relationship between the speaker and the events in the past that he or she is talking about. It might be an event in the past that continues into the present (e.g., A lion *has escaped* from the zoo.) or a past experience with current relevance (e.g., I *have* already *bought* the tickets for tonight's show.).
>
> When the present perfect is used, the focus of interest is on the action rather than the time the action happened.
>
> The simple past is used to describe an event that happened at a specified time in the past.

1 Books closed. Write these two sentences on the board: *Officials have announced the World Cup schedule. Officials announced the World Cup schedule last Friday.* Ask Ss to comment on any differences they notice between the two sentences. Then point out that the first sentence contains no time reference, whereas the second sentence contains a specific time reference (i.e., last Friday).

2 Books open. Lead Ss through the information and example sentences in the grammar focus. Then ask: "Which of the two sentences written on the board uses the present perfect? Why?" Have Ss call out their answer. (answer: The first sentence describes a past event at an unspecified time.) Then ask, "Why does the other sentence use the past tense?" (answer: because it describes a past event at a specified time in the past.).

3 Optional: Have Ss look through the newspaper articles in Exercise 1A again and underline examples of the present perfect tense and the past tense, along with the specific time references.

4 Books open. Explain the task and go over the example. Point out again that this sentence describes an event that happened at an unspecified time in the past and, therefore, takes the present perfect tense. Then have Ss individually complete the rest of the exercise, using either the past tense or the present perfect tense as appropriate. Put Ss in pairs to compare answers before going over them with the class.

Answers

1. has destroyed	**5.** have discovered
2. escaped	**6.** damaged/broke/sprayed
3. vanished	**7.** has won
4. have enjoyed	**8.** realized/have disappeared

Optional activity: *Making news*

Ss use keywords as a springboard for writing their own news stories.

1 *Group work* Books open. Put Ss in groups of four or five, and then write the following on the board:
1. pop singer Madonna/concerts;
2. heavy rains/floods/closed roads;
3. airline pilots/strike/World Cup.
Tell Ss to choose one news item and write a three- or four-line article about it while you circulate to offer assistance with vocabulary.

2 Have selected Ss read their news articles to the class.

Possible answers

1. The famous pop singer Madonna has arrived in New York for the second leg of her world tour. She gave a series of concerts in Los Angeles from October 9 through October 15, which were sold out and got great reviews from music critics.
2. Heavy rains have fallen in southern Florida since last week. Many buildings have flooded, causing billions of dollars worth of damage. Roads have closed in many cities, causing traffic jams all over the area. In some cases it has taken hours to travel only a few miles.
3. The airline pilots of several airlines have gone on strike just before the start of the World Cup. Fans from all over the world have had to find other means of transportation, or miss their games. No agreement has been reached between the airline pilots and management, and the strike is expected to continue for many days.

Past vs. past continuous

grammar focus This grammar focus reviews and contrasts the past tense and the past continuous tense.

> **Grammar notes** The past continuous tense is used to describe an event or action that happened over a period of time in the past (e.g., The dog *was barking* all night long.).
>
> If this action is interrupted or intersected by another action, the second action is expressed in the simple past tense (e.g., She *was walking* home from school when it started to rain.). The action expressed by the past continuous goes on for a longer time than the action expressed by the simple past tense. The time words *while, when,* and *as* are used to show the time relationship between the two clauses.
>
> The past continuous tense is also known as the past progressive tense.

1 Books open. Go over the information and example sentences in the grammar box. Point out that adverbs such as *calmly* and *wildly* can appear before or after the main verb. Provide additional examples by using sentences 2, 3, and 6 from Exercise 3 and having Ss add suitable past continuous actions to each one.

2 Ask Ss to look at the photograph and describe what they think is happening. Explain the task and go over the example. Have Ss work individually to complete each item with either the past continuous or the past tense of the verbs in parentheses, as appropriate. Then have Ss compare with a partner before going over the answers as a class.

Possible answers

1. visited; gave
2. was flying; began
3. was waiting; arrived
4. was waving; climbed
5. said; kissed

You'll find it in the newspaper.

vocabulary In these activities, Ss learn vocabulary for different kinds of news stories, and then use the language to discuss recent events in the news.

A Pair work

1 Books open. Explain the task and have Ss say what is pictured (answer: a volcano). Ask Ss why the photograph is labeled "a natural disaster."

2 Have Ss work with a partner to explain what each item means. Pairs may use a dictionary and can either make notes or write out their answers. Have selected pairs explain one of their items to the class.

Optional activity: *Playing definitions*

Time: 10–15 minutes. Ss continue practicing with the words for news events and their definitions.

1 Books closed. On small cards, write down definitions of the words in Exercise 5. If you have a large class, write the same definition on several cards so that each S will have at least three different definitions. Pass out the definition cards to the Ss, making sure each S has at least three cards and that none are duplicates. Give Ss a moment to look over the definitions they've received.

2 Explain that Ss are going to play a card game and that they should not show the definitions they have to any other S. Explain that the objective is to get rid of the card with the definition of the word the teacher calls out by having another S pick it from their hand.

3 Call out one of the 9 words listed for news events in the Student's Book. As soon as you call out the word, give Ss 30 seconds to pick one card from another S. Ss who have the definition of the word still in their hand should come to the front and present it to the teacher. These Ss get a point for recognizing the correct definition. Ss lose a point if they present an incorrect definition. Ss do not receive or lose any points if they had the definition but did not come to the front of the room. Have Ss keep track of their own scores.

4 Continue as time allows. The game will go rather quickly once Ss get the hang of it. The game ends when all the words have been called. The Ss with the most points by the end of the game win.

B Pair work

1 Books open. Explain the task and have Ss read the sample dialog. Then put Ss in pairs to discuss news events they've read about lately.

2 Have selected Ss or volunteers tell the class about one of their news stories.

6 *On the radio*

listening

In these activities, Ss listen to a radio news broadcast and practice listening for gist and for specific information.

A

1 Books open. Explain the task and have Ss read the list of six possible answers. Point out that the first time Ss listen, they should listen only to determine the type of news story each of the three reports is about. Then play the audio program, and have Ss complete the left side of the chart by writing the number of the type of each news event as they listen. Have Ss compare answers with a partner, and then go over the correct answers with the whole class.

Answers

| 2: epidemic | 3: scandal | 1: natural disaster | 6: human interest story |

2 Optional: Pre-teach items from the following vocabulary list that you think will be helpful for your Ss:

potential possible

epidemic a disease that spreads rapidly and infects many people in an area

untreatable not curable by known methods

cases patients with a particular illness [in this case, TB]

tuberculosis (TB) a disease of the lungs

a sunflower a plant with a large round yellow flower

authenticity the state of being real or true

a fake an object made to look real in order to deceive people

landslide a mass of rock and earth moving suddenly and quickly down a steep slope

an impact an effect

harassed feeling anxious because you have too many problems

brownies chocolate cakelike desserts cut into squares

negotiations formal discussions between people with different opinions in order to reach an agreement

3 Replay the audio program; this time Ss take notes about what happened in each story as they listen. Pause between each report if you wish to give Ss time to write. Have Ss compare notes with a partner, but don't go over the notes as a class until after Exercise B.

Transcript

Listen to an early morning news broadcast. Write down the number of each type of news story you hear. Then take notes about what happened.

Announcer: It's seven o'clock and time for the news. Our top stories today:

First, this from the World Health Organization, or the W-H-O. The W-H-O has reported that we are facing a potential global epidemic due to untreatable cases of tuberculosis, also known as TB. TB is dangerous because it affects the lungs. The number of cases is growing worldwide, and this has researchers worried. According to a study, a third of all known TB cases are untreatable. The drugs normally used to treat TB are simply not working. Researchers are trying hard to find out why this is the case. For now, the W-H-O is planning an international program to educate people about the dangers of TB.

And now we have a report on the artist Vincent van Gogh. Of course, you may know that van Gogh is a famous nineteenth-century painter. You may also be familiar with one of his famous paintings: the one of flowers – sunflowers to be exact. It was painted in 1888 by van Gogh. Well, a scandal erupted in London yesterday over the authenticity of van Gogh's *Sunflowers*. The painting was recently bought by a large multinational company for several million dollars. And now, an art expert is saying that the painting is a fake. Authorities are looking into the matter.

Next, to Mexico. Hurricane Pauline pounded Acapulco and nearby areas last night, leaving many people homeless. The strong winds and heavy rains made for horrible conditions. Floods and landslides destroyed homes and cars, especially in the hillside areas. Rescue is particularly difficult because streets are blocked, in most cases, by mud. It's believed that some people may be trapped inside their homes and cannot get out. Most people have left their homes and are

continued

now safely in temporary shelters. This natural disaster is going to have a big impact on the tourist business in Acapulco this year.

Finally, a story for all you parents out there: How often do your kids push you to your limit, and what do you do about it? One tired and harassed mother from Illinois decided she'd had enough yesterday. Instead of yelling at her children, as she normally would, she decided to leave. She walked out the door and climbed a tree – the tree with her children's tree house in it, that is. She decided to stay in the tree house until her three children stopped misbehaving. She told her children she had decided to stay in their tree house until they started appreciating her more. She put a sign in front of the tree house that said "On Strike – No cooking, cleaning, doctoring, banking, or driving until demands met." The children tried to persuade her to come down, but no luck. Finally, one of them had the smart idea of baking their mother's favorite treat – brownies. Well, they must have smelled good because that did the trick. Mom agreed to come down and meet her children at the bargaining table. No word yet on the outcome of those negotiations, though. That's it for now. We'll be back in an hour with more news.

B

1 Books open. Explain the task and then replay the audio program. Point out that this time Ss should listen for more specific words and ideas and try to take more complete notes about each news report. Have Ss take notes on a piece of paper while you replay the audio program.

2 Have Ss compare notes with a partner. Then ask selected Ss or volunteers to read their notes. Compile a class set of notes for each news story on the board.

Possible answers (Answers will vary depending on the notes Ss took in Exercise A.)

News story	What happened
2. epidemic	WHO worried about global epidemic of tuberculosis. Researchers are worried. Drugs are not working. WHO is planning an international program.
3. scandal	Scandal erupted in London yesterday about Vincent van Gogh's famous painting *Sunflowers,* painted in 1888. Recently bought by a multinational company for several million dollars. Art expert says that the painting is a fake. Authorities looking into the matter.
1. natural disaster	Hurricane Pauline pounded Acapulco in Mexico. Left many people homeless. Strong winds and heavy rains caused horrible conditions. Floods and landslides destroyed homes and cars. Rescue difficult because streets are blocked by mud. People trapped inside their homes. Others in temporary shelters. Natural disaster will be bad for tourism in Acapulco.
6. human interest story	Harassed mother from Illinois had enough of yelling at children. Decided to leave. Climbed into children's tree house and said she would stay until children appreciated her more. Sign in front of tree house: "On Strike." Children tried to persuade her to come down, but no luck. Then they baked mother's favorite, brownies, and she agreed to bargain. No word yet on outcome of negotiations.

C Pair work

Books open. Explain the task and then put Ss in pairs to take turns telling the news stories to each other in their own words. Tell Ss they may use their notes as a reference, but they should try to be creative and tell the story in their own way. Remind Ss to look up from their notes when they are talking.

Preparing a news story

discussion In this activity, Ss work in groups to create a news story of their own.

Group work

1   Books open. Have Ss look at the three pictures and call out the type of news story each is and what each might be about. Then explain the task, and put Ss in groups of four or five. Have groups choose one of the three pictures and then work together to create their own news story about it. Encourage groups to include as much detail as possible and to think of a good headline for their story.

2   After about 10 minutes, have each group choose a spokesperson to present the news story to the class. Alternatively, have each member in each group take turns telling a bit of the news story they created.

3   **Optional:** Have the class vote on the most convincing or creative news story.

"Nutty" news

reading In these activities, Ss practice reading for main ideas and inferring additional information from an existing text.

A

1   Books open. Explain the task and go over the three headlines. Then have Ss silently read the three news articles to match each to the appropriate headline.

2   Ss add information to each headline while you circulate to help. Then have Ss compare answers with a partner.

3   Have a few Ss read one of their complete headlines to the class. Then go over the answers.

Possible answers

> _3_ Vanished Pet   _1_ A Letter from Mom   _2_ Illegal Passenger
> Article 1: A Letter from Mom Sends Bank Robber to Jail
> Article 2: Illegal Passenger Is Furry and Well Behaved
> Article 3: Vanished Pet Recognizes Owner in Court

B Pair work

Books open. Explain the task and then put Ss in pairs to complete the task. Combine pairs to form groups of four to compare answers. Then go over the answers with the class.

Possible answers

3 The bird was taken to the police station to determine its rightful owner.

1 Most of the letter was about how proud she was that Bailey was staying out of trouble.

2 In fact, another passenger commented on how well behaved he was.

Article 1: Unfortunately for Bailey, he had written his note on an envelope that contained a letter from his mother. *Most of the letter was about how proud she was that Bailey was staying out of trouble.* The bank teller noticed Bailey's name and address on the envelope as soon as he handed it to her.

Article 2: Alex caused no trouble when he woke up as he was strapped into his own seat, purchased at the full fare of $400. *In fact, another passenger commented on how well behaved he was.* He was enjoying his lunch when the trouble began.

Article 3: But when she heard the familiar screech "Hello, Raquel!" as she walked past a neighbor's house one weekend, she called the police. *The bird was taken to the police station to determine its rightful owner.* The neighbor denied the bird was Raquel and said he had bought it from a pet store three years ago.

C Group work

1 Books open. Explain the task and then combine pairs to form groups of four. Have Ss take turns sharing unusual news stories, and ask and answer follow-up questions.

2 Each group decides whose story is more surprising. If time permits, have each group share a story with the class.

This unit highlights the past forms of *should, ought to,* and *wish* to refer to wishes and regrets in the past, adjectives of emotion + past time clauses to express feelings about past actions, and noun clauses introduced by *it* and by verbs to evaluate character traits and describe hopes and beliefs.

Growing up

Fond memories and regrets

starting point   In these activities, Ss read about and describe other people's personal values.

Pair work

1   Books closed. On the board write *values, fond memories, regrets.* Work with the class to define each one.

> **values** beliefs a person has that are important in his or her life
> **fond memories** good memories
> **regrets** feelings of sadness or disappointment about something that went wrong
> or a mistake that you made in the past

2   **Optional:** Tell the class about a value, a fond memory, and a regret you have in your own life.

3   Have Ss work alone for some moments to think of a value, a fond memory, and a regret they have in their lives. Then have selected Ss or volunteers share answers with the class.

4   Books open. Explain the task. Have Ss look at the photograph and say what city they see (answer: Hong Kong). Ask Ss to describe the character of Hong Kong, eliciting that it is very international, cosmopolitan, etc. Have Ss read Joe's statement, and then state the value being expressed.

5   Have Ss silently read the texts to find what values each person believes in or rejects, underlining their answers in the text. Then ask Ss to read the model answers in the speech balloons.

6   Put Ss in pairs to discuss each person's values. Have selected Ss or volunteers tell the class about one person's values.

Possible answers

Joe believes it's important to be tolerant of other people's cultures and beliefs.
Sharon believes it's important to get encouragement and support from one's family.
Penny believes you should always put other people's needs before your own.
Stan believes the main thing in life is to have as much fun as possible.
Cal believes it's impossible to be happy without money.
Angel believes you shouldn't take your friends for granted.

Values I learned

discussion   In this activity, Ss compare their own values to those expressed in Exercise 1.

Pair work

1   Books open. Explain the task. Have Ss read the model language in the speech balloons. Then have Ss choose the person from Exercise 1 that they are most like and the values from Exercise 1 that they think are the most important.

2   Put Ss in pairs to share and discuss their answers. Have several students call out and explain their answers. Encourage class discussion.

Optional activity: *Values learned as a child*

Time: 5–10 minutes. Ss further explore the topic of the unit.

Group work Books open. Tell Ss to list two or three values their parents or family tried to instill in them. After a few minutes, put Ss in groups of four or five to share their values and discuss the importance of these values to their lives at the moment.

Should have *and* ought to have; *wishes about the past*

grammar
focus   This grammar focus presents the structures of *should have, ought to have,* and wishes about the past to express regrets.

> **Grammar notes** In American English, *should not have* is more common than *ought not to have*. Also note that the word *that* in sentences with *wish* is optional. Following are some examples of the relationship between structure and meaning for statements with *should, ought to,* and *wish* in the past.

Structure	Meaning
ought to / should + present perfect I ought to/should have spent more time going out with my friends.	I didn't spend a lot of time with my friends in the past. Now I regret it.
wish + (that) + past perfect (affirmative) I wish (that) I had saved some money.	I didn't save money in the past. Now I regret it.
wish + (that) + past perfect (negative) I wish (that) I hadn't been so selfish.	I was selfish in the past. Now I regret it.
shouldn't / ought not to + present perfect I ought not to/shouldn't have been so critical of my best friend.	I was critical of my best friend in the past. Now I regret it.

1 Books closed. Write these sentences on the board: *I should have studied English harder. I ought to have listened to my grandfather's advice. I shouldn't have been so shy when I was a child. I wish (that) I'd been more outgoing. I wish (that) I hadn't been so negative about everything.*

2 Ask the class, "Do these statements describe values, fond memories, or regrets?" Have Ss call out their answer (regrets). Then ask the class several questions, such as: "What's something you should have studied harder? What advice should you have listened to?" Have Ss call out their answers, and write them on the board in full sentences to provide additional examples of the pattern.

3 **Optional:** Have Ss look back at the statements in Exercise 1 on page 66 of the Student's Book and underline examples of regrets using *should, ought to,* and *wish* with the past.

4 Books open. Lead Ss through the information and examples in the grammar focus. Explain as necessary, and have Ss work as a class to come up with some additional example sentences.

5 As a class or in pairs, have Ss try to work out the rule for the use of the present perfect and the past perfect with *should, ought to,* and *wish.* Ss should be able to do this by examining the sentences in the box. Have Ss call out their answers.

Possible answer

Should, shouldn't, and *ought to* are always followed by a verb in the present perfect. *Wish,* in both negative and affirmative statements, is always followed by a verb in the past perfect tense when used to describe regrets.

6 **Optional:** To help Ss better understand this grammar rule, write these five sentences on the board, and tell Ss that each sentence includes one or more errors:

1. I should had paid attention to my grades when I was in school.

2. I ought to have to think more about my future.

3. I wish (that) I have more money when I was on vacation.

4. I shouldn't had been so selfish with my things.

5. I wish (that) I haven't been so talkative at the party last night.

Explain that Ss are to work alone or in pairs to correct all the sentences as quickly as they can. The first Ss to correct the sentences are the winners. To go over the answers, have selected Ss come to the board to correct an error in one of the sentences.

Possible answers

1. I should had paid attention . . .	I should *have paid* attention . . .
2. I ought to have to think . . .	I ought to *have thought* . . .
3. I wish (that) I have . . .	I wish (that) I *had* . . .
4. I shouldn't had been . . .	I shouldn't *have been* . . .
5. I wish (that) I haven't been . . .	I wish (that) I *hadn't been* . . .

7 Books open. Have Ss look at the picture and say what they think is happening. Explain the task and go over the example. Then have Ss individually rewrite the remaining sentences using *should, ought to*, and *wish*, and then check the sentences that are true for them. Point out that the words *any, too much*, and *very* will need to be changed as well (see the following answers). Circulate to offer help where needed.

8 Have Ss compare their answers with a partner and discuss their similarities and differences. Go over the answers with the class.

Possible answers

Note: When negative sentences are transformed into positive sentences, certain adverbs change as well (e.g., in these sentences, *any* changes to *some, too much* changes to *so much*, and *very/very much* changes to *more*).

1. I ought to/should have listened to my parents when I was a child.
I wish I had listened to my parents when I was a child.

2. I ought to/should have paid attention to my schoolwork.
I wish I had paid attention to my schoolwork.

3. I ought to/should have learned to play some sports well.
I wish I had learned to play some sports well.

4. I ought not to/shouldn't have spent so much time by myself when I was a kid.
I wish I hadn't spent so much time by myself when I was a kid.

5. I ought to/should have joined more clubs when I was in school.
I wish I had joined more clubs when I was in school.

6. I ought to/should have traveled more as a kid.

I wish I had traveled more as a kid.

7. I ought to/should have taken my studies more seriously in college.

I wish I had taken my studies more seriously in college.

---

4 Adjectives of emotion + past time clauses

grammar focus This grammar focus presents adjectives of emotion and past time clauses to describe things in one's past that one is happy one did or did not do.

> **Grammar notes** Note that the word *that* is optional. Also note that a verb in any tense (present, past, or future) can follow these adjectives of emotion (e.g., I'm glad I *live*/I'm *living* in a small town, I'm glad I *lived* in a small town, I'm glad I *will be living* in a small town.).

1 Books closed. Ask Ss to call out something they feel good about having done in the past (e.g., learning how to swim). Write several of these sentences on the right side of the board, along with the S's name next to each one. Then ask one of the Ss, "Are you glad (that) you learned how to swim?" When the S responds, complete that S's sentence like this: "I'm glad (that) I learned how to swim." Have Ss help you complete the first part of the sentences expressing their feelings about those actions (e.g., *I'm glad* I learned how to swim when I was a child.).

2 Complete the other sentences on the board in the same way.

3 Books open. Lead Ss through the information and examples in the grammar focus. Point out that the word *that* in these sentences is optional and that people hardly use it in spoken English. It is, however, quite common in written English.

4 **Optional:** Brainstorm with the class other adjectives of emotion that could be used in similar sentences. Have Ss call out their answers (e.g., surprised, afraid, delighted, etc.).

5 Explain the task and do the first sentence with the class if necessary. Then have Ss work individually to complete each sentence with information of their own. Circulate to help and check for accuracy. Then have Ss compare and discuss answers with a partner. Encourage them to give reasons and examples to support their answers. Have several Ss share answers with the class.

Possible answers

> **1.** I'm glad (that) I learned how to speak another language as a child.
> **2.** I'm happy (that) I lived next door to nice people during my childhood.
> **3.** I'm pleased (that) my parents gave me a good upbringing.

continued

4. I'm relieved (that) I didn't fail any of my final exams.

5. I'm happy (that) I never was very sick as a child.

6. I'm relieved (that) my family never moved from my hometown.

7. I'm pleased (that) I always had some spare time after classes.

8. I'm glad (that) my friends helped me with my homework.

Life's ups and downs

discussion   In this activity, Ss discuss some life experiences they are happy about and some of their regrets.

Pair work

1   Books open. Explain the task and have Ss read the model language in the balloons. Then put Ss in pairs to discuss three recent regrets and three recent things they're glad they did. Encourage pairs to give details to support their answers, and to ask and answer follow-up questions.

2   Either have several Ss share one of their own answers with the class, or have several Ss tell the class about one of their partner's answers. The latter would provide a good opportunity for Ss to practice using reported speech.

Optional activity: *Regrets and fond memories; truth or lies?*

Time: 10 minutes. Ss continue practicing with adjectives of emotion + past time clauses, *should have*, *ought to have*, and *wish*.

Pair work Books closed. Ss individually write down six sentences about things they're happy they did or regrets they have. Three of the sentences should be false, and the other three should be true. Then have Ss join together in pairs with a new partner to take turns reading their sentences aloud. Ss should question each other to determine which sentences are true and which are false.

Learning a thing or two

vocabulary   This activity presents nouns often used to talk about values.

Pair work

1   Books open. Put Ss in pairs to discuss what they see happening in the picture. Pronounce the word *perseverance* for the class and have Ss use the picture to define it (answer: the will and determination to achieve a goal).

2   Explain the task and have Ss read the list of words. Check Ss' comprehension of these words:

> **compassion** a feeling of sympathy or pity for the suffering of other people
> **courage** the quality of not showing fear in a dangerous situation
> **forgiveness** the ability to stop being angry with someone for something bad he
>   or she has done
> **loyalty** the quality of being firm in one's support for someone or something
> **patience** the ability to wait for something or to handle suffering
> **perseverance** doing something in a determined way and in spite of difficulties
> **self-discipline** self-control
> **sensitivity** the quality of being concerned for other people's feelings

Alternatively, explain the task and lead Ss through the list of words. Put Ss in pairs to discuss the meanings of the words listed. Tell them to think of examples to illustrate each word. If necessary, have Ss use monolingual dictionaries for this task. Each S can look up half of the words. Then they explain their words to each other.

3 Ss work individually to choose four words from the list (or words of their own) to describe the four most important values one needs to be a good person. Have Ss read the sample language in the speech balloon. Then put Ss in pairs to share and discuss answers with a partner. Encourage Ss to give reasons to support their answers.

4 **Optional:** Combine pairs to form groups of four or six. Have groups compile a list of the single most important value for each S in the group. Then have each group report their results to the class. Compile a class list on the board to discover which values the class thinks are the most important. Lead a class discussion as appropriate.

What values do you think are most important?

listening

In these activities, Ss practice listening for both gist and specific information.

A

1 Books open. Explain the task and lead Ss through the chart, making sure they know what information they need to listen for. Play the audio program once through without stopping. Have Ss only listen.

2 **Optional:** Pre-teach any items from the following vocabulary list that you think will help your Ss:

> **portion** part, section
> **on the air** broadcasting (a TV or radio show) live
> **to respect** to have a good opinion of someone's judgment [to respect one's
>   parents means to listen to them and treat them politely]
> **people's privacy** people's right to keep personal matters secret
> **to sign off** to end a radio or television program

3 Replay the audio program, this time pausing briefly after each speaker has finished. Ask Ss to complete the chart with each person's most important value and their reasons for why it is important. Remind Ss that they only need to write key words for each person.

4 Have Ss compare answers with a partner. Replay the audio program as needed before going over the answers with the class.

Answers

	Values	Why they are important
First person	respect	It's important to show respect to your parents.
Second person	honesty	Honesty is the best policy. You're going to get in trouble if you're not honest.
Third person	privacy	People need to respect each other's privacy.

Transcript

Listen to Randy Simmons interviewing people on the street. What values do they think are most important and why?

Randy: We're back on the street for the "Ask the People" portion of our show. Today our question is "What values do you think are the most important and why?" Now, I just have to find some people who are willing to talk to me. . . . Excuse me, sir?

Man: Yes?

Randy: My name is Randy Simmons. I'm a reporter from WBBQ, and we're on the air. Do you have a moment to talk with us?

Man: Well, I'm on my way to work.

Randy: This should just take a moment.

Man: Well, OK. But make it fast.

Randy: OK. We're asking people what they think are the most important values in today's society and why.

Man: Hmmm, that's a tough one. I guess I think it's important to listen to your parents. Kids these days . . . my kids never listen to anything that I say.

Randy: Ah-hah. So you think it's important to respect your parents?

Man: That's right. I've got to go. Bye.

Randy: Good-bye. Boy, was he in a hurry! . . . Miss. Excuse me. Hello?

Woman 1: Yes?

Randy: Do you have a second? I'm Randy Simmons from WBBQ. I'm doing a radio show.

Woman 1: Yeah?

Randy: We're asking people on the street what values they think are important and why.

Woman 1: I don't really have the time. . . . Well, I don't know. I guess that honesty is important. You know what they say: Honesty is the best policy.

Randy: OK. That's interesting.

Woman 1: Well, I mean, you're just going to get in trouble if you're not honest. At least that's been my experience.

Randy: I see.

Woman 1: Listen. I have to go.

Randy: Thanks. Let's see if I can find one more person. . . . Oops!

Woman 2: Ouch!

Randy: I'm sorry. I-I didn't see you standing there behind me. Are you OK?

Woman 2: You stepped on my toes! What are you doing standing here, anyway?

Randy: Well, actually, I'm interviewing people. I'm Randy Simmons from WBBQ.

Woman 2: What's that?

Randy: I'm Randy Simmons. From the radio station WBBQ. I'm doing on-the-street interviews.

Woman 2: Oh. OK.

Randy: We're asking people about values. What values do you think are most important in today's society?

Woman 2: Privacy. I think people need to respect each other's privacy. Like right now. You should leave me alone. *(continues shouting in the background)*

Randy: Uh, . . . oh, . . . well, . . . uh, sorry. Uh, folks, that's all the time we have today for our show. Today's question was "What values do you think are important in today's society and why?" After this experience, I'd have to say that one thing we all need to work on is being kinder. This sure is a tough job. This is Randy Simmons of WBBQ radio signing off until next time.

Optional activity: *Defending one's values*

Time: 5–10 minutes. Ss think about personal values and justify their choices.

1 *Group work* Books open. Explain that the speakers on the audio program didn't give good reasons for their values because they were in such a hurry. Divide the class into three groups and assign each group one of the values in the audio program. Have each group think up additional reasons why these values are important.

2 Have selected Ss from each group give their reasons while you write them on the board.

B Pair work

1 Books open. Explain the task and then put Ss in pairs to discuss which person they agree with the most and why. After a few minutes, have selected Ss share their answer with the class.

2 **Optional:** Have Ss pair up with someone new. Then have pairs discuss which person they agree with least and why.

Making the most of it

discussion   In these activities, Ss give each other good advice and justify their choices.

A Pair work

1   Books closed. Ask the class to call out any advice they think teenagers need. Write these ideas on the board.

2   Explain the task and have Ss read the model dialog. Put Ss in pairs to discuss what they think teenagers need to know to make the most of their lives.

B Class activity

Books open. Explain the task and have Ss form groups of six to eight, with one person acting as secretary for the group. Each group reports their list of advice while you, or another S, write it on the board. The class votes on the most important pieces of advice. Lead a class discussion about the reasons why the most popular answers got the most votes.

Optional activity: *Changes*

Time: 10 minutes. Ss discuss how their values have changed over time.

1   *Pair work* Books open. Ask Ss to think of how they have changed over the last few years. (If most of your Ss are no longer teens, ask them to think of how they have changed since they were teens.) Tell Ss to consider what they used to think was important but no longer do.

2   Put Ss in pairs or small groups to discuss how their values have changed over the last few years and why. Tell Ss to say what made them see things differently. Encourage partners or group members to ask follow-up questions.

A multi-paragraph composition

writing   These activities present a multi-paragraph composition and introduce the concept of *thesis statement* (i.e., the sentence of a composition that introduces the overall topic).

Books open. Lead Ss through the information in the box about thesis statements. Point out that a thesis statement not only introduces the topic, but it also often includes an idea or opinion that is explained in the rest of the composition.

A

Books open. Explain the task and ask Ss to read the three possible thesis statements. Then have Ss silently read the composition and choose the best thesis statement. Ask Ss to compare their answer with a partner. Then go over the best answer with the class.

Possible answer

> When I think about high school, I have both good and bad memories.
>
> This statement introduces all the information the writer talks about. The other two choices are too narrow and only introduce certain parts of the information in the composition.

Optional activity 1: *The best title*

Time: 5–7 minutes. Ss think about the composition in Exercise A as a whole.

1 *Pair and group work* Books open. Put Ss in pairs to come up with a good title for the composition. Then combine three pairs to form groups of six to take turns reading their titles. Have the groups vote on the title that best reflects the contents of the composition.

2 Have the pair who wrote the best title in each group share their title with the class.

Optional activity 2: *Positive or negative?*

Time: 10 minutes. Ss look more carefully at how information is arranged in paragraphs according to the topic.

1 *Class activity* Books open. Put the following question on the board: *From the thesis statement, do you think the author's high school experience was mainly positive or negative?* Ask Ss to discuss the question in pairs.

2 Lead a class discussion about the question on the board. Ask Ss to list all the positive and negative experiences under two headings. Then put Ss in groups to compare lists. Go over the lists as a class, and discuss how the experiences support the thesis statement.

B

1 Books open. Explain the task and then lead Ss through the guidelines in the box. If time permits, have Ss write their compositions in class so that you can circulate to provide help and guidance as they are writing. If there is not enough time to write in class, have Ss produce a possible thesis statement for their compositions, and share their thesis statements with other Ss. They can complete the composition at home.

2 **Optional:** Have Ss write a title for their compositions.

C Group work

Books open. Explain the task and remind Ss of the value of peer feedback. Ss should just listen to their peers' comments rather than defend themselves. Then have Ss form small groups of four or five to take turns reading their compositions aloud and listening to other people's feedback.

Lesson B   *The wisdom of age*

1   Generation gap

starting point   In these activities, Ss discuss ideas that older people often have about younger people.

> **Culture note** The concept of a generation gap is widely accepted in Canada and the United States. It was a concept that grew in prominence in the 1960s and 1970s, when a common belief among young people was "Never trust anyone over thirty," and many older people felt they could no longer understand younger people. These days, many people think that the generation gap is lessening because the baby-boom generation (those born between 1946 and 1961) has moved past the age of thirty.

A

1 Books closed. Ask Ss if they understand the term *generation gap*. Have Ss call out their answers, and encourage them to give examples. Then ask the class, "Do you think there really is a generation gap between older people and younger people?" Have Ss respond with a show of hands. Then ask volunteers to give reasons for their opinions.

2 Books open. Have Ss look at the three photographs. Ask them how old they think each person is. Explain the task and check that Ss understand the following:

> **elders** people who are older than you are [in this case, it refers to one's parents and grandparents]
>
> **to talk back** to talk in a disrespectful way to a person of authority, such as a parent or teacher

3 Have Ss silently read the three texts carefully and think about whether they know anyone who has similar ideas and whether they agree with any of the three statements. Have several Ss share their answer(s), and lead a class discussion as appropriate.

B Pair work

Books open. Explain the task. Then, in groups of four, have Ss discuss the questions. Ask selected Ss to share their group's best answers, and have the class vote on which statements they agree with the most.

Optional activity: *Stereotypical ideas about different generations*

Time: 10 minutes. Ss explore their opinions about the generation gap.

Group work Books open. Put Ss in small groups to discuss which comments they think are true about older people and which are true about younger people. Have the groups make lists of the two categories (true and false) for the two generations. Tell Ss to come up with some reasons why younger and older people might have these misconceptions about each other.

Values and attitudes

discussion

These activities present some adjectives that are often used to describe people's beliefs and values.

A

1 Books open. Explain the task and lead Ss through the list of adjectives. Clarify the meaning of any words that may be new to Ss, such as:

> **closed-minded** unwilling and unable to accept new ideas or opinions
> **conservative** not liking or trusting change, especially sudden change
> **conventional** acting in ways that are usual and socially acceptable
> **intolerant** disapproving or refusing to accept ideas that are different from one's own
> **liberal** respecting and allowing many different types of beliefs

2 Have Ss individually match each word with its opposite and to add two more words to the list. Circulate to help. Have Ss either call out an answer or come to the board to write it.

Possible answers

> closed-minded/open-minded, conservative/liberal, conventional/unconventional, intolerant/tolerant, modern/old fashioned, optimistic/pessimistic, realistic/unrealistic

Suggested answers for additional pairs

> moderate/radical, spontaneous/reserved, thoughtful/thoughtless, skeptical/gullible

B Pair work

1 Books open. Explain the task and have Ss read the model language in the speech balloon. Give Ss a few moments to work alone to choose words from Exercise A that describe their best friend, parents, grandparents, and teacher. Then put Ss in pairs to take turns sharing and discussing their answers. Remind Ss that they should give reasons and examples to support their choices. Also encourage Ss to ask and answer follow-up questions.

2 Have selected Ss or volunteers share one or more answers with the class.

Noun clauses introduced by it

grammar focus This grammar focus presents the structure *it* + noun clause, which is often used to describe one's opinion or feelings about a present situation.

> **Grammar notes** In these sentences, *that* is not a relative pronoun, but introduces the noun clause that follows. The word *it* is the grammatical subject of the sentence, taking the place of the noun clause that is the true subject of the sentence. The sentence would be equally grammatical without using *it* (e.g., That kids today don't respect their elders is sad.). However, this structure is more formal and less common in spoken English.
>
> Using *it* to begin the sentence gives more emphasis to the noun clause that ends the sentence (e.g., It's sad that *kids today don't respect their elders.*).

1 Books open. Go through the information and example sentences in the grammar focus.

2 On the board write *It's sad that . . . some people don't listen to others.* Ask Ss to finish the sentence in as many other ways as they can. Have Ss call out their answers, and write these on the board. Ask Ss to think of other adjectives to replace *sad.* Brainstorm with the class, and write all possible answers offered on the board (e.g., *wonderful, true, obvious, fortunate, unfortunate, good*).

A

1 Books open. Explain the task and go over the sample answer. Then go through the list of adjectives with the class, clarifying meaning as necessary:

> **apparent** clear, easy to see
> **obvious** easy to recognize or understand
> **a shame** a disappointment

2 Have Ss individually use the cues to write sentences that follow the pattern in the grammar box. Encourage them to write more than one sentence for each item. Circulate to help and check for accuracy. Then have Ss compare answers with a partner.

3 Have selected Ss or volunteers either read one of their answers aloud or come to the board to write it. Lead a class discussion as appropriate, and correct and revise sentences as necessary.

Possible answers

> **1.** It's apparent that a child's character is strongly influenced by his or her parents. However, it's also likely that there are other influences, such as his or her friends.
> **2.** It's obvious that a happy person makes a better parent. However, it's also likely that being too friendly with children will make them harder to control.

3. It's unfortunate that age doesn't always bring wisdom. Some older people act foolishly.

4. It's true that most elderly people think the world was a better place when they were young. However, there were probably many bad things about living in those times that they don't remember.

5. It's sad that many teenagers are afraid they may grow up to be like their parents. However, it's likely that they will be like their parents, since parents have a strong influence on their children's personalities.

6. It's not true that most people have learned all they need to know by the time they are 20. Actually, it's likely that they have only begun to learn the most important things.

B

1 Books open. Explain the task and have Ss work individually to write three sentences about younger people and three sentences about older people. Circulate to help and check for accuracy.

2 Have Ss form pairs to take turns reading and discussing their sentences. Encourage pairs to give reasons and examples to support the ideas in their sentences, and to ask and answer follow-up questions. Then have selected Ss or volunteers share their most interesting sentence with the class.

Noun clauses introduced by verbs

grammar focus   This grammar focus presents verbs such as *hope* and *believe* + noun clauses to speculate about people's beliefs or future events.

> **Grammar notes** Verbs such as *hope* and *believe* are used to speculate or guess about things or events. Other common verbs of this type include *imagine, guess,* and *suppose.*
>
> These sentences have a main clause (e.g., *I hope*) and a dependent clause (e.g., *that schools will do something about teaching respect*). The dependent clause is a noun clause that functions as the direct object of the verb *hope.*
>
> In these sentences, *that* functions as a subordinate conjunction that introduces the dependent clause and shows that it is a noun clause.
>
> The present or future tenses can be used after verbs of supposition when speculating about the present or future.

1 Books open. Go over the information and example sentences in the grammar box. Point out that these verbs are used to speculate or guess about hopes, beliefs, or events. Elicit other verbs of supposition, such as *imagine* and *guess.*

2 Put Ss in pairs. Explain the task and go over the example under the first picture. Then have Ss individually write one more statement about this person and two about each of the other people. Remind them to use the sentence pattern modeled in the grammar box. Point out that there's no way to know for sure what the values and beliefs of these people might be. Tell Ss that they should guess based on each person's picture.

3 Have Ss compare and discuss their answers in small groups before going over them with the class.

Possible answers

> **professor**
> I hope that people will spend more money on education.
> I believe that parents understand the value of a good education better than their children do.
>
> **businesswoman**
> I hope that more women will enter the business world.
> I believe that women can be as effective as men in business.
>
> **rock musician**
> I hope that people recognize that rock musicians are serious artists.
> I believe that rock music is one of the best ways to unite people from around the world.

 Changing beliefs

discussion In these activities, Ss talk about how their beliefs have changed and practice using noun clauses introduced by verbs.

Group work

1 Books closed. Ask Ss to think of a belief they had as children but which they no longer believe in. Have Ss call out their answers.

2 Books open. Explain the task and go over the sample language in the speech balloon. Put Ss in groups of four to six to discuss the questions. Circulate to help and to keep Ss on task.

3 Have one or more Ss from each group report the most interesting things they learned about the others in their group.

Optional activity: *Childhood dreams*

Time: 10–15 minutes. Ss reflect on how their hopes and dreams have changed since they were children.

1 *Class activity* Books open or closed. Tell Ss to think back to the dreams and hopes they had as children. On a slip of paper have Ss write at least one dream they no longer have; they should not put their names on the paper. Then collect the papers and redistribute them to the class. Give Ss a few minutes to read and try to guess whose childhood dream they have. Tell Ss they will be walking around the room addressing Ss they think wrote their dream.

2 Have Ss memorize the dream and then stand up without their paper and try to find the author of their dream by walking around the class and asking other Ss. Once they have found the author of their dream, have them sit down and find out what had happened to change the person's dreams. Ask a few volunteers to report back about their discussions.

6 · Role models

listening

In these activities, Ss listen to people talking about the role models in their lives and then discuss their own role models.

A

1 Books closed. Tell the class about an older person who influenced your own life. Then ask for volunteers to tell the class about someone who has had an influence on theirs.

2 Books open. Explain the task and lead Ss through the chart, making sure they know what information they need to listen for. Point out that Ss need to write a few words only about each person in order to complete the chart. Then play the audio program once through without stopping. Ask Ss to fill in as much information as they can.

3 Replay the audio program, this time pausing briefly after each speaker has finished to allow Ss time to complete the chart. Then have Ss compare answers with a partner. Replay the audio program as necessary before going over the answers with the class.

Answers

	Who	**What they learned**
Cristina	parents: mother and father	From her mother, she learned about trying her best. She also learned that anything was possible. From her father, she learned not to take things too seriously and to laugh at life.
Vince	third-grade teacher a high school teacher	From his third-grade teacher, he learned to enjoy going to school and to have fun at school. From his high school teacher, he learned to write well.
Brian	people who have changed society (e.g., John Lennon and Martin Luther King Jr.)	He learned to speak up for what he believes in and to accept and work with other people, regardless of their race.

Transcript

Listen to Cristina, Vince, and Brian talking about people who have had an influence on them. Who is each person talking about? What did they learn from these people?

Cristina: My parents had a big influence on me. I don't think I could say it was just my mother or my father – it was more like a combination of them both. My parents are so different. I learned from both of them.

continued

Copyright © Cambridge University Press 1998

Lesson B The wisdom of age   **177**

My mother was very serious, and she worked really hard. She was one of the first women to work in the computer industry back in the fifties. You could say she was a working woman before it became fashionable. I learned a lot about trying my best. I guess she taught me that anything was possible.

From my father, I learned to laugh at life. He always used to say that if you waited long enough, a bad situation would change for the better. My parents used to have some interesting conversations, believe me! Somehow they always managed to get along, though.

Vince: Well, the first person I think of is my third-grade teacher. It's funny, isn't it? She made school fun. I'd had a real problem with school before that – I didn't like to go, I had trouble making friends. . . . I wonder where she is now. Gosh, that was a long time ago!

I also owe a lot to one of my high school teachers. He was really tough, but he taught me how to write well. That's a skill that's helped me in every single job I've had. I mean, at the time, I hated his class, but looking back I realized just how much it's helped me.

Brian: This is kind of different, but I've been most influenced by people who have made a change in society. I really respect those people who have spoken up about what they believed in. I guess John Lennon was kind of my hero. I mean, I liked the Beatles, and I loved his music, but John also believed in a lot of issues that I support. I was so shocked when he was killed. I've also been deeply affected by the words of people like Dr. Martin Luther King Jr. He tried to get people to work together – to accept each other whether they were black, white, or whatever.

Optional activity: *Details, details*

Time: 5–10 minutes. Ss listen more intensively for selected details.

1 Books open or closed. Write the following questions on the board:

1. How are Cristina's parents different?

2. What field of work was Cristina's mother in, and when did she work?

3. What was Cristina's father's attitude about hard times?

4. What were Vince's problems with school before the third grade?

5. What was Vince's high school writing teacher like?

6. At the time, how did Vince feel about the writing teacher's class?

7. Why is John Lennon Brian's hero?

8. How did he feel about the Beatles' music?

9. What did he especially like about Dr. Martin Luther King Jr.?

2 Put Ss in pairs to answer any questions they can before listening again. Then replay the audio program for Ss to check the answers they remembered, as well as listen for the questions they weren't able to answer. Go over the answers as a class.

Possible answers

1. Her mother is serious and hardworking, and her father laughs at life and is an optimist.
2. She worked in the computer industry in the fifties.
3. He used to say that if you wait long enough, a bad situation would change for the better.
4. He didn't like to go and had trouble making friends.
5. He was tough, but he taught Vince how to write well.
6. He hated his class.
7. John Lennon believed in a lot of issues that Brian supports.
8. He loved it.
9. He likes that Martin Luther King Jr. tried to get people to work together and accept each other, whether they were black or white.

B Pair work

1 Books open. Explain the task and have Ss read the sample dialog. Then put Ss in pairs to discuss the questions. Encourage Ss to provide as much detail as possible about the people who have influenced them, and to ask and answer follow-up questions. Circulate to keep Ss on task and to provide vocabulary help as needed.

2 Either have selected Ss or volunteers tell the class about the person who influenced them most, or about the person who influenced their partner most.

Collocations

vocabulary These activities present verbs and nouns that often form collocations, and which can be used to talk about how people can influence each other.

A

1 Books open. Put Ss in pairs to discuss the two pictures. Explain the task and have Ss read the list of nouns and verbs, clarifying meanings as needed.

2 Give Ss one or two examples of nouns and verbs that can go together (e.g., give an opinion, have a positive effect). Then have Ss individually combine the verbs and nouns in as many ways as they can, and then think of two more nouns to go with each verb. Point out that most of the verbs can be combined with more than one noun.

3 Have Ss compare answers with a partner or in small groups. Then go over possible answers with the class.

Answers

> **give:** advice, an example, an opinion, support
> **have:** an influence, an opinion, a positive effect
> **make:** a contribution, a donation, an effort, a good impression
> **set:** an example

Sample answers for additional nouns

> **give:** a speech, notice, (someone) a piece of your mind
> **have:** faith, a belief, an idea
> **make:** a speech, a statement
> **set:** a goal

Optional activity: *More collocations*

Time: 10–15 minutes. Ss continue practicing the vocabulary.

Group work Books closed. Have Ss form small groups of four to six. Explain that Ss should work together to create a short dialog that includes at least two of the collocations from the exercise. Tell them that the dialog can be about any topic. Then have a S from each group perform the group's dialog for the class.

B Pair work

1 Books open. Explain the task and go over the example. Then have Ss work in pairs to write sentences using the phrases they made in Exercise A to describe relations between younger people and older people. Encourage creativity as well as accuracy. Encourage Ss to write sentences that describe their true opinions.

2 Have two or three pairs join to compare and discuss their answers. Then have selected Ss or volunteers share one or more of their answers with the class. Lead a class discussion as appropriate.

Optional activity: *Influencing others*

Time: 5–10 minutes. Ss discuss the influence they have had on other people.

Group work Books open. Ask Ss to think of a younger person that they have influenced or would like to influence. Put Ss in small groups to tell each other about their experiences. Write *responsibility* on the board. Tell Ss to discuss in what ways we must be responsible when we influence others. Then ask selected Ss to report back to the class about their discussions.

reading In these activities, Ss read an article about middle age and how society's views about aging are changing. Ss also practice the skills of prediction, inferencing, summarizing, and extending the theme of the reading.

A Pair work

1 Books open. Explain the task and have Ss read the questions. Then put Ss in pairs to discuss them. If you wish, have them cover the article while they have their discussion. Have several Ss share answers with the class. Then have Ss silently read the article to compare their ideas with the author's.

2 Put Ss back in pairs to compare their ideas with those of the author. Then go over the author's ideas with the class. Lead a class discussion as appropriate.

Possible answers

> **1.** It's a time when people deepen their relationships and care more about other people.
> **2.** fruitful, growing, developing, altruistic, peaceful, generous, experienced, exciting, rewarding, mature, secure, aware, caring
> **3.** Middle age is a more peaceful time because people are settled in their careers, and they can look back at the many good things they have done.
> **4.** A middle-aged person can give more attention to friends and can give more advice owing to his or her life experiences.

B Group work

1 Books open. Explain the task and have Ss read the three questions. Then put Ss in small groups of four to six to discuss the questions. Circulate to keep Ss on task, and encourage them to give reasons and examples to support their answers. Have Ss ask and answer follow-up questions.

2 Have a spokesperson from each group report the group's answers to the class. Make a note of interesting answers on the board, and then lead a class discussion as time allows.

Possible answers

> **1.** Middle age is not something to fear; rather, it can be the most fruitful time of life.
> **2.** Answers will vary.
> **3.** Answers will vary.

In this unit, students talk about the nature of creativity and the ways in which people are creative in their personal and professional lives. The unit focuses on reduced relative clauses and non-defining relative clauses.

Exploring creativity

Qualities of creative people

starting point   In these activities, Ss are introduced to the qualities that creative people have and the types of creativity needed for several different jobs.

A

1   Books closed. Ask Ss if they think they are creative people. Have Ss respond with a show of hands. Then brainstorm with the class some adjectives to describe the qualities of creative people. Write all responses on the board.

2   Books open. Have Ss look at the list of words to see if any of the ones they mentioned are listed. Check that Ss understand the following:

> **curiosity**   an eager desire to know or learn something
> **decisiveness**   the ability to make decisions easily and stick to them
> **determination**   the quality of not giving up on a task even if it is very difficult
> **resourcefulness**   the ability to find creative solutions to difficult problems
> **thriftiness**   the ability to save money

3   Explain the task and have Ss work individually, first to decide which of the qualities creative people usually have, and then to rank the qualities they chose from most to least important. Have Ss add other qualities of their own.

4   Have Ss compare answers with a partner. Then have selected Ss or volunteers share their ideas with the class.

5   **Optional:** Write the most popular answers on the board. Then have the class discuss which of the top three or four answers is really the most important quality for creative people to have.

B   Pair work

1   Books open. Explain the task and have Ss read the model language in the speech balloon. Then put Ss in pairs to discuss whether or not each job requires a high degree of creativity and what qualities are needed for each job. Encourage Ss to give reasons and examples to support their answers, and to ask and answer follow-up questions.

2 Have several Ss share their answers for each of the six jobs. Lead a class discussion as appropriate.

Optional activity: *Creativity – only for the arts?*

Time: 15–20 minutes. Ss have a debate about creativity in jobs.

1 *Group work* Books closed. Write on the board: *Creativity is only necessary for people who work in occupations such as design, photography, and the arts.* Split the class into groups A and B. Tell Ss in group A to think of as many reasons as they can in favor of the statement. Tell Ss in group B to think of as many reasons as they can against the statement.

2 Have Ss work individually before putting Ss in groups of three to compare answers and think of additional reasons. Then form groups of six by combining three Ss from group A and three Ss from group B. Have Ss take turns presenting and discussing their ideas, for and against. Then have two Ss from each group present their most convincing statements to the class.

Creativity at work

listening

In these activities, Ss listen to people talking about why creativity is needed for the kinds of jobs they do.

A

1 Books open. Explain the task and lead Ss through the chart, making sure they know what information they need to complete it. Remind Ss to fill in the chart in note form. Play the audio program. Encourage Ss to take notes, but allow them to only listen at this point.

2 **Optional:** Pre-teach any items from the following vocabulary that you think will help your Ss:

> **essential** necessary
> **architect** a person who designs buildings as a profession
> **trends** general developments or changes in the way people do things
> **potential** possible
> **interior designer** a person who plans the decoration of the inside of
>   buildings as a profession

3 Replay the audio program, this time pausing briefly after each speaker has finished so that Ss can fill in the chart. Remind Ss that they only need to write a few words for each person. Have Ss compare answers with a partner. Replay the audio program as necessary before going over the answers with the class.

Answers

	Occupation	Why creativity is important
Angela	architect	Creativity is important because she needs to make old things look new, recycle ideas and adapt them, and keep on top of new trends.
Simon	small business owner	Creativity is important because he has to do everything: solve his problems alone, identify customers, and think about the competition.
Naomi	interior designer	Creativity is important because she has to look at homes and decide what looks best, match the appropriate idea to the right place, come up with new ideas, and communicate them.

Transcript

Listen to Angela, Simon, and Naomi talking about their jobs. What are their occupations? Why is creativity important in their work?

Angela: Well, I guess I'd have to say that creativity is essential to my work. I'm an architect, and the creative part is trying to look at old things and make them look new. I mean, we recycle a lot of ideas and then adapt them to fit our needs. And we also have to keep on top of new trends: We have to know all about new building styles and efficient ways to use energy – you know, the kinds of things that homeowners worry about. No one wants a house that is heated inefficiently or looks old-fashioned. And we work long hours, but I must say, the job's pretty interesting. You never know what to expect next!

Simon: Well, I have my own small business. I think all business owners, especially small business owners, have to be pretty creative. We have to do everything. I do the work, answer the phones, take care of the accounting . . . you know, there are so many potential problems, and there's no one else to turn to. I mean, I can't ask my boss for help – I am the boss! The hardest part is figuring out how to identify your customers. Who are they? Where are they? How can you get to them? You also need to think creatively about the competition. How can you make your business services more attractive than what the competition has to offer? Well, it's challenging, and I think it requires a lot of creativity.

Naomi: I'm an interior designer, so what I do is go into people's homes and create a suitable environment for them. You know – my clients – they don't know what they want, so I have to look at their homes and decide what would look best. Not every idea works in every home. You have to match the appropriate idea with the right place. After I come up with an idea, I present it to my client. Sometimes they don't like my first idea, and boy, that can be frustrating. You have to start all over again. So I need creativity to both come up with the ideas and to communicate them. Creativity also comes in handy when I want to convince a client that my idea is the best one. I don't always succeed, but I do manage to get my way a lot of the time.

B Pair work

1 Books open. Read the questions aloud to the class. Then put Ss in pairs to discuss the questions.

2 **Optional:** Have selected Ss share their answers with the class. Write responses on the board in note form. Then check how many other Ss in class have the same or similar answers.

Reduced relative clauses

grammar focus   This grammar focus presents reduced relative clauses that define or describe the subject.

> **Grammar notes** These relative clauses consist of a subject + relative pronoun *(who/that/which)* + *be* + verb. To reduce a relative clause, the relative pronoun and *be* are deleted and the verb is changed to the *-ing* form (e.g., a person [who is] working as a screenwriter). Once reduced, the clause becomes an adjective phrase.
>
> The adjective phrase is bound within a noun phrase and defines and describes that noun phrase (e.g., a person [noun phrase] working as a screenwriter [adjective phrase]).
>
> These reduced relative clauses (or adjective phrases) must come immediately after the nouns they describe because they give essential information about that noun or noun phrase. They are not separated from the noun phrase by commas.

1 Books closed. Ask Ss to call out a few occupations while you write them on the board. Now ask Ss to write a sentence for each occupation, describing the qualities or abilities a person needs to do the job well. Provide this example: *A person who works as an interpreter should be able to think fast and effectively.* Have volunteers write their sentences on the board.

2 Rewrite your example on the board to contain a reduced clause (i.e., *A person working as an interpreter should be able to think fast and effectively.*).

3 Books open. Lead Ss through the information and example sentences in the grammar box. Then have Ss convert the other sentences on the board in the same way.

A

1 Have Ss look at the photograph and say what job the man on the left does (answer: journalist). Explain the task and go over the example. Then have Ss individually rewrite each of the sentences and reduce the relative clauses.

2 **Optional:** Have Ss add a statement to each of the seven sentences in order to provide additional information. For example, for the first item, Ss could add the statement "Also, anyone working for a newspaper has to be willing to work late hours." Circulate to help and check for accuracy.

3 Have Ss compare answers with a partner. Then go over the answers with the class, either by calling on selected Ss to read a sentence aloud or by having selected Ss write one of their sentences on the board.

Answers

1. Anyone wanting to become a journalist should be able to write under pressure.
2. Anyone hoping to succeed in business needs to have original ideas on how to market products.
3. A person working as an inventor is always looking for new ways of solving common problems.
4. A person working as a detective has to try to get inside the mind of a criminal.
5. Anyone trying to become a successful actor will find that there is a lot more to it than he or she first thought.
6. Someone working in advertising needs to be able to write catchy slogans.
7. A person responsible for a large staff has to be creative with scheduling.

B

1 Books open. Explain the task and go over the example. Then have Ss individually rewrite the sentences in Exercise 3A with their own ideas. Circulate to help and check for accuracy. Then have Ss compare and discuss their answers with a partner or in small groups.

2 Ask several selected Ss to read their most interesting sentences to the class.

Optional activity: *The matching game*

Time: 10–15 minutes. Ss continue discussing the match between qualities and jobs.

1 *Group work* Books closed. Have Ss form groups of three and take out one sheet of paper per group. Ask one S in the group to think of two adjectives, and write down the beginning of a sentence like this: *Someone who is (adj.) and (adj.) . . . .* Write this on the board, if necessary. Have these Ss fold their papers (so that the others can't see what they've written) and then pass them to the S on their left.

2 The next S, without unfolding the paper, completes the sentence like this: *. . . should be a (profession).* These Ss pass their papers to the third S in the group. Ask this S to unfold the paper and decide if the two clauses make sense together. If not, this S should correct either clause. Have the other Ss check the revised sentence to make sure it makes sense. Then have the group call you over to check. If the sentence is coherent and accurate, have Ss begin again and follow the same procedure. Continue as time permits.

Jobs that demand creativity

discussion   In these activities, Ss discuss the role creativity plays in various occupations.

A Pair work

1 Books open. Explain the task and have Ss read the list of jobs. Have Ss individually rank the jobs from most to least creative.

2 Have Ss read the sample dialog. Then put Ss in pairs to share and discuss their answers. Encourage Ss to give reasons to support their answers and to ask and answer follow-up questions. Have the pairs share their most and least creative jobs with the class while you write them on the board. Tally the jobs as they are mentioned. Use this list as the basis for a class discussion.

B Group work

1 Books open. Explain the task and then combine pairs to form groups of four. Have Ss describe one more job that requires a high degree of creativity, one that requires a medium degree, and one that requires little creativity.

2 **Optional:** Have pairs think of the jobs they are going to describe before having Ss form groups.

3 Ss explain their choices and give reasons for their answers. Encourage Ss to ask and answer follow-up questions. Have groups decide which jobs require the most and the least creativity. Then have groups tell the class the jobs they think require the most and the least creativity, and why.

Possible answers

> High degree of creativity: fashion designer, painter, filmmaker, writer
> Medium degree of creativity: gardener, teacher, tour guide
> Low degree of creativity: shop assistant, receptionist, telephone operator

Creativity quiz

discussion   In these activities, Ss complete a questionnaire to find out how creative they are.

A

1 Books closed. Ask Ss where questionnaires or personality quizzes can often be found (answer: popular magazines). Then ask Ss how many of them take the time to fill out these kinds of questionnaires.

2 Books open. Explain the activity and have Ss read the list of questions and look at the pictures to say what they see in each one. Check Ss' comprehension of the following vocabulary:

> **to take risks** to try and do dangerous things
> **to excel** to do very well
> **sense of humor** the ability to see the funny side of things

3 Have Ss individually add two more creative and interesting questions to the list. Circulate to help and check for accuracy. Then have several Ss share their most interesting questions with the class.

B Group work

1 Books open. Explain the task and then have Ss individually answer the questions about themselves.

2 Have Ss read the model language in the speech balloon. Then put Ss into groups of four or six to take turns asking and answering the questions in pairs. Encourage Ss to give detailed answers and examples, and to ask and answer follow-up questions.

3 When pairs have finished asking and answering the questions, have them decide who is the more creative person. Then have Ss compare their answers in the group and say who is the most creative person, and why.

Creative solutions

discussion   In these activities, Ss practice finding creative solutions to problems.

A Pair work

1 Books open. Have Ss look at the photographs and describe what they see. Ask Ss how old the children in the bottom photograph seem to be. Explain the task and have Ss read the four situations and the sample dialog.

2 Have Ss form pairs to discuss the situations and brainstorm many possible solutions before deciding which three are the best.

B Group work

1 Books open. Combine pairs to form groups of four to share and discuss their answers. Ask groups to decide on the most creative suggestion presented for each situation.

2 Have spokespeople from each group present their best suggestions to the class.

3 **Optional:** Write each group's suggestions on the board, and have the class vote on the most creative suggestion for each situation.

Possible answers

1. Pay a famous athlete to do an advertisement for the club.
   Send invitations to the public offering a free day to use the facilities.
   Send brochures to people's houses showing what the club looks like.
2. Take them to a children's museum that features hands-on activities.
   Show them an exciting video and read them stories.
   Take them on a picnic and play games.
3. Buy your friend a gift certificate from his or her favorite department store.
   Give your friend a surprise party and invite one hundred guests.
   Invite your friend out for dinner somewhere unusual, like a riverboat.
4. Change it into a meditation room with soft lighting and mood music.
   Use it as a small library for books and videos.
   Take the door off and use the space to display your best photos or artwork.

Optional activity: *Designing ads*

Time: 15–20 minutes. Ss use their ideas on creativity to write an advertisement.

1   *Group work* Books open. Tell Ss they are going to use the ideas they came up with in Exercise 6A to write a magazine or television advertisement for a sports club. Explain that Ss can use both pictures and words.

2   Put Ss in groups of three or four to work on their advertisement. Have groups decide whether their ads will be for a magazine or television. For the groups making ads for a magazine, provide colored markers and plain paper, if possible. Tell Ss that television ads will be performed.

3   Have Ss who wrote magazine ads present and explain them to the class. Have Ss who wrote television ads perform them for the class.

   ## Beginning new paragraphs

writing   These writing activities help Ss work out when to begin a new paragraph in a composition.

A

1   Books open. Go over the information in the box. Explain that *focus* is the central idea or topic of a paragraph, and that writers begin a new paragraph each time they change focus. Remind Ss that each paragraph should contain only one central idea or topic.

2   Explain the task and have Ss silently read the composition about Lucy Gomez to determine the central ideas or topics. Put Ss in pairs to compare the central ideas they found.

3   **Optional:** If Ss need help, tell them that there are only three central ideas.

4   Go over the answers with the class.

Possible answers

> 1. The creative things Lucy Gomez did in the past
> 2. How Lucy is creative now
> 3. Lucy's personality

5 Have Ss reread the text to find exactly where the writer changes focus. Have Ss write a ⓟ at this place to show where they think a new paragraph should begin.

6 Have Ss compare answers with a partner. Ask pairs to discuss the reasons for their answers. Then go over the answers with the class.

Answers

> Her parents were very proud of her. ⓟ Now Lucy works as a sitcom writer for a popular TV show.
> She starts work late in the morning and often works until 7 or 8 at night. ⓟ Lucy is very curious.

B

1 Books open. Explain the task and go over the three questions.
Ss may use either these questions or others of their own to guide their composition.

2 Have Ss individually write their three-paragraph composition about someone they know who is creative or unique. Circulate to help and check for accuracy. Assign the composition for homework if there is not enough time to write it in class.

C Pair work

1 Books open. Explain the task and lead Ss through the three questions. Then put Ss in pairs, and have them exchange compositions. If necessary, remind Ss of the value and purpose of peer feedback. Have pairs read each other's compositions in order to answer the peer feedback questions. Have Ss make notes about their answers as they read.

2 Have Ss return their partner's composition. Then have Ss take turns sharing and discussing their answers to the three questions. If you wish, have Ss revise their compositions for homework, based on their partner's suggestions.

3 Have Ss display their compositions on a bulletin board for other Ss to read.

Ideas that work

1 Everyday objects

starting In these activities, Ss talk about what makes everyday household objects useful
point and successful.

A

1 Books closed. Ask Ss to think of everyday objects that they find useful, such
as matches, flashlights, or cell phones. Have selected Ss or volunteers call
out their answers. List them on the board, and then lead a brief class
discussion about their usefulness and why they are so successful.

2 Books open. Explain the task and have Ss look at the six inventions and
read the model language in the speech balloon. Have Ss silently think of
reasons why each object has been so successful. If you wish, have Ss make
notes of their answers. Then have Ss compare answers with a partner before
having selected Ss share answers with the class.

Possible answers

Microwave oven: People need a quick and easy way to cook food.
Buttons: People want a decorative, easy, and durable way to fasten their clothes.
Matches: People need to be able to start fires easily.
Post-it® Notes: People need an easy way to place short notes in places where they
   will be noticed.
Aluminum foil: People need a way to wrap food and keep it fresh.
Paper clips: People need a way to keep documents organized.

B Pair work

Books open. Explain the task and then put Ss in pairs to discuss the questions.
Have selected pairs share answers with the class.

2 Great ideas?

listening In these activities, Ss listen to people talking about great ideas for inventions.

A

1 Books closed. Ask Ss if they have ever thought up an invention, either a
whimsical and impractical one or an invention they thought would be
successful. Write Ss' answers on the board.

2 Books open. Explain the task and lead Ss through the chart, making sure
they know what information they need to complete it.

3 **Optional:** Pre-teach any items from the following vocabulary that you think will help your Ss:

> **to broadcast** to send out sound or pictures
>   (on radio or television) by radio waves
> **device** an object or machine that does a specific job
> **to monitor** to watch something carefully
> **to glide** to move easily across something

4 Play the audio program. Encourage Ss to take notes, but allow them to only listen at this point. Then replay the audio program, this time pausing briefly after each speaker has finished. Have Ss complete the chart with the thing each person would like to invent and what these things would do. Remind Ss that they need to write only a few words for each person.

5 Have Ss compare answers with a partner. Replay the audio program as necessary before going over the answers with the class.

Possible answers

	What are the inventions	What would they do
John	an invention for ordering TV programs	It would allow you to watch a program anytime, without having to wait for the show to be broadcast.
	a system on the TV to wake you up when you fall asleep	A voice from the TV would wake you up when you start to fall asleep.
Sandra	device to monitor car parts	It would tell you if the engine was not working well, or if there were problems with the brakes, so that you could get them fixed right away.
	a car that could roll over other cars	It would rise up 20 feet in the air and roll over the other cars.
Ted	a cooking robot	It would cook for you while you were at work or school so that the meal would be ready by the time you got home. It could be given instructions by phone.

Transcript

Listen to John, Sandra, and Ted talking about what they would invent to make their lives easier. What are the inventions? What would they do?

John: Well, I love to watch TV. So, I'd like to see an invention that would allow us to watch programs anytime, you know what I mean? We wouldn't have to wait until the show is broadcast. Each TV screen would have a list on it, and you would order the program you want to watch, like ordering from a menu. You could watch any program at any time of the day.

And I often fall asleep late at night while I'm watching TV. Then I miss the end of my program! It would be great if the TV could somehow have a system that would wake you up when you start to fall asleep. You know, you'd hear this voice from the TV shouting, "Wake up! You're falling asleep!" And the TV would somehow know that you were falling asleep. Well, on second thought, maybe some people wouldn't like this invention. They wouldn't be able to enjoy their nap with the TV screaming at them.

Sandra: My car is always breaking down. I have so much trouble with it! I wish there were some kind of device that would monitor the different parts of your car. You know, some kind of machine that would tell you when the engine is not working well or if there are problems with the brakes. That way I wouldn't have to worry about my car. I could just take it to the garage right away and get it fixed.

Oh, another idea: I drive to work. And I'm always sitting in traffic jams. I sometimes wish I had a special car, you know, one that could rise up ten or twenty feet in the air and just roll over the other cars. You know, everyone else would be sitting there, and I'd be gliding by overhead. Isn't that a weird thought? Well, uh, . . . these are the kinds of things I think about when I'm sitting in traffic!

Ted: My idea would be useful for when you get home hungry. Well, if you got home from work or school and you didn't want to cook, you'd have this cooking robot. You could program certain menus into the robot – each menu would have a number – and you could punch in that number. Then the robot would start cooking. . . . I mean, the robot would do everything! Oh yeah, and you could call the robot from an outside phone – from school or work, from your car, wherever – and the robot would start cooking. The meal would be ready by the time you got home. Wouldn't that be great? I'd probably stop filling up on junk food after school if I had a robot like that!

Oh, I've got to go. I think my dinner's ready.

B Pair work

1 Books open. Explain the task and put Ss in pairs to discuss which of the inventions described in the audio program would be the most useful for them and why. Then have selected Ss or volunteers share answers with the class.

2 **Optional:** Take a tally of the Ss' preferences to use as the basis of a class discussion.

Optional activity: *Creative inventions*

Time: 15–20 minutes. Ss come up with an invention of their own.

1 *Group work* Books closed. Ask Ss: "What would you like to invent if you had a chance? What would this thing be used for? Why would it be successful?" Have Ss work in small groups to come up with one invention and to explain why their invention would be necessary and successful. If you wish, have groups draw a picture of their invention.

2 Have each group present their invention to the class. Have the class vote on which invention is the most interesting.

Non-defining relative clauses as sentence modifiers

grammar focus

This grammar focus presents non-defining relative clauses with *which* to modify the entire sentence.

> **Grammar notes** In these relative clauses, the relative pronoun *which* refers not to a particular noun, but to the whole idea in the main clause (e.g., The floods have damaged the vegetable crops, *which means that the price of vegetables will go up this summer.*).
>
> Non-defining relative clauses are always the second clause in a two-clause sentence. Because these clauses are non-defining, they are set off from the main clause by commas.
>
> This type of non-defining relative clause adds information or a comment that applies to the entire sentence, but is not essential information to the meaning of the sentence.
>
> Only *wh-* relative pronouns (*who, whom,* or *which*) can be used in non-defining relative clauses. *That* cannot be used.

1 Books closed. On the board, write:

A.	B.
1. Lap-top computers are easy to carry,	a. which means new software titles come out all the time.
2. People enjoy playing computer games,	b. which is why many people travel with one.

Read the sentences aloud, and have Ss match the clauses and call out their answers (answers: 1/b, 2/a). Then put Ss in pairs to think of another clause that begins with *which is why* to complete the "A" part of each sentence. Have Ss call out their answers and write them on the board. Revise and correct as necessary. Ask Ss if they know what kind of relative clauses these are (answer: non-defining relative clauses).

2 Books open. Lead Ss through the information in the grammar box, and go over the examples. Provide additional explanations and examples as necessary. Then have Ss compare these sentences with the non-defining relative clauses in Exercise 3 on page 19 of the Student's Book, and ask how they are different (answer: these clauses make a comment on the complete sentence as opposed to commenting on a noun).

A

1 Explain the task and go over the example. Clarify the meanings of the following vocabulary:

> **to dispose of** to get rid of, to throw away
>
> **terrorism** violent action or threats of violence for a political purpose
>
> **inadequate** not good enough
>
> **express delivery service** a business that delivers packages and mail, usually in less time than the postal service
>
> **nicotine** a poisonous and addictive chemical in tobacco products
>
> **nicotine patch** a small piece of material with nicotine on it that helps a person stop smoking when it is stuck to his or her skin
>
> **personal navigation system** an electronic device in a car that helps the driver plan the best route to a destination
>
> **childproof bottle cap** a lid for a bottle containing dangerous substances that children cannot open
>
> **vaccine** a substance often injected into the blood that protects you from getting a particular disease
>
> **metal detector** a piece of equipment used to find metal objects that are hidden from view

2 Have Ss individually match each problem with an appropriate non-defining relative clause. Then have them compare answers with a partner before going over them with the class.

Answers

1. i	**2.** b	**3.** e	**4.** j	**5.** g
6. c	**7.** d	**8.** a	**9.** f	**10.** h

3 Next have Ss work with the same partners to write their own non-defining relative clause for each of the ten sentences. Circulate to help and check for accuracy. Then combine pairs into groups of four to compare and check each other's answers. Have these groups of four decide upon the two most interesting sentences. Then have groups share these two sentences with the class.

Possible answers

> **1.** AIDS kills thousands of people each year, which is why more money should be spent on research.
> **2.** Cities are running out of safe places to dispose of trash, which means that new locations will need to be found.
> **3.** It's very difficult to quit smoking, which is why it is better not to start smoking in the first place.

continued

4. Air travel became more dangerous in the 1980s because of terrorism, which is why stricter airport security rules were put into effect.

5. Children used to get sick after opening medicine bottles and taking pills, which is why it is important to store medicines safely.

6. There are thousands of accidents in the workplace each year, which is why many companies have safety training for their employees.

7. The postal service in many countries is not very efficient, which means that one needs to be cautious when mailing important letters.

8. People already find today's computers inadequate, which is why new and faster models are being launched all the time.

9. It's easy to get lost when driving in a new city, which is why it's important to study a good map before setting out.

10. It used to be that people couldn't drive in the rain, which meant that people's lives were much more dependent on the weather.

B

1 Books open. Explain the task and have Ss read the five sentences. Have Ss individually add creative non-defining relative clauses beginning with *which is why* or *which means that* to each sentence. Circulate to offer assistance. Then have Ss compare answers with a partner and check each other's work for accuracy.

2 Have selected Ss or volunteers share answers with the class. Write them on the board for later revision and correction.

Sample answers

1. People today watch TV more than they buy books, which is why they understand visual information far better than written information.

2. The Internet is used by millions of people, which means that it is becoming a good way for companies to advertise and sell products.

3. Airplane design has improved tremendously, which is why people are less afraid to fly than they used to be.

4. There have been many advances in medicine in recent years, which means that money used for medical research has been well spent.

5. It's becoming less expensive to use cellular phones, which means that everybody will have one in the future.

Optional activity: *The sentence modifying race*

Time: 10 minutes. Ss practice modifying sentences with non-defining relative clauses.

1 *Pair work* Books closed. Write these non-defining clauses on the board:

. . . which is why they have become so popular

. . . which means that prices fell drastically

. . . which is why people are living longer these days

. . . which is why people don't have to depend on the postal system anymore

. . . which means that bookstores may one day become a thing of the past

. . . which is why no one buys them anymore

. . . which is why it was an incredibly successful product

2 Have Ss work with a partner to write at least one opening clause to complete each sentence. The first pair to complete each sentence with at least one accurate and appropriate clause is the winner.

Inventions and discoveries

discussion In this activity, Ss discuss great inventions of the twentieth century.

Group work

1 Books closed. Brainstorm with the class about inventions that have had a big impact on life in the twentieth century. Have Ss call out their answers, and list them on the board.

2 Books open. Have Ss look at the photograph and say what they see. Explain the task and ask Ss to read the model answer in the speech balloon. Then put Ss in groups of four or five to come up with three inventions they think have had the greatest impact on life in the twentieth century. Remind Ss to give reasons and that their statements should include a non-defining relative clause.

3 Have groups report their ideas to the class while you write their sentences on the board and work with the class to revise and correct them, if needed. Alternatively, use the sentences as the basis for a class discussion.

5 Collocations

vocabulary These activities present some common verb + noun collocations for describing how people come up with ideas.

A

1 Books open. Explain the task and have Ss read the list of verbs and nouns in the box, clarifying meaning as necessary. Go over the examples. Then have Ss individually combine the verbs and nouns. Point out that some of the verbs can be combined with more than one noun.

2 Have Ss compare answers with a partner. Then go over the answers with the class.

Possible answers

> analyze: a problem, a situation, information
> explore: alternatives, possibilities
> find: a mistake, a solution, alternatives, information
> make: a mistake
> organize: information
> solve: a problem

B Pair work

1 Books open. Explain the task and have Ss read the sample answer in the speech balloon. Then put Ss in pairs to discuss the question. Circulate to help Ss use the expressions from Exercise A in their answers.

2 Combine pairs to form groups of four to take turns reading and discussing their statements. Then have each group share one or more sentences with the class. Lead a class discussion as appropriate.

6 Making life better

discussion In these activities, Ss talk about how inventions can help improve our lives.

A Pair work

1 Books open. Put Ss in pairs to look at the photograph and describe to each other what they see and why they think this product was invented. Explain the task and have Ss read the list of reasons why new products are invented. Then have the pairs add two more reasons to the list. Tell Ss that it may be helpful for them to also think of examples of products that were invented for the reasons they listed.

2 Have pairs share their answers with the class. Lead a class discussion as appropriate.

Possible answers

> to help people use time more efficiently
> to make information available more quickly
> to help people with disabilities

B Group work

1 Books open. Explain the task and have Ss read the list of inventions, checking that they are familiar with each one. Then have Ss read the sample answer in the speech balloon.

Combine pairs to form groups of four to match each invention to a reason from Exercise A. Have selected Ss or volunteers share an answer with the class.

2 **Optional:** Ask Ss for examples of things invented to protect the environment (or things they would like to see invented). Have Ss call out their suggestions and give reasons for their choices. Lead a class discussion as appropriate.

Possible answers

> air bags for cars: to save lives
> fax machines: to make business more efficient / to make
>   information available more quickly
> handheld computers: to make business more efficient / to
>   make computers easy to carry with you
> lie detectors: to gather accurate information
> life preservers: to save lives
> jet engines: to make long-distance travel easier
> overnight delivery services: to make business more efficient
> the Walkman: to make life more enjoyable
> virtual reality: to make life more enjoyable

Optional activity: *Inventing reasons*

Time: 10–15 minutes. Ss practice giving reasons for inventions.

1 *Class activity* Books closed. Prepare two papers using the following headings, leaving ten places for inventions and reasons.

Inventions	Reasons

2 Split the class into two groups: A and B. Give a copy of the paper to each group. Tell the groups to appoint a secretary. Then have Ss work in their groups to brainstorm ten inventions while their secretary lists them on the left side of the paper. Tell Ss to think of unusual inventions different from those in Exercise 6B, while you circulate to help with vocabulary.

3 Collect the papers from the groups. Then have Ss form two circles, one inside the other so that a S from group B is standing in front of a S from group A. Give group A's list of inventions to one S from group B and vice versa. Give each S up to 30 seconds to write a possible reason why the first invention on the list was invented. As soon as the first Ss are finished, have them pass the paper to the next person to complete the reason for the second invention, and so on.

4 Ss who cannot write a reason within 30 seconds pass the paper to the next S to complete this blank. The first group to complete the chart with reasonable and appropriate reasons next to each of the ten inventions on their list is the winner.

Innovative products and services

reading   The reading text provides information about the ideas behind three famous inventions, and the activities allow Ss to practice reading for main ideas and drawing inferences.

A Pair work

Books open. Have Ss cover the article with a piece of paper. Then explain the task, and put Ss in pairs to look at the photos of the three products and discuss what they are, why they were invented, and why they have been so successful. After about 5 minutes, have several pairs share an answer with the class. Lead a class discussion as appropriate.

B

1 Books closed. Tell Ss that the three products began when their inventors were inspired by simple questions. Ask Ss to try to think of what the question was for each product. Have Ss call out their answers, but don't comment on them.

2 Books open. Explain the task and have Ss silently read the article to check their predictions and find out what questions inspired the development of each product.

3 **Optional:** Have Ss underline up to five words that are new to them as they read. Then, when Ss are finished, have them compare underlined words with a partner to try to come up with definitions before asking you to clarify meaning.

4 **Optional:** Have Ss underline the inventors' questions as they read.

5 Go over the answers with the class.

> Sony Walkman: What would happen if Sony removed the recording function and speaker and sold headphones with a tape player instead?
> NIKE athletic shoes: What would happen if one poured rubber into a waffle iron?
> Federal Express: Why couldn't there be a reliable overnight mail delivery service?

C Group work

1 Books open. Explain the task and lead Ss through the list of questions. Then put Ss in groups of four or five to discuss them. Encourage Ss to give examples from the text and reasons of their own to support their answers.

2 Have selected Ss from each group share an answer with the class. Lead a class discussion as appropriate.

Possible answers

> 1. Because it looked funny and they weren't used to it.
> 2. Maybe the professor didn't think his business idea was a practical one.
> 3. NIKE athletic shoe soles
> 4. Answers will vary.

Optional activity: *This may be a silly question*

Time: 5–10 minutes. Ss further discuss the concept of originality and inventions.

1 *Pair work* Books open. Have Ss reread the last paragraph of the text. Then put Ss in pairs to define "an open-ended question" and say why the questions these inventors asked were "open-ended."

2 Ask each pair to come up with at least one "silly and open-ended" question about something that is not usually questioned in daily life (e.g., "Why do people have to work from 9 to 5 every day?"). Then combine pairs to form groups of four to compare their questions. Have groups share their best questions with the class and decide if any of the questions might lead to a great idea for an invention or service.

Students review ways of talking about events in the past (such as news and personal stories and regrets) using the simple past, past perfect, present perfect, and past continuous tenses.

Using the grammar structures *should have* and *ought to have*, noun clauses introduced by *it*, and reduced relative clauses, students also practice talking about personal values, beliefs, and character traits, as well as about the role of creativity in our personal and professional lives.

1 Adverbs with the past and past perfect

In these activities, Ss review adverbs used with the past and past perfect to describe events that happened at two different times.

A

1 Books closed. On the board, draw this time line:

```
        two                          last
◄----- months ago ----------------- month -------------------- now ----------►
```

Ask Ss to call out any actions, and write them on the board under *two months ago* or *last month* (e.g., ate at a restaurant, I met them). Have Ss make sentences with the information on the time line, such as "I had eaten at that restaurant before I met them." Circle the word *before* and ask Ss if they remember any other adverbs of time; write them on the board as Ss call them out. Then have Ss make sentences with the different adverbs and actions on the board. Ask Ss to explain why the action on the left side of the line is in the past perfect while the more recent action is in the simple past (answer: the past perfect is used to describe something that happened or something that was true *before* another event in the past).

2 Books open. Explain the task and have Ss read the four events. Ask Ss to underline the time expressions in each one (answers: 1. since, Before that; 2. last year, Until that time; 3. last summer, Before that; 4. a few months ago, Up until then).

3 Have Ss complete the sentences describing an event that occurred at an earlier time.

Possible answers

> 1. Before that, I'd always worn glasses.
> 2. Until that time, I'd always taken a train or driven a car.
> 3. Before that, I'd only traveled around my own country.
> 4. Up until then, I'd always lived with my parents.

B

1 Books open. Explain the task and then have Ss look at the picture and say what change it depicts. Ask Ss to read the model language and then choose two of the events from Exercise A to write more about. Remind Ss to use the expressions listed.

2 Put Ss in pairs to compare answers and to ask each other follow-up questions. Have selected Ss or volunteers share one event with the class.

Present perfect vs. past continuous vs. past

In this activity, Ss review the different uses of the present perfect, past continuous, and the past in a news article.

1 Books open. Explain the task and check that Ss remember the form and use of the three tenses mentioned.

2 Have Ss read the articles. Check that Ss understand the meaning of the following vocabulary:

> **fare** the price of a ticket
> **to drop dramatically** to decrease a lot
> **site** place, location

3 Have Ss complete the sentences with the verbs in parentheses. Then put Ss in pairs to compare answers before going over them as a class.

Answers

> **Article on the left:** announced; has developed; listened/were listening; made; has dropped; took place
> **Article on the right:** occurred; ran; were traveling; lost; were; has been

Should have *and* ought to have; *wishes about the past*

In this activity, Ss review the use of *should have* and *ought to have* to talk about regrets.

1 Books closed. Tell Ss of a regret you have about something you did or didn't do in the past. Write the word *regret* on the board, and ask Ss to think of the kinds of things people usually regret, such as not studying for an important test or not applying for a particular job. List their ideas on the board.

2 Books open. Explain the task and have Ss read the example. Then have Ss individually complete the sentences with their own regrets while you circulate to check Ss' progress.

3 Put Ss in pairs to tell each other about their regrets. Encourage them to ask and answer follow-up questions. Have volunteers share one of their regrets with the class.

Optional activity: *Guess my age*

Time: 10 minutes. Ss practice expressing regrets about the past.

Group work Books closed. Write on the board: *childhood, early teens, late teens* (if your Ss are older than early twenties, use the ages of *childhood, teens,* and *twenties*). Tell Ss to think of a personal regret they have for each age on the board. Using *wish, ought to have, should have,* or *shouldn't have,* Ss write a statement for each without referring to their age. Then put Ss into groups of three or four to take turns telling each other their wishes about the past while the rest of the group guesses which age the S is referring to.

Noun clauses introduced by it

In this activity, Ss review sentences in which the structure *it* + adjective + noun clause is used to describe one's opinion or feelings about a topic.

1 Books closed. Write *wonderful* on the board, and then ask a S to make a sentence, starting with *it's,* about something current in his or her life. Write the sentence on the board. If the S doesn't produce the target structure, ask other Ss for ways to say the same thing, until you have the sentence beginning "It's wonderful that . . . ," on the board.

2 Books open. Explain the task and have Ss read the adjectives and the five statements. Give Ss a few minutes to decide which adjective they would use and how to comment on each statement. Then have selected Ss share their comments with the class. Ask them to give reasons, and then have other Ss respond to their classmates' ideas.

Possible answers

> 1. It's wonderful/fortunate that children today have far more opportunities.
> 2. It's unfortunate that young people don't pay much attention to their parents' advice.
> 3. It's interesting that teenagers everywhere face the same problems.
> 4. It's true that schools don't always prepare students to succeed in the real world.
> 5. It's obvious that young people have to learn about computers if they are going to survive in this world.

Optional activity: *Commenting on life*

Time: 5–10 minutes. Ss use the adjectives and sentence structure in Exercise 4 to describe their own feelings about the topics.

Pair work Books open. Tell Ss to write comments about anything in their lives using the six adjectives in Exercise 4. Put Ss in pairs to compare and explain their comments. Have pairs share their most interesting ones with the class.

5 Reduced relative clauses

In these activities, Ss use reduced relative clauses to talk about qualities required for different professions.

A

1 Books closed. Write the following professions on the board: *fashion designer, accountant, forest ranger, taxi driver*. Ask Ss to call out some of the qualities required by each of these professions.

2 Books open. Have Ss look at the photograph, and ask which profession is represented. Explain the task and have Ss read the sentence parts in the two columns. Have Ss match the professions with the qualities listed. Explain that each profession has two qualities. Put Ss in pairs to compare answers before going over them with the class.

Answers

1. b, d	**2.** e, h	**3.** c, g	**4.** a, f

B

Books open. Explain the task and go over the example. Ask Ss if the example contains a defining or non-defining relative clause (answer: defining). Then have Ss rewrite the sentences from Exercise A with reduced relative clauses.
Put Ss in pairs to compare answers before going over them with the class.

Possible answers

1. A person working as a fashion designer should be aware of trends and familiar with different styles.
2. A person working as an accountant has to be good with numbers and very accurate.
3. A person working as a forest ranger needs to be knowledgeable about plants and animals and be physically fit.
4. A person working as a taxi driver must be a good driver and familiar with city streets.

Optional activity: *Having what it takes*

Time: 5–10 minutes. Ss continue practicing reduced relative clauses while exploring their own professional choices and abilities.

1 *Pair work* Books open. Tell Ss to think about their own abilities and characteristics. Then have them choose the profession listed in Exercise A that most closely matches their abilities. Put Ss in pairs to tell each other which profession they chose and why. Remind them to use reduced relative clauses.

2 On the board, tally the number of Ss who chose each profession. Then have pairs discuss additional qualities that might be helpful for the professions they chose. Circulate to help with vocabulary and to observe Ss' fluency levels.

6 Tell me a story.

In these activities, Ss use the past tenses to tell each other stories about events in their lives.

A Pair work

1 Books open. Explain the task and have Ss read the situations. Check that Ss understand the following vocabulary:

> **fascinating** very interesting
> **to laugh hysterically** to laugh uncontrollably

2 Give Ss a few minutes to think about times when the things listed happened to them. Then put Ss in pairs to tell each other about those times.

B Group work

Books open. Explain the task and then combine pairs to form groups of four. Go over the sample dialog, and have Ss tell their stories again. Circulate to listen to Ss, encourage group members to ask and answer follow-up questions, and offer help when needed. Have selected groups share one of their stories with the class.

7 Headline news

In these activities, Ss write about news events using reduced and defining/non-defining relative clauses and past tenses.

A

1 Books open. Have Ss look at the two photographs and say what is happening in each and why each is labeled in the way that it is. Explain the task and have Ss read the six headlines and the six news story types. Check Ss' comprehension of the following vocabulary:

> **triumphant** achieving great success
> **exhibit** a show
> **impressionism** a style of painting developed in the late nineteenth
> century, mainly by French artists (e.g., Monet)
> **impressionist** done in the style of impressionism
> **to draw (someone to something)** to attract
> **breakthrough** an important discovery

2 Have Ss match the headlines with the news story types. Then have Ss write a news item using one of these topics, or one of their own. Tell them to write about three to five lines.

Answers

> **1.** c   **2.** d   **3.** f   **4.** b   **5.** e   **6.** a

B Group work

1 Books open. Explain the task and put Ss in groups of four or five. Tell Ss to hand their paper to the S on their right and then to read the article. Have them continue this way until each S has read each article. Tell them to choose which article they found the most interesting.

2 **Optional:** Put Ss in groups to add more information to an article that most of the group found interesting. Then collect the papers, and post them on the bulletin board for Ss to read over the next couple of days. Attach a slip of paper and a pencil to each article, and have Ss put a check mark under the article they liked best. Then after everyone has had a chance to read all the articles, see which article received the most votes.

Optional activity: *And now, the news*

Time: 25–30 minutes. Ss continue practicing language relating to the news.

1 Books closed. Write on the board: *Reporting the news*. Then ask Ss to call out common phrases used by news anchors to introduce and conclude their reports while you write them on the board. Elicit or produce the following, and write them on the board: *Good evening. Welcome to the seven o'clock news. Our top story tonight . . . , This just in . . . .*

2 Have groups use their news articles to create news broadcasts. Tell them to choose two anchors and decide on the order of their news reports. If they need to, have them write additional news articles. Give Ss time to rehearse their broadcasts. Then have them present their news broadcasts to the class using the phrases on the board. If possible, record the news broadcasts with a camcorder to show Ss for evaluation and error correction.

8 *Teaching values*

In these activities, Ss review the vocabulary used to talk about personal values and social issues.

A Group work

1 Books open. Explain the task and have Ss read the values in the box. Check Ss' comprehension of the following vocabulary:

> **tolerance** the ability to allow other people to have their own beliefs
> **generosity** a willingness to give money or help beyond what is usually expected
> **charity** the act of giving food and money to people who need it

2 Have Ss read the model dialog. Put Ss in groups of four or five to design a lesson to teach the values listed. Have them choose a group secretary to take notes on their ideas.

B Class activity

Books open. Explain the task and have groups share their lesson ideas with the class. Have the class put together a collection of the best ideas for one of the problems.

9 Learning from others

In this activity, Ss continue talking about values and personal beliefs.

Pair work

1 Books open. Put Ss in pairs to look at the photograph and describe what they see. Explain the task and have Ss read the pairs of groups in the box and the model language in the speech balloon. Tell Ss to decide the two most important values each group learns from another group. Circulate to listen and observe Ss' fluency levels.

2 Have selected pairs share their thoughts on the values learned and taught by one of the pairs of groups.

Possible answers

Children learn from their parents how to distinguish right from wrong.
Parents learn from their children how to live each day more fully.
Teenagers learn from their peers about friendship and loyalty.
Employees learn from their bosses about responsibility and time management.
Bosses learn from their employees about loyalty and dedication.

Optional activity: *And the award goes to . . .*

Time: 15–20 minutes. Ss role-play an awards ceremony to recognize people who have had important influences on them.

1 *Group work* Books open or closed. Tell Ss to think of people who have influenced them in important ways. Explain that Ss are going to stage an awards ceremony for the people who have influenced them most. First, have each group choose a master of ceremonies to introduce Ss. Then have Ss write presentations based on the group discussions and practice their presentations.

2 Have groups present their awards programs to the rest of the class.

10 *Give us your ideas.*

In these activities, Ss practice talking about solutions to problems.

A Pair work

1 Books open. Explain the task and have Ss read the situations. Check Ss' comprehension of the following vocabulary:

> **in stock** available for purchase in a store
> **to promote** to advertise

2 Put Ss in pairs to suggest solutions for each situation. Circulate to listen to Ss' suggestions and offer assistance when needed.

B Group work

Books open. Explain the task and then combine pairs to form groups of four to share their suggestions. Encourage group members to ask each other follow-up questions. Then have groups present their most interesting suggestion to the class.

Optional activity: *What's the solution?*

Time: 10–15 minutes. Ss practice talking about problems and offering solutions.

1 *Pair work* Books open or closed. Have Ss work in pairs to think of a situation similar to the ones in Exercise A. Tell Ss to write the situation on a piece of paper while you circulate to help with vocabulary and accuracy. Then have Ss exchange papers with another pair; pairs write solutions to each other's problems.

2 Have pairs who exchanged situations form groups of four, and have Ss explain their solutions to each other. Encourage them to ask and answer follow-up questions. Have selected groups share a problem and solution with the class.

This unit focuses on everyday annoyances, community issues, and consumer complaints. Students use noun clauses containing relative clauses and noun clauses as subjects and objects to talk about complaints and ways of dealing with them.

 Lesson A   *That really bugs me!*

1   *Everyday annoyances*

starting point

Pair work

1   Books closed. Write the word *annoyance* on the board, and tell the class to think of some things they find annoying in their daily lives. Have Ss call out their answers.

2   Books open. Have Ss look at the four pictures while they cover the text below each one. Ask them what they think is happening in each picture. Have Ss call out their answers. Then have Ss read the text under each picture. Ask Ss to raise their hands if any of these annoyances are also annoyances for them.

3   Explain the task and put Ss in pairs to share and discuss their answers. Then have selected Ss or volunteers share an answer with the class.

Optional activity: *Dealing with annoyances*

Time: 5–10 minutes. Ss talk about common annoyances and how to deal with them.

1   *Pair work* Books open. Put Ss in pairs, and have them look again at each picture and discuss the best way to respond in each situation, and why. Then ask Ss to discuss what their natural response is likely to be, and why it is sometimes difficult to respond to situations in the right way.

2   Have pairs role-play one of the situations pictured. Then have selected Ss or volunteers perform their role plays for the class. Tell the class to call out which picture the Ss are role-playing.

2   *It gets on my nerves!*

listening

In these activities, Ss listen to people talking about something irritating that happened to them.

A

1   Books closed. Ask Ss if they know what the title of the exercise means. If not, provide examples such as, "It gets on my nerves when my neighbors make noise late at night." Put Ss in pairs to tell each other two things that get on their nerves.

2 Books open. Tell Ss they are going to listen to two people talk about what annoys them. Then explain the task, and make sure Ss know what information to listen for to complete the chart.

3 **Optional:** Pre-teach any items from the following vocabulary that you think will help your Ss:

> **to act up** to behave badly
>
> **to stomp** to make a loud noise with your feet when walking
>
> **a movie review** an article about the good and bad points of a movie
>
> **to get good (great) reviews** to receive positive comments in a movie review
>
> **an usher** a person working at an event who shows people to their seats
>
> **out of hand** out of control

4 Play the audio program, and have Ss complete the chart as much as they can.

5 Ss compare answers with a partner. Replay the audio program, and have Ss add more information to the chart. Then ask selected Ss to share answers with the class.

Answers

	What happened
Jane	The neighbors went onto the roof of Jane's apartment (they wanted to show an out-of-town visitor the view) and made a lot of noise on her roof. She got dressed and went up onto the roof to tell them to be quiet. After that she couldn't fall back asleep.
Bob	A man and a woman ruined the movie for him: They came in late, took a while to get into their seats, and started talking. The man was telling the woman the entire story of the movie. Another person asked them to be quiet. They started arguing and the usher had to be called because it was getting out of hand.

Transcript

> **Listen to Jane and Bob talking about something that irritated them. What happened in each situation?**
>
> **Man:** Hi, Jane. . . . Say, are you OK? You're looking a bit tired.
>
> **Jane:** Oh, I am. It's my neighbors.
>
> **Man:** Oh, so they're acting up again. Huh?
>
> **Jane:** Unfortunately, yes, they are.
>
> **Man:** Loud music?
>
> **Jane:** Not exactly. You've been to my apartment, right?
>
> **Man:** Yeah. I've been there once. It's a nice place.

continued

Jane: Well, thank you. So you remember I live on the top floor. Well, last night, around eleven, my neighbors decided to go up on the roof of my apartment building!

Man: The roof? Really?

Jane: Yeah. They had this guy in from out of town and they wanted to show him the view! Can you believe it? I'm fast asleep, and all of a sudden I hear "stomp, stomp, stomp!" They're walking around on the roof. It sounded like my ceiling was going to fall in.

Man: So what did you do?

Jane: Well, after about ten minutes, I got dressed and went up there to tell them to be quiet. I was so mad. Then of course after that, I couldn't go back to sleep.

Man: Oh, don't you hate when that happens? You can't fall asleep, and then before you know it, it's morning and the alarm clock is going off.

Woman: Hey, Bob! So how was the movie?

Bob: Well, I didn't really enjoy it very much.

Woman: Why? That film got great reviews. It's really popular.

Bob: Oh, the movie was fine. I just got irritated by the people sitting in front of me.

Woman: What happened?

Bob: Well, first they came in late. It took them a while to get into their seats. All this was happening during an exciting part of the movie. And then they started talking.

Woman: Oh, I hate when that happens!

Bob: There were two of them: a man and a woman. The man had seen the movie before. He was telling the woman the entire story.

Woman: Unbelievable!

Bob: Well, you won't believe what happened next! Another person asked them to be quiet. Politely, of course.

Woman: Right.

Bob: And they started arguing! Their voices were getting louder and louder. One guy was saying, "You shouldn't talk in the movie," and the other guy was saying, "You can't tell me what to do!"

Woman: Well, what finally happened?

Bob: The usher had to be called in because it was getting out of hand. Everyone quieted down eventually, but it was too late. They had ruined the movie for me.

Optional activity: *Details, details*

Time: 5–10 minutes. Ss listen for details.

1 Books open. Write the following questions on the board, and have Ss listen to the audio program again while they write their answers.

Jane: 1. What time did Jane's neighbors go onto the roof?
2. Why did her neighbors go up on the roof?
3. Why couldn't Jane sleep after telling her neighbors to be quiet?

Bob: 1. How did he enjoy the movie?
2. Who had seen the movie before?
3. What were the irritating people talking about?

2 Go over the answers as a class.

Answers

> **Jane: 1.** around 11:00
>
>   **2.** to show their out-of-town visitor the view
>
>   **3.** She was too angry.
>
> **Bob: 1.** He didn't enjoy it very much.
>
>   **2.** the man who came in late
>
>   **3.** The man was telling the woman the entire story of the movie.

B Pair work

Books open. Ask Ss whether or not they sympathize with the irritation Jane or Bob felt and the way they responded. Then ask, "What other situations irritate you?" Put Ss in pairs to make a list. Have some Ss share their answer with the class.

Noun clauses containing relative clauses

grammar focus This grammar focus presents noun clauses containing relative clauses in both subject and object positions.

> **Grammar notes** These clauses are noun clauses because they occupy noun slots in a sentence.
>
>   In the first two examples in the grammar focus box, the noun clause consists of an indefinite pronoun followed by an adjective clause (e.g., Something [indefinite pronoun] that really bothers me [relative clause with an adjective function]).
>
>   In the third and fourth examples in the grammar box, the noun clauses are introduced by a relative adverb (*when, why*). Nevertheless, they are noun clauses because they occupy noun slots in these sentences, in this case, the subjective complement slot. (Note: A subjective complement is a noun or noun phrase that renames the subject of a sentence with the verb *be*.)
>
>   These noun clauses with *wh-* words are sometimes called *indirect questions*.

1 Books closed. On the board, write:

Something that really bothers me about my neighbors . . .

What I can't stand about people with dogs . . .

2 Have Ss work in pairs to complete the sentences. Then have selected pairs call out answers. Write their answers on the board, and explain that the phrases you are writing are relative clauses functioning as nouns. Rewrite the Ss' answers to illustrate how phrases can also occur as the object of the sentence, for example:

The loud music my neighbors play late at night is something that really bothers me.
People who let their dogs bark late at night is one thing that really irritates me.

3 Books open. Lead Ss through the information and example sentences in the grammar box. Point out how the relative clauses are acting as nouns and that they can serve as either the subject or the object of a sentence.

A

Books open. Explain the task and have Ss individually complete the eight sentences with their own information. Circulate to help and check for accuracy.

B Pair work

1 Books open. Explain the task and have Ss read the sample dialog. Put Ss in pairs to compare answers. Encourage Ss to correct each other's work if they find any errors.

2 Have selected Ss or volunteers call out answers.

3 **Optional:** Have Ss come to the board to write one of their answers. Provide feedback and correction as necessary.

Possible answers

1. Something that really annoys me in restaurants is when the waiters ignore me.
2. When I'm waiting in line, one thing that gets on my nerves is when people try to cut in front of me.
3. Something that bothers me about people on buses and subways is when they push.
4. When I'm riding in a car, something that irritates me is when others in the car smoke.
5. Something that gets on my nerves at the movies is parents that don't take their babies outside when they start to cry.
6. Family members who don't wash their own dishes after meals is something that bothers me at home.
7. Driving their car too fast on our street is one thing that bothers me about my neighbors.
8. A clock that ticks too loudly is something that bothers me when I'm trying to go to sleep.

4 Ask some Ss to tell the class what most surprised them about their partner's answers.

Optional activity: *More complaints*

Time: 5–10 minutes. Ss continue practicing using noun clauses containing relative clauses to talk about things that annoy them.

1 *Pair work* Books open. Write the following on the board: *at school, at the supermarket, at the post office, during English class.* Tell Ss to think of a complaint for each situation using noun clauses containing relative clauses. Then put Ss in pairs to compare their complaints.

2 Have several Ss share answers with the class. Provide feedback and correction as necessary.

Possible answers

One thing that annoys me at school is when teachers give out too much homework.

Students cheating on tests is something that irritates me at school.

People trying to get into the express check-out line with too many items is the thing I hate most at the supermarket.

One thing that annoys me at the supermarket is products with no prices on them.

Stamp machines that don't work is one thing that irritates me at the post office.

What I hate is how the post office always seems to be closing just as I arrive.

One thing that irritates me during English class is people who always forget to bring their textbooks to class.

What I can't stand during English class is when other students ask me for an answer.

 Pet peeves

discussion These activities extend the theme of the lesson and give Ss additional practice with the grammar.

A

Books open. Explain the task and have Ss individually list at least four things they wish their friends or family members wouldn't do. Circulate to help.

B Pair work

Books open. Explain the task and have Ss read the sample language in the speech balloon. Then put Ss in pairs to compare and discuss their pet peeves. Have pairs decide how similar or different their complaints are. Then have selected pairs tell the class about their most similar or different complaints.

 What type of complainer are you?

discussion In these activities, Ss examine different types of complainers.

A Pair work

1 Books closed. On the board write a situation that might elicit a complaint (e.g., *The flowers you ordered were never delivered, but you were charged for them.*). Brainstorm with Ss what they would do in such a situation. Have Ss indicate with a show of hands who would complain and who would not. Point out that different people have different viewpoints on complaining.

2 Books open. Explain the task and have Ss read the text under the four pictures and the sample dialog. Put Ss in pairs to take turns explaining which of the four descriptions fits them best, and why. Have Ss ask and answer follow-up questions. Then have several Ss share their answers with the class.

3 Optional: Take a survey to find out the most common type of complainer in the class.

B Group work

1 Books open. Put Ss in pairs to describe to each other what is happening in the picture. Explain the task and have Ss read the four situations. Clarify meanings as necessary, checking that Ss understand the following:

> **to chat** to talk to someone in a friendly, informal way
>
> **to litter** to throw garbage on the ground

2 Have Ss read the sample language in the speech balloon. Then combine pairs to form groups of four to discuss whether or not they would complain in each of the situations, and if so, what they would do or say. Encourage Ss to give examples to support their answers, and have them ask and answer follow-up questions.

3 Have at least one S in each group report the group's most interesting answers to the class.

Possible answers

> **Situation 1:** No, I wouldn't complain, but I would stare at the person to make him or her feel really uncomfortable.
>
> **Situation 2:** Yes, I'd give them a call and politely explain that they are keeping me awake.
>
> **Situation 3:** Yes, I'd tell the person that their store had just lost my business, and then I would walk out.
>
> **Situation 4:** Yes, I'd approach them and tell them to throw their litter away in the trash can.

6 *Responding to complaints*

role play In these activities, Ss practice complaining about things and responding to complaints.

A Pair work

Books open. Explain the activity and lead Ss through the situations and the language in the box. Have Ss work with a partner to write a short dialog for each of the three situations. Circulate to help and check for accuracy. Then have pairs practice acting out their dialogs several times until they feel they can do it without reading their notes.

B Group work

1 Books open. Explain the task and then put pairs in groups of eight to ten, and have pairs within the groups take turns performing their dialogs for each other. Ask Ss to vote on the best dialog in their group for each situation. Then have the pairs with the best dialogs from each group perform them for the class.

2 Have the class decide which complaints are the most effective and which responses are the most polite.

Optional activity: *Guess my type!*

Time: 10–15 minutes. Ss practice making complaints and responding to them.

1 Put Ss in pairs and tell them to list on a piece of paper five more situations that warrant complaints. Then tell them to choose one of the situations and plan a role play using one of the types of complainers from Exercise 5A, without indicating it on their paper.

2 Combine pairs to form groups of four. Tell Ss that each pair will role-play their chosen situation while the other pair tries to guess both the situation and the type of complainer.

Writing a letter of complaint

writing These activities present Ss with the appropriate elements and correct order of a letter of complaint.

> **Culture note** A commonly held belief of businesspeople in the United States and Canada is that the customer is usually right, and any complaints from customers should be taken seriously. This approach encourages U.S. and Canadian consumers to complain when they feel they have not gotten their money's worth.

1 Books closed. Ask Ss if they have ever written a letter to complain about something. Have Ss respond with a show of hands. Then ask a few Ss who have written such a letter to say what they wrote about and the kind of information they included. If no one has written a letter of complaint before, have Ss look back at the situations in Exercise 5B and say for which situation they might write a letter of complaint (e.g., the rude salesclerk). What information would they want to include in such a letter?

2 Books open. Go over the information in the box. Explain that *relevant background information* could be any information leading up to the situation that caused the complaint.

A

1 Books open. Ask Ss to look at the postcard of the Bayview Inn, and brainstorm with the class about the kinds of problems one could have staying there.

2 Explain the task and have Ss read the three sentences. Then have Ss silently read the letter of complaint to decide in which paragraph each sentence belongs.

3 **Optional:** Have Ss decide where in the paragraphs each sentence should go.

4 Have Ss compare answers with a partner before going over them with the class.

Possible answers

> 2 Despite these problems, . . .   1 Unfortunately, . . .   3 Until things change at your inn, . . .
>
> 1. On July 16 my friends and I arrived at your inn hoping to spend an enjoyable weekend. **Unfortunately, because of your poor service, our weekend was a disaster.** Since your ad says "have a fabulous time or get your money back," I am requesting that you refund our money.
> 2. . . . The room, which had a view of a parking lot instead of the bay, had not yet been cleaned, so we found dirty towels on the beds and cigarette butts in the ashtrays. **Despite these problems, none of your employees apologized to us.** This was not the weekend we had been looking forward to.
> 3. . . . My previous visits were always enjoyable because of the courteous service and clean rooms with beautiful views. **Until things change at your inn, I will never recommend it to anyone.** I expect to receive my refund shortly.

B

Books open. Explain the task and have Ss read the four situations. Then have Ss choose one of the listed situations, or one of their own. Either in class or for homework, have Ss individually write a three-paragraph letter of complaint. Have Ss use the format of the letter to the general manager of the Bayview Inn as a model.

C Group work

1 Books open. Explain the task and put Ss in small groups of four to six to take turns reading their letters. Have groups decide which of the letters would be the most effective.

2 **Optional:** Have the S with the best letter of each group read his or her letter to the class and post it on the bulletin board.

Optional activity: *Peer editing*

Time: 10 minutes. Ss give each other suggestions for ways to improve their writing.

1 *Pair work* Books open or closed. Put Ss in pairs, and tell them to exchange their letters of complaint. Then have Ss read each other's papers and offer suggestions for improvement in organization, explanation, choice of words, and grammar.

2 Have Ss return each other's papers and discuss their suggestions while you circulate to help.

Let's do something about it!

  Why don't they do something about it?

starting point These activities give Ss a chance to think about what problems exist in their town or city and what can be done about them.

1 Books closed. Write this list of complaints about a city on the board:

There aren't enough parks.

Public transportation isn't very good.

There's nowhere for young people to go.

It's hard to find a parking spot.

The city doesn't take complaints seriously.

The materials in the libraries are old and out of date.

Have Ss work in pairs or groups to list as many additional complaints as they can in 5 minutes.

2 Have Ss call out some of the complaints they thought of, and write them on the board. Then ask the class questions like these: "Which of these things are serious problems in our city? Which is the most serious? What do you think should be done about it?" Lead a class discussion.

A

1 Books open. Explain the task and have Ss read the list of problems, checking Ss' comprehension of the following:

> **recklessly** dangerously, carelessly
> **to pick up after (someone)** to clean up for (someone)
>   [in this case, a dog's waste]
> **to enforce a law** to make people obey a law

2 Have Ss individually read the list and check (✓) which of the issues are problems in their city and which are not. Ask Ss to compare and discuss their answers with a partner.

3 Have selected Ss tell the class about some of the problems in their city. Lead a class discussion as appropriate.

B Pair work

1 Books open. Explain the activity and have Ss read the sample dialog. Then put Ss in pairs to identify the four most serious problems in their own city and discuss what they think should be done. Encourage Ss to give reasons and examples to support their answers. Also encourage them to come up with ideas to solve the problems.

2 Either have pairs join together to form groups to share their ideas, or have several pairs share ideas with the class.

Optional activity: *Press conference*

Time: 15–20 minutes. Ss practice making complaints and suggesting solutions.

1 *Class activity* Books closed. Tell Ss they will be part of a city team – either citizens, judges, or candidates for mayor. Explain that they will role-play a press conference to question the mayoral candidates, and the judges will decide on the winner of the election.

2 Choose five volunteers as candidates for mayor. Then choose three volunteers to be judges. The rest of the Ss will be citizens.

3 Divide the class into their groups. Have each citizen write one or more questions to ask the candidates about how they would solve problems in the city (e.g., What are you going to do about kids writing graffiti all over the buildings?). Have the candidates think of what problems they might be asked about.

4 Have mayoral candidates sit in front of the class and judges off to the side. Then have citizens call out their questions one at a time from their seats. Give each candidate a chance to answer. Have each judge take his or her own notes of the best answer for each question.

5 Have judges decide on and announce the "winner" of the press conference. Have another press conference with different candidates and judges, if time allows.

Problems where I live

listening

In these activities, Ss listen to people talking about the problems in their neighborhoods.

A

1 Explain the task and tell Ss that they should listen for the problems Mike and Rosanna discuss and what should be done about them. Play the audio program twice. The first time, have Ss listen without writing. The second time, have Ss complete the chart as they listen. Remind Ss that they need to write a few words only.

2 **Optional:** Pre-teach any of the following vocabulary that you think will help your Ss:

> **to report** to give a formal description of something
> [in this case, to the police]
> **a plus** an advantage
> **neck of the woods** neighborhood
> **to sleep in** to sleep later than usual in the morning

3 Ask Ss to compare answers with a partner. Then replay the audio program, if necessary, before going over the answers with the class.

Answers

	Problem	What should be done
Mike	graffiti	report the people doing it to the police
	noise	feels that nothing can be done about it
Rosanna	graffiti	report the people doing it to the police
	parking shortage	rent space in a garage

Transcript

Listen to Mike and Rosanna talking about problems where they live. What are the biggest problems? What do they think should be done about them?

Mike: Hey, Rosanna. Over here!

Rosanna: Hi, Mike. How are you? Been waiting long?

Mike: No, not at all. Have a seat.

Rosanna: Oh, it's great to see you.

Mike: Same here. So, how's the new apartment working out?

Rosanna: Good, good. I like it. The neighborhood, though, is . . .

Mike: Oh, what's the matter?

Rosanna: Well, there's a real graffiti problem. Some of the buildings down the street are covered with it, and it looks terrible.

Mike: I know what you mean. My neighborhood is the same way. I think we need to report people who are writing the graffiti to the police.

Rosanna: Yeah. That would really help, except I never see them doing it!

Mike: Well, other than that, how's the new neighborhood?

Rosanna: Well, I like all the stores. It's convenient for shopping. . . . And it's pretty quiet at night. That's definitely a plus.

Mike: Sounds like you're pretty satisfied.

Rosanna: Yeah, I guess so. Uh, the only other problem is that it's impossible to find parking. I have to drive around the block six or seven times to find a space. Usually I can find one, but sometimes I have to park really far away.

Mike: Well, is there any way you can rent space in a garage?

Rosanna: Yeah, that's a good idea. I'm thinking about doing just that. . . . So, how are things in your neck of the woods?

Mike: Well, there's a bit of a noise problem where I live. I live right down the street from a school. The bell rings every morning at seven thirty. It's impossible to sleep in.

Rosanna: Oh, what a drag!

continued

Mike: Yeah, and when school lets out, the kids are really noisy. I mean, they're nice kids, just loud!

Rosanna: Well, I don't know what you could do about that situation. . . .

Mike: Yeah. There's really nothing I can do, I guess. I . . . I just have to live with it. I don't know. . . .

Waitress: Excuse me. Are you ready to order?

Mike: Uh, could you give us a few more minutes? Thanks. I guess we'd better look at these menus first and talk later.

Rosanna: Yeah. So, what's good here?

Mike: Well, . . . um, . . . I think the fish is pretty good. Uh, I've also tried the turkey club, which isn't bad . . .

Optional activity: *Details, details*

Time: 5 minutes. This activity checks Ss' comprehension of the details of the listening text.

1 Books open or closed. Write the following questions on the board, and have Ss write down their answers:

1. Where are Mike and Rosanna?

2. What features of her neighborhood does Rosanna like?

3. What does Rosanna do when she can't find a parking space for her car?

4. What happens every morning in Mike's neighborhood, and why is it a problem?

2 Go over the answers as a class. Replay the audio program if necessary.

Answers

> **1.** in a restaurant
> **2.** She likes all the stores, it's convenient for shopping, and it's quiet at night.
> **3.** She drives around the block six or seven times to find one.
> **4.** The school bell rings every morning at 7:30. It's impossible for him to sleep in.

B

1 Books open. Explain the task and then put Ss in pairs or small groups to brainstorm other solutions for the problems Mike and Rosanna discussed.

2 **Optional:** Establish an amount of money Ss have to solve the problems; that is, Ss must think of a solution for each problem that won't cost too much.

3 Have Ss compare their ideas. Then ask selected Ss or volunteers to present one of their solutions to the class.

Noun clauses beginning with question words, *whether, and* if

grammar focus This grammar focus presents embedded noun clauses formed from *Wh-* and yes/no questions with statement word order.

Grammar notes As mentioned in the grammar notes earlier in this unit, noun clauses that begin with *wh-* words are called *indirect questions.* In these noun clauses, the word order of the underlying question is changed to the statement word order (e.g., the question *Why aren't there* more youth centers? changes to I don't know *why there aren't* more youth centers.).

Noun clauses with *wh-* words can function as the subject or object of a sentence.

Yes/no questions are changed into noun clauses by introducing the clause with *whether* or *if* followed by the statement word order rather than the inverted word order (e.g., I wonder *if they're going* to build more parking garages?).

Noun clauses that begin with *whether* or *if* can only occupy the object slot in a sentence.

A

1 Books open. Lead Ss through the information and example sentences in the grammar box. Have the class compare these noun clauses with the ones they studied in Lesson A, and have Ss call out any differences they notice (answer: initial words such as *something, one thing,* or *what* versus *why, if,* and *whether).* Point out that the connecting word is a question word, *whether,* or *if,* and that this connecting word is not optional. Also point out the statement word order by providing other examples of the transformation of questions into embedded noun clauses.

2 Explain the activity and go over the example. Have Ss read the eight sentences and phrases in parentheses. Check that Ss understand that some noun clauses function as the subject and others as the object. Also check that Ss understand that when questions with *would,* such as number 6, are transformed into noun clauses, they begin with *if.* Then have Ss individually rewrite each sentence. Circulate to help and check for accuracy. Have Ss compare answers with a partner before going over them as a class.

Answers

1. I wonder whether or not it's possible to stop people from littering.
2. I'd like to figure out how we can convince people to pick up after their dogs.
3. Why motorcycles have to be so loud is a mystery to me!
4. I'd like to know when they are going to help the homeless people.
5. I want to find out how I can help to maintain the city parks.
6. I wonder if hiring more police would help to lower crime.
7. I don't understand why the city can't add more streetlights.
8. Why drivers honk their horns so much is something I can't understand.

Optional activity: *Community concerns*

Time: 10 minutes. Ss write their own sentences using noun clauses beginning with question words, *whether*, or *if*.

Group work Books open or closed. Write the following topics on the board: *safety on the streets, the neighborhood, the educational system, traffic*. Then put Ss in groups of three or four to write two statements of concern about each topic using noun clauses beginning with question words, *whether*, or *if*. Provide the following example: "I don't understand why the city doesn't add more streetlights." Also explain that they can use the phrases listed in parentheses in Exercise 3A.

Possible answers

> **Safety on the streets:** I wonder whether the streets will ever be really safe or not.
> I wonder if the streets will be safer when the city hires more police to patrol them.
>
> **The neighborhood:** I'd like to know why the neighborhood is so noisy all the time.
> Whether this neighborhood will ever be clean is a question nobody can answer.
>
> **The educational system:** Teachers often wonder if what they're teaching is really getting through.
> I want to know why there is such an emphasis at school on preparing for examinations.
>
> **Traffic:** Why drivers need to constantly honk their horns is something I'll never understand.
> I'd like to know why they haven't built any new roads recently.

B Pair work

Books open. Explain the task and then put Ss in pairs to take turns reading and commenting on each other's sentences. Encourage Ss to ask follow-up questions, as well. Have several Ss share their sentences with the class. Write them on the board for revision and correction as needed.

Taking action

role play   These activities consolidate the grammar while Ss discuss solutions to community problems.

A Pair work

1   Books open. Put Ss in pairs to discuss what they see in the photograph. Explain the task and have Ss read the three problems. Have pairs brainstorm possible solutions for each one and take notes, listing as many possible solutions as they can.

2   Have pairs decide which solutions are workable and which are not for each problem. Then have them present their best solutions to the class.

3 **Optional:** Write conflicting solutions on the board, and have Ss debate them. Then have the class vote on which one seems best as a result of the debate.

Possible answers

> How can the police build a good relationship with the citizens?
>> Have regular community meetings between the police and citizens.
>> Sponsor sports events between the police and community groups.
>
> How can we stop people from littering?
>> Make fines higher.
>> Run an advertising campaign to discourage littering.
>
> How can the city keep young kids out of trouble?
>> Build a sports center for kids.
>> Offer free counseling at school.

B Group work

Books open. Explain the task and have Ss read the sample dialog. Put Ss in groups of three or four to take turns playing the roles of citizens making complaints and city officials offering suggestions. Then have Ss switch roles. Encourage Ss to play their roles realistically and to ask and answer follow-up questions.

I want to return this!

discussion In these activities, Ss talk about consumer complaints.

A

1 Books closed. Write on the board, *"This doesn't work right."* Ask Ss what kinds of things this sentence might refer to, and in what situations have they heard this statement before. Have Ss call out their answers.

2 Books open. Have Ss look at the photos and say what the two things are. Explain the task and have Ss read the complaints. Check that Ss understand the following vocabulary:

> **to shrink** to become smaller
>
> **to install software** to put a program into a computer so that the computer can use it

3 Have Ss think of a product that the complaint could refer to. Have Ss compare answers with a partner or in small groups. Then have Ss call out their answers. List them on the board, if you wish.

Possible answers

1. a pair of shoes or boots	**3.** a computer	**5.** a vase/a teapot
2. any item of clothing	**4.** a camera	

B Pair work

Books open. Explain the task and then put Ss in pairs to discuss consumer complaints they've made recently. Encourage Ss to give details about the problems and to say what they did to solve them. Have Ss ask and answer follow-up questions. Then have several Ss or volunteers either tell the class about a consumer problem of their own or report about one of their partner's complaints.

Optional activity: *Making real complaints*

Time: 15–20 minutes. Ss practice making consumer complaints.

1 *Class activity* Books open or closed. Put Ss in pairs and distribute pictures or ads of products, or other things people could purchase (such as a leisure cruise); each pair should have a picture. Tell pairs to write a statement of complaint about their picture on a slip of paper. Then collect the papers and the pictures.

2 Divide the class in half. Redistribute the pictures to one half, making sure no S gets the one he or she had. Redistribute the complaints to the other half, again making sure no one receives a complaint that he or she has written.

3 Explain to Ss that those who received a picture are the store owners who sold that item. The Ss who received a complaint are the buyers. Have Ss stand up. Tell them not to show each other their pictures or complaints. Buyers should walk around the room asking store owners if their store sells the product they are complaining about. Once buyers and store owners find each other, have them sit down and role-play the situation, trying to resolve their problem.

4 Have selected pairs perform their role plays for the class, and have the class vote on the best resolution.

Advice for consumers

vocabulary   These activities present more vocabulary related to consumer issues and advice.

A

Books open. Explain the task and have Ss read the list of vocabulary items on the left. Then have Ss individually match each word on the left with its definition on the right. Circulate to provide help as needed. Have Ss ask you questions to help them complete the task, if necessary. Ss could also use an English dictionary. Have Ss compare answers with a partner before going over them with the class.

Answers

1. b	**2.** e	**3.** h	**4.** d	**5.** a	**6.** c	**7.** f	**8.** g

B Pair work

Books open. Explain the task and have Ss read the model language in the speech balloon. Put Ss in pairs to use two of the words from Exercise A to give consumer advice. Have selected Ss or volunteers share answers with the class.

Optional activity: *Building vocabulary*

Time: 10 minutes. Ss use newspapers and magazines to build their vocabulary for talking about consumer goods.

Group work Books open or closed. Bring a few newspapers and magazines to class and distribute them to groups of three or four Ss. Tell Ss to look through the advertisements in their newspapers or magazines for new consumer-related vocabulary. Have them compile a list of terms on a piece of paper. Then have selected Ss share their words with the class while you make a list on the board, going over the meaning of words as needed.

A word to the wise

discussion These activities expand and consolidate the theme of consumer complaints.

A

1   Books closed. Brainstorm with the class about advice they might offer to help people prevent consumer complaints. Have Ss call out their answers.

2   Books open. Explain the task and have Ss read the list of advice. Check that Ss understand the following vocabulary:

> **reputation** how much something is liked or respected
> **reputable** having a good reputation
> **a return policy** a store's rules about how and when you can return something
>   you no longer want (that you bought from that store)
> **comparison shopping** going to different shops to compare their merchandise
>   and prices

3   Have Ss individually add two more pieces of advice to the list. Then have Ss compare answers with a partner. Have several Ss each share one piece of advice with the class.

Possible answers

> Make sure you get the clerk's name so that you can ask for him or her again.
> Have the clerk write down any information he or she gives you.
> Open the box to make sure the product you're taking home is the one you
>   ordered.
> Always keep your receipt.

B Group work

1 Books open. Explain the task and have Ss read the sample dialog. Put Ss in groups of three or four to take turns telling each other about a problem they had with something they bought. They should also say whether the advice in Exercise A would have helped prevent the problem. Encourage Ss to give detailed accounts of their problems and to ask and answer follow-up questions.

2 Have one S from each group tell the class about the most interesting problem presented in their group.

8   *Consumer complaints*

reading   These activities include a pre-reading activity and a post-reading inferencing activity.

1 Books closed. Tell Ss they are going to read an article that offers advice about problems people sometimes face when traveling. Brainstorm with the class what some of these problems might be and what advice might be offered in the article. Write these things on the board as Ss suggest them.

2 Books open. Give Ss about 1 minute to scan the article to see if it mentions any of their predictions.

A Pair work

1 Explain the task and have Ss read the two questions. Put Ss in pairs to discuss them. Have several pairs share answers with the class. Then have Ss silently read the article to compare their ideas with the information presented.

2 **Optional:** As Ss read, have them underline up to five words that are new to them and which they feel they need to know to understand the article. After they finish reading, have Ss ask each other about their words before asking you. Help Ss understand meaning from context, as appropriate.

B Pair work

1 Books open. Explain the task and have Ss read the list of five consumer problems. Put Ss in pairs to decide what each person should do. Suggest that Ss match each problem with an appropriate piece of advice from the article. Also, have pairs discuss what they would do in each situation.

2 Combine pairs to form groups of four to compare and discuss their answers. Then have selected Ss or volunteers share answers with the class. Lead a class discussion as appropriate.

Possible answers

> **Situation 1:** Celia should first ask the flight attendant if she can be reseated in a window seat.
>
> **Situation 2:** Russ should call the front desk and ask to be moved to a different room.
>
> **Situation 3:** Carl should have written a letter of complaint immediately and sent the toy back with it.
>
> **Situation 4:** Leslie should have asked to speak to the manager.
>
> **Situation 5:** Marissa should have written her letter of complaint right away.

This unit focuses on the themes of international travel, culture shock, and travel experiences. The students use future perfect tenses, gerunds as the objects of prepositions, and mixed conditionals to talk about culture and customs, and to give advice.

Lesson A *Culture shock*

Moving abroad

starting point

These activities introduce the theme of culture shock.

1 **Optional:** Books closed. For classes being taught in the Ss' home country, ask how many Ss have traveled abroad. Have Ss respond with a show of hands. Then ask how many have ever thought about living or studying in a foreign country. Again, have Ss respond with a show of hands.

2 Books closed. Brainstorm with the class about the kinds of problems a person has when living abroad for an extended period. List answers on the board, and lead a class discussion as appropriate. Write the term *culture shock* on the board, and ask how many Ss are familiar with the term. Have these Ss define it for the others. Then provide the following definition: *Culture shock is the feeling of disorientation and confusion that occurs when faced with differences in a new culture.*

A

Books open. Explain the task and have Ss read the two questions. Encourage Ss to give reasons and examples to explain their feelings.

B

1 Books open. Explain the task and have Ss look over the chart. Put Ss in pairs to discuss the chart and the meaning of each part. Check that Ss understand the following:

> **(a feeling of) emptiness** (a feeling of) incompleteness or that nothing is worthwhile
> **recovery** improvement

2 Have Ss read the four stages of culture shock, and point out that the stages are listed out of order. Have Ss individually match the stages with their descriptions. Then put Ss in pairs to compare answers before going over them with the class.

Answers

> **2** the emptiness stage; **4** the acceptance stage; **1** the tourist stage;
> **3** the recovery stage

C Pair work

1 Books open. Explain the task and put Ss in pairs (with other Ss from their country, if possible) to discuss what they would do to help a visitor to their country deal with the emptiness stage. Encourage Ss to give reasons to support their answers.

2 Have selected Ss or volunteers share answers with the class. Lead a class discussion as appropriate.

Possible answers

> Encourage the person to concentrate on the familiar rather than unfamiliar aspects of your culture.
>
> Reassure the person by telling him or her that it's normal to feel this way and that it is a stage everyone goes through.
>
> Suggest that the person keep a journal and write about what he or she is feeling.
>
> Encourage the person to get involved in free-time activities so that he or she is busy and has less time to feel depressed.

Optional activity: *Different perspectives*

Time: 5 minutes. Ss think about the topic from another perspective.

Group work Books open. Put Ss in groups of three or four (with other Ss from the same country, if possible), and ask them to think of some incorrect opinions tourists often have about their country. Ask Ss to discuss what they would say to a tourist who held these opinions. Ask selected Ss to report what their group discussed.

How did they fare?

listening

In this activity, Ss practice listening both for gist and specific information.

1 Books open. Explain the task and lead Ss through the chart, making sure they know what information they need to listen for. Point out that Ss need to take notes on which parts of each person's overseas experiences were negative and which were positive.

2 **Optional:** Pre-teach any items from the following vocabulary that you think will help your Ss:

> **to speak one's mind** to say very directly what you think about something
> **assertive** forceful
> **appetizers** small amounts of food eaten before the main course of a meal; snacks
> **dramatically** greatly
> **to be overwhelmed** to feel powerless because of a situation that is difficult to fight against
> **living in a bubble** living separate and feeling isolated from people around you

3 Play the audio program once through without stopping. Have Ss listen and take notes.

4 Replay the audio program, this time pausing briefly after each speaker has finished. Have Ss complete the chart with notes about the feelings the three speakers had. Were these feelings positive or negative? Then have Ss compare answers with a partner. Replay the audio program if necessary before going over the answers with the class.

Answers

	Experiences	Positive or negative
Andrew	tried to listen more and not be so assertive	positive
	went out for afternoon tea	positive
	enjoyed the old buildings	positive
	watched comedy TV shows; enjoyed British sense of humor	positive
Amy	felt homesick and missed her family	negative
	couldn't communicate well in Spanish	negative
	went to *tapas* bars and made Spanish friends	positive
	Spanish improved dramatically	positive
	eating dinner late at night	negative
Layla	everything seemed so different (e.g., using a pay phone or going to the doctor)	negative
	overwhelmed and didn't feel comfortable	negative
	made friends with only people from her own country	negative
	started feeling more confident about her English	positive
	started meeting Americans	positive
	Americans talked about themselves too much	negative
	learned to talk about herself	positive

Transcript

Listen to Andrew, Amy, and Layla talking about their experiences abroad. Were they positive or negative experiences?

Andrew: When I was in college, I spent a semester studying in London. Even though we speak the same language, English people and Americans are very different. I guess I felt that Americans have a bad reputation. Some people think we're loud and that we speak our minds too much. So I tried to listen a bit more and not be so assertive, if that makes sense. I wanted to make a good impression. I shouldn't have worried about it, but I did.

I loved the lifestyle there. Going out for afternoon tea was fun, and I really loved the old buildings. We don't have anything that old in the United States, so it was pretty amazing! The

continued

British also have a different sense of humor. . . . I really like it. Their comedy shows on TV are really funny!

I'd have to say my experience was a positive one overall. In fact, I'm saving up money so I can go back there again!

Amy: I lived in Madrid for a whole year. And I have to be honest and say that at first, well, . . . I wasn't very happy. You see, I was homesick. I missed my family and I just wanted to go home. Part of the problem was my Spanish. I couldn't communicate very well.

But I love to eat! And that's what really saved me. You see, once I discovered *tapas*, . . . oh, let me explain – these delicious appetizers you eat. So, I made some Spanish friends, and we'd go out to *tapas* bars. So, I got to eat a lot of delicious food, and of course, my Spanish improved dramatically as well. But there was one thing that was difficult to adjust to, and that was that dinner was always served at a late hour. I wasn't used to eating at eleven at night!

Layla: I came over to the U.S. from the Middle East. My family opened up a restaurant here. At first I found it difficult. Everything seemed so different. Just using a pay phone, for example, or going to a doctor, was different. I was pretty overwhelmed. And I guess because I wasn't feeling comfortable, I tended to make friends only with people from my country. I felt like I was living in a bubble, separated from the Americans. But once I started feeling more confident about my English, I started meeting Americans. I found them very friendly and open, and it turned out to be very easy to make friends.

But there was one thing about Americans that bothered me at first. I found it hard to get used to the way they talked so much about themselves. It took me a long time to understand that you were supposed to talk about yourself, too, because that is how people get to know one another. It's still hard for me to talk a lot about myself, but I'm getting better at it.

Optional activity: *Details, details*

Time: 5 minutes. Ss listen intensively for detailed information.

1 *Pair work* Books open or closed. Write the following questions on the board, and put Ss in pairs to discuss the answers.

Andrew: 1. Where did Andrew go, and why? How long did he live there?
2. Why did Andrew try to change himself?

Amy: 1. Where did Amy go? How long did she live there?
2. Why was Amy so homesick?

Layla: 1. Where is Layla from? What did her family do in the U.S.?
2. How did she like living in the U.S. at first? What changed her feelings about living in the U.S.?

In general: 1. What was the main factor that seemed to make living overseas a better experience for all three people?
2. What two stages did each person talk about?

2 Go over the answers as a class.

Possible answers

> **Andrew:** 1. He went to London to study for a semester.
> 2. He wanted to be more like the English/to be liked by the English.
>
> **Amy:** 1. She lived in Madrid for a year.
> 2. She missed her family.
>
> **Layla:** 1. She's from the Middle East. Her family opened a restaurant.
> 2. She found living in the U.S. difficult at first, but once she started meeting Americans, she felt better.
>
> **In general:** 1. Meeting and making friends with the people who lived there.
> 2. The emptiness stage and the recovery stage.

Future perfect and future perfect continuous

grammar focus This grammar focus presents the future perfect and the future perfect continuous tenses.

> **Grammar notes** These tenses are used to express the completion (future perfect) or duration (future perfect continuous) of an action or event at some time in the future. They can be used to talk about an event or action that started in the past but will not be completed until the future (e.g., By the middle of next year, *I will have paid off* all my loans.).
>
> The future perfect is made up of the simple future (*will*) + present perfect (*have* + past participle). The future perfect continuous is made up of the simple future (*will*) + present perfect continuous (*have* + *been* + present participle).
>
> There are various time phrases used with this tense. Some of the more common ones are: *after* (an amount of time), *by then*, *by* (a specific date), *before* (a specific date), *when*, and *by the time (that)* (e.g., *By the time* [*that*] you finish the project, you will have been living in your new home for a year.).

1 Books closed. Ask Ss to think of something they think they will have completed by this time next year. Have Ss call out their answers, and write some of them on the board. Then on the board, write: *By this time next year, I will have . . .* and complete the sentence orally with some of the phrases listed on the board. Write these complete sentences on the board so that you have sentences such as: *By this time next year, I will have graduated from school.* Explain that this is the future perfect tense, which is used to talk about actions or events that will be completed at a future time.

2 Next, on the board, write: *By this time next year, I will have been studying English for . . . .* Have Ss call out an answer that is true for them. Write one of the answers on the board to complete the sentence. Explain that this is the future perfect continuous tense, which is used to talk about the ongoing duration of an event by a certain point in the future.

3 Books open. Lead Ss through the information and example sentences in the grammar box. Provide additional explanations and examples as necessary. Ask Ss to take note of the use of commas in these sentences.

A

1 Books open. Explain the task and have Ss individually complete each sentence with either the future perfect or future continuous. Point out that two of the sentences could be completed with either form. Check Ss' comprehension of the following vocabulary:

> **the person of my dreams** the romantically ideal person for you

2 Have Ss compare answers with a partner before going over them with the class.

Answers

> **1.** By the end of next year, I *will have learned* another foreign language.
> **2.** In a year's time, I *will have been living* in this city for 20 years.
> **3.** Within two years, I *will have opened* my own business.
> **4.** In five years' time, I *will have settled down* with the person of my dreams.
> **5.** By this time next year, I *will have been studying* English for more than half my life.
> **6.** Within six months or so, I *will have paid off* all my loans.

B

Books open. Have Ss complete the sentences in Exercise 3A that are true for them. Ask Ss to share and discuss their answers with a partner. Then have several Ss each share one of their corrected sentences with the class.

Optional activity: *Predicting the future*

Time: 10 minutes. Ss continue practicing the grammar point.

1 *Class activity* Books open or closed. Have Ss individually write three sentences about what they think they will or will not have accomplished by some time in the future. Tell Ss not to put their names on the papers. Circulate to help with vocabulary and to check for accuracy.

2 Collect the papers and redistribute them. Tell Ss to stand up and find the author of the paper by asking questions, such as: Do you think you will have had children by this time next year? Tell Ss to answer truthfully (e.g., if a S didn't write that sentence but the answer is yes, he or she should say "Yes, but I am not the author of that sentence."). When Ss find the author of their paper, have them sit down and ask a couple of follow-up questions, and then get up again until they themselves are found.

4 Gerunds as the objects of prepositions

grammar focus This grammar focus presents gerunds as the objects of prepositions to talk about feelings associated with future events.

> **Grammar notes** A verb that follows a preposition must be in gerund form (e.g., I am excited about *traveling* overseas.).
>
> The prepositions most commonly found in these structures are: *of, about, on, in, to, against, for,* and *with.*

1 Books open. Lead Ss through the information and example sentences in the grammar box. Point out that in these sentences, the gerunds are objects of the prepositions. Also point out that the verb and preposition combinations are fixed (i.e., they do not change).

2 Explain the task and have Ss read the example and the five remaining expressions. Have Ss individually write two true sentences for each expression. Circulate to help. Then have Ss compare and discuss their answers with a partner.

3 Ask several Ss to share one or more of their sentences with the class. Lead a class discussion as appropriate.

Possible answers

> **1.** I would be afraid of leaving all my friends and family behind.
> I would be afraid of getting lost all the time.
> **2.** I would be excited about visiting new places.
> I would be excited about making new friends.
> **3.** I would be interested in visiting all the museums.
> I would be interested in learning a new hobby.
> **4.** I would insist on not being treated like a tourist.
> I would insist on finding my own apartment.
> **5.** I would look forward to having a lot of interesting stories to tell.
> I would look forward to seeing new places.
> **6.** I would worry about not being able to communicate well.
> I would worry about being lonely.

discussion   In this activity, Ss practice giving advice to someone who is preparing to travel abroad, using gerund phrases.

Pair work

1   Books open. Explain the task and have Ss read the list of items and the sample language in the speech balloon. Check Ss' comprehension of the following:

> **words of encouragement** reassuring words to make someone feel more confident
>
> **language barrier** an obstacle to communication that happens when people don't speak the same language

2   Put Ss in pairs to think of two pieces of advice. Tell Ss to use gerunds as the objects of prepositions in their answers. Then put Ss in pairs to compare answers.

Possible answers

> You should introduce yourself to everyone at your new job./You should have your lunch with the people you work with. Within a couple of weeks or so, you will have met many people and feel comfortable in your job.
>
> You can break the language barrier quickly if you study hard./Don't worry about breaking the language barrier. It will happen gradually. After a year, you will have had much more practice speaking, and you will find it easier to communicate.
>
> You shouldn't worry about making new friends./If you get involved in activities, you will make friends sooner than you expect. By this time next year, I'm sure you will have made many new friends.
>
> You shouldn't worry too much about getting used to the food. I'm sure you will find some foods that you like./You should try out lots of different kinds of food. Just don't try them out all at the same time. Within a few months, you will have acquired a taste for many of the regional specialties.
>
> You should look forward to learning the new customs, since that can be very interesting./ You will be surprised about how soon you will feel comfortable with many of the new customs. Within a few months, you will have accustomed yourself to many of the things that seemed strange at first.
>
> Don't be preoccupied with missing your friends and family. It is a feeling that will pass./You can count on missing your friends and family, but everyone will be waiting for you when you get home. After a year, you will have passed the worst period of homesickness.

Customs and traditions

discussion   In these activities, Ss talk about cultural differences and compare their own customs with customs in the United States and Canada.

A

1   Books closed. Ask Ss what cultural differences between people of their culture and people of Canada or the United States they are aware of. Have Ss call out their answers.

2   Books open. Have Ss look at the two photographs, and ask them to say who they think the people are and what they are doing. Then ask if these scenes would be common in their countries. If not, how would they be different? Have Ss call out their answers, and lead a brief class discussion about cultural differences.

3   Explain the task and have Ss read the list of Canadian and U.S. customs. Have Ss work alone to check (✓) whether the customs are the same or different in their country. Then have Ss compare answers with a partner. Ask selected Ss or volunteers to share answers with the class.

4   **Optional:** Take a tally on the board of Ss' responses to use as the basis for a class discussion or debate.

B   Pair work

Books open. Explain the task and put Ss in pairs to discuss those customs that are different in their countries. Have Ss discuss what each difference is and how it might affect visitors to their countries. Then have Ss tell the class about the one difference they think would have the greatest effect on visitors to their country. Lead a class discussion as appropriate.

Crossing cultures

discussion   In this activity, Ss think about how living abroad would affect them.

Group work

Books open. Explain the task and have Ss read the items in the circles. Give Ss a few moments to individually think of an example for each item. Then put Ss in groups of four or five to take turns sharing their information. Encourage Ss to ask and answer follow-up questions. Circulate to hear Ss' comments and to ask follow-up questions of your own.

writing These writing activities focus on brainstorming as a technique for planning a composition.

A Group work

1 Books closed. Ask Ss if they know what brainstorming is. Have Ss call out their answers. Then ask the class how brainstorming might be useful when planning a composition. Again, have Ss call out their answers (e.g., Brainstorming helps a writer generate ideas.).

2 Explain the task and have Ss read the sample topic lists of advantages and disadvantages and the overall conclusion. Then put Ss in groups of three or four to choose one of the topics and brainstorm ideas of their own. Remind Ss to share any idea that occurs to them, even if it seems silly or off track. Tell Ss to assign a secretary to keep a list of the ideas. Give Ss 3 to 5 minutes to brainstorm ideas on their topic. Then have selected Ss from each group share their best ideas with the class.

B

1 Explain the task and have Ss read the sample composition. Have Ss individually create a thesis statement from their overall conclusion in Exercise 8A, as well as a list of ideas to support it. Circulate to help Ss with their thesis statements and list of ideas.

2 Either in class or for homework, have Ss individually write their compositions. Remind Ss to include reasons, examples, and additional information to support their ideas. Ask them to make sure that all information in the composition supports the thesis statement.

C Pair work

Books open. Explain the task and put Ss in pairs. Remind Ss of the value of peer feedback, and then have Ss exchange compositions to give feedback on the content of the composition.

Globe-trotting

Travel troubles

starting point

These activities introduce the theme of giving advice to people traveling abroad.

A Pair work

1 Books closed. Ask Ss if they have ever had any problems, such as losing money or airline tickets, while traveling. Have Ss call out their problems, and list them on the board.

2 Books open. Explain the task and put Ss in pairs to think of tips for each category. Then combine pairs into groups of four to compare tips and to take turns asking and answering follow-up questions about their tips.

Possible answers

> **air travel:**
> Leave yourself plenty of time in case there are long lines at the check-in counter.
> Keep relevant phone numbers on hand in case you are delayed and need to call anyone.
> Bring a sweater because many airplanes are heavily air-conditioned.
> **packing:**
> Pack clothes that won't wrinkle easily.
> Pack clothes for both hot and cold weather.
> Take less than you think you will need so that your luggage won't be too heavy.
> **money:**
> Don't carry cash. Use traveler's checks and credit cards.
> Write down all the important numbers of your checks and credit cards, so if you lose them you can get them back quickly.

B Pair work

1 Books open. Put Ss in pairs and have them cover the statements under the pictures. Have Ss tell each other what they think is each person's problem. Then explain the task, and have Ss uncover and read the three statements. Tell Ss to discuss what advice they would give each person and what they would have done in each situation.

2 Have selected Ss or volunteers share an answer with the class. Lead a class discussion as appropriate.

3 **Optional:** Have Ss vote on the best piece of advice offered for each situation.

listening

In this activity, Ss listen for specific information.

1 Books open. Explain the task and lead Ss through the chart, making sure they know what information they need to listen for. Remind Ss to complete the chart in note form.

2 **Optional:** Pre-teach any items from the following vocabulary that you think will help your Ss:

> **destination** the place a person is going to
>
> **to apologize** to tell someone you are sorry for something you did or said
>
> **layover** a stop somewhere between your departure point and your destination [usually refers to air travel]
>
> **departure gate** the place from where a plane leaves
>
> **drowsy** tired, sleepy
>
> **to cut short** to shorten the amount of time
>
> **to go standby** in this case, to put your name on a waiting list with the hope of getting on a flight that is full

3 Play the audio program. Encourage Ss to start taking notes, but allow them to only listen at this point.

4 Replay the audio program, this time pausing briefly after each speaker has finished. Have Ss complete the chart with a few words to describe what happened to and what went wrong for each person. Ask the Ss to listen for how each situation was resolved (answers: Cindy returned the suitcase and apologized; Scott stayed overnight and caught a flight out the next morning; Kate had to go standby and got on the flight after all). Then have Ss compare answers with a partner. Replay the audio program as necessary before going over the answers with the class.

Possible answers

	What happened	**What went wrong**
Cindy	She went on a business trip. The flight was long, and when she arrived at her destination, she was eager to get her baggage and go to her hotel to relax.	She was in a hurry. She picked up someone else's suitcase and didn't realize her mistake until she got to the hotel.
Scott	He had a layover in Toronto, and his flight was delayed. He went to sit away from the departure gate to avoid the crowds.	He fell asleep and missed his flight.
Kate	She was going on a short vacation to the beach on a long holiday weekend.	She got to the airport and discovered there was a problem with her ticket: The travel agent had printed the wrong date on her ticket.

Transcript

Listen to Cindy, Scott, and Kate talking about their travel experiences. What happened during each one? What went wrong?

Cindy: You'll probably be surprised to hear what I did! I was on a business trip. . . . The flight was a long one, and when I arrived at my destination, I was eager to get my bags and get to my hotel to relax. Well, you know, they always tell you to be careful to get the right bag, but I was in a hurry. You can guess what happened: My black suitcase looked just like every other one, so I picked up someone else's. I didn't realize my mistake until I got to the hotel. Well, I immediately called the airport, and fortunately it all worked out. I had to go back to the airport, though, to pick up my suitcase and return the other one. And of course, I also had to apologize!

Scott: This is kind of a funny story. I was in Toronto and had a layover between flights. I'd arrived at about six P.M., and my flight out wasn't until about eight thirty. Well, my flight was delayed . . . and delayed. It got really crowded at the departure gate. I was getting tired, and there were so many people around – I hate crowds – so I went to sit away from the departure gate to escape the crowds. I was reading my newspaper, feeling drowsy, and then . . . the next thing I know, I wake up and there's no one around! The crowd is gone! I'd fallen asleep and missed my flight! They must have made lots of announcements, and I missed them all! Boy, did I feel stupid. I had to stay in Toronto overnight and catch a flight out the next morning.

Kate: Let's see, my travel experience was a truly frustrating one. I was going on a short vacation to the beach. We had a long holiday weekend, so it was going to be a short trip. You know, fly out on a Friday night and come back on a Sunday afternoon kind of thing. Well, when I got to the airport and checked in at the counter, there was a problem with my ticket. It turned out the travel agent had printed the wrong date on my ticket! My ticket was for a flight at the same time, but on the following day! I couldn't believe it!

I didn't want to leave the next day because my trip was already such a short one. Why should I have to cut my vacation short when it wasn't even my fault? I complained to everyone at the counter, including a manager. But there was nothing they could do. I had to go standby on that flight. In the end, I was very lucky that they had an extra seat on the plane. So I got to enjoy the beach after all.

Now you can bet that I always double-check my tickets to make sure all the information is printed correctly!

Optional activity: *Giving advice*

Time: 10–15 minutes. Ss give advice about what the people in the listening should have done.

Group work Books open. Put Ss in groups of three or four, and ask them to brainstorm advice they would like to offer each of the three people about what they should have done. Have each group share their most interesting advice with the class.

Mixed conditionals

grammar focus This grammar focus presents mixed conditionals in which present and past time are mixed to talk about hypothetical situations.

> **Grammar notes** Conditional sentences are made up of condition clauses (*if* clauses) and result clauses (e.g., If I had listened to the morning news, *I would have heard about the traffic jam on the freeway.*). They are used to describe imaginary or hypothetical situations.
>
> Mixed conditionals are conditional sentences where different times are referred to in the condition clause and the result clause. They are used to describe hypothetical or imaginary situations such as the following:
>
> How the real past affects the future (e.g., If they haven't been in trouble yet, they won't get in trouble this time.).
>
> How the unreal present affects the past (e.g., If he had the money, he wouldn't have had to go to the bank.).
>
> How the unreal past affects the present (e.g., If we hadn't eaten so much, we would be feeling better right now.).
>
> How the unreal present affects the present (e.g., If you weren't always late, you wouldn't be out of a job.).

1 Books closed. Write the following on the board:

   1. I forgot my passport, so I'm not on the plane right now.

   2. I'm not organized, so I'm looking for my wallet right now.

   Ask volunteers to underline the verbs in the sentence. Have Ss tell you what times they express (1. past/present, 2. habitual present/in the moment present). Explain that these are real situations. In the first sentence, the speaker is stating what happened and what's happening now. In the second sentence, the speaker is talking about a personal characteristic in the first clause to explain the present situation in the second clause.

2 Now write these sentences on the board:

   1. If I hadn't forgotten my passport, I would be on the plane right now.

   2. If I were more organized, I wouldn't be looking for my wallet.

   Ask volunteers to underline the verbs in each clause. Tell Ss that these are hypothetical or imaginary situations. In both sentences, the speaker is explaining in the second clause what would be true if the information in the first clause was not true. Explain that because the times expressed in these sentences are not the same in both clauses, the sentences are called mixed conditionals.

3   Books open. Lead Ss through the information and example sentences in the grammar box. Write this sentence on the board, and ask Ss to turn it into a mixed conditional: *I got up late, so I missed the bus.* (Answer: If I hadn't gotten up late, I wouldn't have missed the bus.) Explain that when the conditional clause appears as the first clause, the clauses are separated by a comma. When it appears as the second, no comma is needed. Provide additional explanations and examples as necessary.

A

Explain the task. Then have Ss read the sentences. Check that Ss understand all of the vocabulary. Have them rewrite the information as conditional sentences. Circulate to help and check for accuracy. Then have Ss compare answers with a partner and discuss whether they have ever been in similar situations. Go over the answers with the class.

Possible answers

1. If Mark and Steve had made a hotel reservation, they wouldn't be spending the night in a train station.
2. If my mother spoke some English, she wouldn't have been afraid to explore New York on her own.
3. If I hadn't forgotten to bring my camera with me to Thailand, I would be taking pictures of the beautiful temples.
4. If the airline hadn't lost my luggage, I wouldn't have to wear the same clothes for two days.
5. If Elizabeth had packed a bathing suit, she would be spending the first day of her vacation at the beach right now.
6. If my father had liked to fly, he would have visited me when I lived overseas.

B Pair work

1   Books open. Explain the task and have Ss individually complete each sentence with a mixed conditional. Then have Ss compare and discuss their answers with a partner. Encourage pairs to take turns reading each other's sentences. Ask them to check for mistakes as well as respond to the content.

2   **Optional:** Have selected Ss each write one of their sentences that is not wholly correct on the board. Work as a class to revise the sentences as necessary.

Possible answers

1. People wouldn't be so concerned with air travel if there weren't so many terrorist problems in the world.
2. If there were more tourists in my country, people would have opened more restaurants and hotels.
3. There would be fewer communication problems in the world if more people were better listeners.
4. If more Americans and Canadians spoke foreign languages fluently, they might have a better understanding of some of the world's problems.
5. If I could speak several languages fluently, I would enjoy traveling more.
6. I would have spent my last vacation differently if I had had more money.

 Your own trip

discussion   In this activity, Ss continue practicing mixed conditionals while discussing travel.

Pair work

1   Books open. Explain the task and have Ss read the list of topics and the model dialog. Then put Ss in pairs to take turns telling each other about a travel experience they had that didn't work out the way they had planned, and saying what they could have done better. Encourage Ss to give as much detail as possible. Also remind them to use mixed conditionals where appropriate, and have them ask and answer follow-up questions.

2   Either have a few Ss tell their own stories to the class, or have Ss report their partner's story.

 Compound adjectives

vocabulary   In these activities, Ss are presented with some adjectives used to talk about characteristics of a good traveler.

A

1   Books open. Explain the task and have Ss read the list of words and prefixes in the box. Check that Ss understand the following:

> **assured** in this case, confident
> **conforming** behaving according to society's usual standards of behavior
> **judgmental** judging things and people quickly and often negatively
> **reliant** dependent

2 Explain that these adjectives are formed by a prefix such as *non* (meaning *not*), an adverb, an adjective, or a noun + an adjective. Point out that some of these adjectives have a hyphen (-).

3 Have Ss individually combine the prefixes and words to make as many adjectives as they can.

4 **Optional:** Have Ss use a monolingual dictionary to check their answers.

5 Have Ss compare answers with a partner before going over them with the class.

Answers

> culturally aware, culturally sensitive
> nonconforming, nonjudgmental
> open-hearted, open-minded
> self-assured, self-motivated, self-reliant

B Pair work

Books open. Explain the task and go over the example in the speech balloon. Then put Ss in pairs to describe the meaning of each compound adjective. Have pairs try to work out meanings on their own first before they check them in a dictionary. Then have Ss discuss why these characteristics are important for travelers. Go over the answers by having selected Ss each share one of their definitions and examples with the class.

Possible answers

> If you are culturally aware, you'll find it easier to accept cultural differences/to be able to understand how culture affects people.
> Being nonjudgmental is helpful because you are more likely to accept the behavior or attitudes of others/to be tolerant about differences in people from different cultures.
> It's important to be self-assured when you are in a foreign country because you will need to feel comfortable going out by yourself/you may have to deal with unfamiliar problems.
> Being open-hearted is important because you will be able to make new friends more quickly/to get into conversations with strangers more easily.
> If you are self-reliant, you'll be able to enjoy yourself better in an unfamiliar place/to find it easier to see and do the things that interest you most.

C Pair work

Books open. Explain the task and put Ss in pairs to think of three more characteristics of a good traveler. Encourage Ss to give reasons and examples to support their answers. Have Ss ask and answer follow-up questions. Then have several Ss share their characteristics with the class.

Optional activity 1: *Designing the perfect traveler*

Time: 5–10 minutes. Ss discuss important characteristics for travelers.

Group work Books closed. Write the following on the board: *curiosity, organization, sense of humor, flexibility.* Tell Ss to write these words on a piece of paper in order of importance as characteristics for a traveler. Then put Ss in groups of four or five to discuss their ratings and create a group ranking of the characteristics. Encourage Ss to give reasons for ranking these characteristics the way they did and to try to persuade their group members to agree with them. Then have selected groups share their rankings with the class. Write answers on the board to use as a basis for a class discussion.

Optional activity 2: *Describing yourself*

Time: 5–10 minutes. Ss practice the vocabulary of Exercise 5A.

Pair work Books open. Ask Ss to think about the type of traveler they are or might be if they had the chance to travel. Then tell them to choose words from Exercise 5A and characteristics from Exercise 5C and Optional Activity 1 that apply to them. Put Ss in pairs to tell each other about the words they chose. Encourage Ss to ask follow-up questions. Have selected Ss share the words they chose with the class and say why.

6 Travel options

discussion   In this activity, Ss talk about their own travel preferences.

Pair work

1   Books open. Put Ss in pairs to look at the two photographs and say what they see and what kinds of trips they depict.

2   Explain the task and have Ss read the travel options in the box. Clarify meanings as necessary, especially:

> **itinerary** a detailed travel plan, including dates and locations

3   Have Ss read the sample language in the speech balloon.

4   Put Ss in pairs to discuss the travel options and talk about how they prefer to travel. Encourage Ss to explain their reasons and give examples of what they mean. Then have selected Ss or volunteers share answers with the class.

reading   In these activities, Ss practice prediction and inferencing skills.

A Pair work

1   Books closed. Write the title of the reading on the board. Ask Ss what they think *smooth talking* might mean and how it might relate to the topic of travel. Then put Ss in pairs to discuss the question.

2   Have Ss silently read the article to compare their ideas to the author's. Have Ss underline up to five new words they feel they need to know. Then have them discuss their words with a partner or in groups. Circulate to help, if needed.

B Group work

1   Books open. Explain the task and have Ss read the two questions. Then put Ss in small groups of four to six to discuss whether or not they think the author's ideas are useful, and what additional advice they would give to a foreign traveler.

2   Have selected Ss from each group share answers or pieces of advice with the class. Lead a class discussion as appropriate.

Unit 12 Dilemmas

This unit focuses on important issues of public concern and some personal and ethical dilemmas. It introduces conjunctions such as *moreover* to link ideas; the passive continuous; and *if, only if, unless,* and *even if* to express conditions.

Lesson A *Public concerns*

Important issues

starting point In these activities, Ss are introduced to some common issues of public concern around the world.

Pair work

1   Books closed. On the board, write the word *issues,* and underneath it write *animal, punishment, energy, television,* and *women.* Ask Ss to define the meaning of the word *issue* (answer: a subject or problem that people are thinking or talking about). Then put Ss in pairs to think of and list as many issues as they can involving these topics. Have selected Ss call out their answers while you write them on the board. Answers might include: animal rights, animals being used in medical tests, the death penalty, nuclear energy, alternative energy, violence on television, unfair employment practices for women, etc.

2   Books open. Explain the task and have Ss read about the issues. Check Ss' comprehension of the following vocabulary:

> **to downsize** to reduce the number of people that a company employs
>
> **retirement** the point at which someone stops working
>
> **early retirement** retirement at a younger age than usual, but with the usual retirement benefits
>
> **day-care centers** facilities that take care of children while their parents are at work
>
> **a demand** a forceful request
>
> **to clear** to remove (something) so that an area is unblocked
>
> **to develop land** to build houses on land to make it more useful or profitable

3   Put Ss in pairs to discuss whether or not the issues they read about are problems in their countries. Have selected pairs share their responses with the class.

Optional activity: *Current issues*

Time: 5–10 minutes. Ss consider issues of public concern that affect their country.

Group work Books open. Tell Ss to think about the three most important issues facing their country at the moment. Then put Ss in groups to compare their lists and discuss their reasons for these choices. In a class where all Ss are from the same country, tell groups they have 5 minutes to all agree on the three most important issues facing their country. Then have groups present their issues to the class.

2 In my opinion

listening

In these activities, Ss listen to three people talking about issues they feel strongly about.

A

1 Books open. Tell Ss they are going to listen to three people each talk about an issue they feel strongly about. Then have Ss look at the chart to make sure they know what information they will be listening for.

2 **Optional:** Pre-teach any items from the following vocabulary that you think will help your Ss:

> **to censor** to monitor the content of something in order to remove anything found to be offensive in it
>
> **to have access to** to have the opportunity to use (something)
>
> **to decide on a case-by-case basis** to make a decision based on the specific details of a situation

3 Play the audio program, and have Ss complete the chart as they listen, writing in note form. Then have Ss compare answers with a partner. Replay the audio program as necessary before going over the answers with the class.

Answers

	Issue	How they feel
Charles	the environment	need to take care of world we live in need to recycle plastics and be careful not to waste water and electricity
Melissa	freedom of speech	should always be allowed to say what we believe doesn't agree with censoring the Internet need to decide everything on a case-by-case basis
Brian	world peace	need to learn to live and work together as a planet we are dependent on one another, and the world is becoming a smaller place supports the United Nations

Transcript

Listen to Charles, Melissa, and Brian talking about issues they feel strongly about. What are the issues, and how do they feel about them?

Charles: You know, the one issue that I feel the strongest about is the environment. Well, maybe it's a little bit expensive to change our ways, but we have to try. We need to take care of the world we live in. So I think we can all do small things: like recycle plastics and be careful not to waste water and electricity. You know what they say: We only have one world, so we shouldn't mess it up.

Melissa: For me, freedom of speech is very important. We should always be allowed to say what we believe – especially now. You know that people want to censor the Internet. They want to limit what we have access to on our computers. Well, I don't agree with that at all. Of course, I know, it's a tricky question. Where do you draw the line on what should be controlled? What limits should be placed on our freedom of speech? I suppose that there have to be some limits set, but I say the fewer the better. Maybe the best thing is just to decide everything on a case-by-case basis.

Brian: I guess I'd have to say the issue I think most about is world peace. It's time we all learned to live together and work together as a planet instead of as separate nations. Now, I'm not saying that it's easy. Of course, we all come from different cultures and speak different languages. It's just that we're so dependent on one another. The world is becoming a smaller place, so to speak. We have to learn to get along. I believe in this issue strongly, and I support the United Nations because I think they do good work.

B Pair work

Books open. Explain the task and put Ss in pairs to discuss whether or not they agree with each opinion mentioned in the audio program. Encourage Ss to give reasons and ask each other follow-up questions about those reasons. Then have Ss say which opinions they agree and disagree with while you tally the responses on the board.

 Adding information and showing conclusions

grammar focus This grammar focus presents conjunctions that are used to link or join ideas.

1 Books open. Lead Ss through the information and example sentences in the grammar box. Provide additional explanations and examples as necessary.

2 Books open. Explain the task and go over the example. Have Ss read the six sentences, and check Ss' comprehension of the following:

> **to target** to aim at or to focus on something or someone
> **high school dropout** a student who stops attending school before finishing the requirements for graduation

3 Have Ss individually complete the sentences. Then put Ss in groups of four or five to compare and discuss their answers. Go over the answers by having selected Ss or volunteers come to the board to write one of their sentences.

Possible answers

1. Drunk drivers should be sent to jail. Moreover, their licenses should be taken away.
2. Children eat more junk food than they used to. In addition, they don't exercise enough.
3. It's becoming more and more expensive to stay in a hospital when you're sick. Furthermore, insurance is paying less of the cost.
4. More people are wearing seat belts when they drive. Consequently, there are fewer deaths caused by accidents.
5. Cigarette advertisements are being targeted toward young people. Therefore, young people are tempted to try them.
6. There are more high school dropouts than before. Thus, there are more unqualified young people looking for jobs.

The passive of the present continuous

grammar focus

This grammar focus presents the passive of the present continuous as it is used to describe ongoing actions.

Grammar notes As with all passive structures, the passive of the present continuous emphasizes the action (what happened) rather than the agent (who did it). Note that the passive of the continuous aspect can be used only in the present and the simple past tenses.

1 Books closed. Write these sentences on the board: *They deny women advancement in many companies. Women are being denied advancement in many companies.* Have Ss call out the difference in structure, and also the difference in meaning between the two statements. Ask Ss who *they* refers to in the first sentence. (Answer: We don't know.) In this sentence, however, the emphasis is on *they* rather than on the fact that women are being denied advancement. Show Ss that in the second sentence, the emphasis is on the action taking place: *women are being denied advancement.* Also point out that this is an ongoing action. Explain that if we don't know who is causing an action, or if we want to emphasize the action that is ongoing, we use the passive of the present continuous tense.

2 Books open. Lead Ss through the information and example sentences in the grammar box. Provide additional explanations and examples as necessary.

3 Explain the task and go over the example. Then have Ss read the five sentences, checking their comprehension of the following:

> **to endanger** to put (something) at risk of being destroyed
> **endangered animals** animals that are at risk of becoming extinct (due to pollution, hunting, deforestation, etc.)
> **ozone layer** the gaseous layer of the atmosphere that stops dangerous sun rays from getting through to the earth
> **to deplete** to use up

4 Have Ss write sentences about the environment using the words in parentheses and then match them with the expressions listed. Have Ss compare their work with a partner before going over them with the class.

Possible answers

1. <u>d</u> The drinking water is being poisoned, causing people to catch diseases.
2. <u>a</u> Endangered animals are being killed off despite the government's efforts to protect them.
3. <u>e</u> The ozone layer is being destroyed, allowing the sun's harmful rays to come through.
4. <u>c</u> The air is being polluted because not enough people are carpooling or using public transportation.
5. <u>b</u> The water supply is being depleted, causing shortages in some areas.

5 Optional: Have Ss use a conjunction to add a statement of their own to each of the sentences in the exercise.

Hot topics

discussion In this activity, Ss talk about current issues while practicing the passive of the present continuous tense.

Group work

1 Books open. Explain the task and then put Ss in small groups of four or five to work out descriptions of each of the five issues listed. Have groups assign a secretary to take notes, and encourage them to discuss their own opinions on each issue.

2 **Optional:** Tell Ss to prepare one written group statement about each issue they discussed.

3 Have each group describe what they feel is the hottest issue to the class and explain how they feel about this issue. Lead a class discussion as appropriate.

Optional activity: *Getting the scoop*

Time: 10–15 minutes. Ss practice presenting an important issue and using the grammar presented.

1 *Group work* Books closed. Divide the class into groups of four or five. Explain that each group consists of a TV news crew trying to get a spot on the evening news by reporting on the hottest, most controversial issue of the day. Have groups choose one issue to present to the class. Tell Ss the aim is to present the issue in such a convincing way that the TV producer (you, the teacher) will decide to focus on this issue on the news tonight.

2 Give groups 5 minutes or so to prepare a statement. Encourage them to use the passive of the present continuous and conjunctions to show results and add information. Then have each group choose a spokesperson to present their issue. Give each group time to present their issue, then decide which issue was the hottest and most convincing.

3 Tell the group with the hottest issue that they have a spot on the evening news!

6 The way they view the world

vocabulary   In these activities, Ss practice using adjectives and nouns that describe people and how they view the world.

A

1 Books open. Explain the task and then have Ss read the words listed in the chart. Check Ss' comprehension of the following:

> **a cynic** a person who doesn't trust the goodness in other people and thinks they always behave selfishly
> **fanatical** extreme
> **a fatalist** a person who believes that the future is predetermined and cannot be altered
> **pragmatic** practical, sensible
> **a realist** a person who is reasonable and focuses on realistic goals
> **skeptical** doubtful

2 Have Ss individually complete the chart with the correct form of the missing words. Then have Ss decide whether the words are positive, negative, or neutral. Explain that a couple of the words may be viewed differently by different people. Have Ss compare answers with a partner before going over them with the class.

Possible answers

cynic	*cynical*	negative
fanatic	*fanatical*	negative
fatalist	*fatalistic*	neutral or negative
optimist	*optimistic*	positive
pessimist	*pessimistic*	negative
pragmatist	*pragmatic*	positive
realist	*realistic*	neutral or positive
skeptic	*skeptical*	neutral

B Pair work

1   Books open. Explain the task and go over the model answer in the speech balloon. Then put Ss in pairs to take turns saying which words from Exercise A describe them and to think of other people they know who could be described by these words. Encourage Ss to give reasons and examples to support their answers and to ask each other follow-up questions.

2   Have selected Ss or volunteers tell the class which words describe them best, and why.

Speak your mind.

discussion   This activity presents and practices verbs that are used to express opinions and beliefs.

Group work

1   Books open. Explain the task and have Ss read the statements in the chart and then complete it. Then have Ss read the verbs of opinion in the box and the model dialog.

2   Put Ss in groups of three or four to discuss their answers. Remind Ss to use verbs of opinion and to give reasons for their answers. Have each group share one of their more intriguing opinions with the class. Lead a class discussion as appropriate.

writing These writing activities introduce Ss to persuasive writing and the idea of writing for a specific audience.

A

1 **Optional:** Books closed. Bring some persuasive magazine advertisements to class. Ask Ss why they think the ads are particularly persuasive. Have Ss say who they think each advertisement appeals to most (e.g., young people, senior citizens, etc.). Explain that this is really an example of persuasive writing. The writer of the advertisement is attempting to convince a specific audience that a product is worth buying. In most persuasive writing, the writer tries to persuade the reader that his or her belief or opinion is worth accepting.

2 Books open. Lead Ss through the information in the box. Explain that in persuasive writing the writer's aim is to convince a specific audience that his or her opinion is valid. To do so, the writer must present convincing evidence that appeals to that audience.

3 Explain the task and have Ss silently read the three paragraphs to establish the intended audience for each one. Then have Ss underline the words and sentences in each paragraph that helped them make their choices. Have Ss compare answers with a partner before going over them with the class.

Answers

1. parents B	**2.** a teacher A	**3.** classmates C

B Pair work

Books open. Explain the task and put Ss in pairs to discuss which paragraph is the most effective and which two need improvement. Tell them to give reasons for their choices and to make suggestions for how the other two paragraphs could be improved. Then bring the class back together, and have selected Ss share their ideas and suggestions.

C

Books open or closed. Explain the task and tell Ss to look back through the lesson to find an issue they feel strongly about. Then, either in class or for homework, have Ss individually write a persuasive paragraph about this issue. Remind Ss to keep their intended audience in mind.

D Pair work

1 Books open or closed. Explain the task and have Ss read the feedback questions. Put Ss in pairs, and have them exchange papers. Remind Ss of the purpose and value of peer feedback. Then have partners read each other's compositions and consider if it is clear who the intended audience is, whether or not the evidence presented is effective, and what improvements they would suggest to make the paragraph better. Ss take notes about their comments and suggestions as they read.

2 Have pairs return their partner's paragraphs and take turns sharing and discussing their answers to the three questions.

3 **Optional:** For homework, have Ss revise their compositions based on their partner's suggestions.

  How honest are you?

What would you do?

starting point This activity introduces the theme of the lesson and has Ss examine their own honesty.

Pair work

1 Books closed. Ask the class if they think they are honest people. Have Ss respond with a show of hands. Then ask other questions about honesty, such as: "Do you think it's possible to be honest all the time? Is it ever OK to tell a lie, such as a white lie?" (If necessary, explain that a white lie is an unimportant lie that is meant to avoid causing hurt feelings.) "Have you told a lie of any kind today?" Have Ss respond by raising their hands. Choose volunteers to explain one of their answers, and lead a class discussion as appropriate.

2 Books open. Have Ss look at the picture and ask them to describe what is going on. Then go over the model language in the speech balloons. Check that Ss understand the meaning of the following:

> **a rumor** unconfirmed information that might be true and that spreads from person to person
> **to confront** to present information or evidence to someone that he or she doesn't want to hear

3 Explain the task. Put Ss in pairs to discuss what they would do in the two situations. After about 5 minutes, ask how many Ss would pick up the money and how many would confront their friend. Tally the answers on the board, and use this as a basis for a class discussion.

Finders, keepers?

listening

In these activities, Ss listen to two people talk about their experiences with moral dilemmas and then discuss how they would have handled similar situations.

A

1   Books open. Explain the task and lead Ss through the chart, making sure they know what information they need to listen for. Remind Ss to complete the chart in note form.

2   **Optional:** Pre-teach any items from the following vocabulary that you think will help your Ss:

> **to pace** to walk back and forth repeatedly because you are anxious about something
>
> **to mutter** to talk quietly, usually to yourself
>
> **relieved** feeling good because a worry or pain has gone away
>
> **a good deed** a kind gesture done to help someone else

3   Play the audio program. Have Ss listen and take notes on what Aaron and Leanne found and what they decided to do. Then replay the audio program, this time pausing briefly after each speaker. Have Ss complete the chart.

4   Have Ss compare answers with a partner, and then go over them with the class.

Answers

	What they found	**What they did**
Aaron	a wallet with $100 at the supermarket	told his son that they couldn't keep it found the owner and returned his wallet
Leanne	an inexpensive book on a train	read it on the train and took it home to finish it

Transcript

> **Listen to Aaron and Leanne talking about what they did when they found something. What did they find? Did they keep it?**
>
> **Aaron:** I was with my son at the supermarket – he was about eight years old at the time – and he found a wallet on the floor. Inside it was a hundred-dollar bill! A hundred dollars! He picked it up and got all excited. In fact, neither of us could really believe it. He started talking about all the things we could buy. Right away I told him that we couldn't keep it. He seemed disappointed at first. We started asking people if they had lost anything. After asking around for a while, we hadn't found anyone, and I was beginning to think we'd asked everyone.

continued

Copyright © Cambridge University Press 1998

Lesson B How honest are you? 257

But then, as we were walking to the front of the store, I noticed a man – actually my son noticed him – who was pacing back and forth, shaking his head, and muttering something. I thought it was probably his wallet, so we asked him and – it was. My son felt better when he saw how relieved the man was about getting his money back. That was our good deed for the day, and the man gave my son ten dollars as a reward for returning the wallet.

Leanne: I was on a train from Washington to New York last month when I found a book lying under my seat. It was so strange. It was just a little book, not an expensive one. It was probably only worth a few dollars. Well, I really wanted to read it. It was pretty interesting, and by the end of the trip I was still reading it, so I decided to keep it. I took it home and finished it.

Now, every time I see it on my bookshelf, I wonder if I should have taken it or not. I mean, do you think I should have returned it to the train conductor? Who knows? Like I said, it wasn't a very expensive book, so I didn't really feel guilty about taking it.

B Pair work

Books open. Read the questions aloud to the class and give Ss a moment to think about them. Then put Ss in pairs to discuss their opinions about whether or not they agreed with the way Aaron and Leanne handled the situations, and why. Encourage Ss to ask each other follow-up questions.

Optional activity: *The great debate*

Time: 10–15 minutes. Ss debate both sides of a moral dilemma.

Pair work Books open. Have Ss sitting on the left side of the class work together to think of arguments against what each person did in the previous listening. Have Ss sitting on the right side of the classroom think of arguments to support what each speaker did. Then have Ss form pairs with one person from each group, and ask them to present their arguments in a convincing way. Have selected Ss share their most convincing argument with the class.

Conditions with *if, only if, unless, and* even if

grammar focus

This grammar focus presents and practices expressing conditions with *if, only if, unless,* and *even if.*

Grammar notes Note that the likelihood of an event in the main clause happening is expressed by the conjunction in the condition clause. The conjunction *if* expresses the most likelihood, followed by *only if* and *unless*, and finally *even if*, which expresses contrast with the event in the main clause (e.g., I won't eat *even if* I'm hungry.).

Structure	Meaning
if I would take the money *if* I didn't know who had dropped it.	This is a straightforward conditional sentence.
only if I would take the money *only if* I didn't know who had dropped it.	I would take the money only under these particular circumstances (i.e., not knowing who had dropped it). If any conditions *other than this one* existed, the person would *not* take the money.
unless I wouldn't take the money *unless* I didn't know who had dropped it.	If I *didn't know* who had dropped the money, I *would* take it. In this sentence, *unless* means *except if*. This sentence has the same meaning as the *only if* sentence.
even if I wouldn't take the money *even if* I didn't know who had dropped it.	Under no circumstances would I take the money. In this situation, the person would not take the money, no matter what conditions existed.

1 Books closed. Put the following sentences on the board:

   a. Sam won't go to the beach unless it is sunny.

   b. Sam will go to the beach if it is sunny.

   c. Sam won't go to the beach even if it is sunny.

   d. Sam will go to the beach only if it is sunny.

Ask Ss to rate the sentences from 1 to 3 to indicate how likely it is (1 being the most likely) that Sam will go to the beach. (answers: a. 2, b. 1, c. 3, d. 2) Ask Ss what words or phrases change the likelihood. Have Ss call out their answers *(if, only if, unless,* and *even if)*. If necessary, ask Ss the following questions for each statement to help them understand the conditions expressed: "Will Sam go to the beach if it is cloudy? Will Sam go to the beach if it is sunny?"

2 Books open. Lead Ss through the information and example sentences in the grammar box. Put Ss in pairs to discuss how likely it is that this person will take the money. Then go over these sentences with the class, explaining that in the first sentence, the likelihood is quite high; in the second and third sentences, it is less likely; and in the fourth sentence, there is no likelihood that the person would take the money.

A

Explain the task and have Ss individually decide the differences in meaning between each pair of sentences. Ss select the one that they agree with. Then have Ss compare and discuss answers with a partner before going over them with the class.

Possible answers

1. The second sentence has a stronger emphasis (*only if*).
2. The first and second sentences have no difference in meaning.
3. These sentences express completely different meanings. In the first sentence, the person *wouldn't* be polite under the stated condition. In the second sentence, the person *would* be polite *in spite of* the stated condition.

B Pair work

1 Books open. Explain the task and have Ss individually complete each sentence with information that is true for them. Circulate to help with vocabulary as needed. Then put Ss in pairs to compare and discuss their answers. Tell Ss to take turns reading their sentences and saying whether or not they agree with each other. Have Ss give reasons to support their opinions.

2 Have several selected Ss or volunteers read a sentence to the class. For each sentence shared ask other Ss to raise their hands to say whether or not they agree. Have one or two Ss explain their opinions about each question.

Possible answers

1. If a store clerk gave me too much change, I wouldn't keep the money even if it was a small amount.
2. If a friend unexpectedly stopped by to visit just as I was planning to go to bed, I wouldn't ask my friend to leave unless I had to get up early the next morning.
3. I wouldn't complain about the service in a restaurant unless it was so bad that I couldn't enjoy my meal.
4. I wouldn't "temporarily borrow" an unlocked bicycle on the street to go a short distance even if the owner would find it quickly.

Optional activity: *The "if only" quiz*

Time: 10 minutes. This activity gives Ss practice with the grammar structure.

1 *Pair work* Books open or closed. Tell Ss to write four true sentences about different topics using each of the conjunctions *if, only if/unless,* and *even if.* Then have them rewrite their sentences leaving a blank for the conjunctions. Put Ss in pairs to exchange papers and decide which conjunction best completes each sentence.

2 Have Ss return their papers to each other and go over the answers. Encourage Ss to ask and answer follow-up questions.

Difficult decisions

discussion   In this activity, Ss talk about their personal principles and practice using adverbs of condition.

Pair work

1   Books open. Explain the task and have Ss read the list of situations and complete the chart. Then have Ss read the sample dialog and pair up to compare and discuss their responses. Encourage Ss to give reasons and examples for their responses and to ask each other follow-up questions.

2   **Optional:** Ask Ss to call out their responses to each question while you keep a tally on the board to use as the basis of a class discussion.

 Ethical dilemmas

discussion   In this activity, Ss use the grammar and vocabulary they've learned to solve some ethical dilemmas.

Pair work

1   Books open. Explain the task and have Ss read the three dilemmas. Check Ss' understanding of the following vocabulary:

> **an outing** a day trip
> **depressed** extremely unhappy; feeling that life is without hope
> **to shoplift** to steal merchandise from a store or shop

2   Have Ss individually circle what they would do and then get into pairs to discuss and compare their choices. Remind Ss to use the structures they learned in the lesson and to try and use as much new vocabulary as they can. Then have selected Ss or volunteers share answers about the situations with the class. Lead a brief class discussion about each of the dilemmas.

 Talking about values

discussion   In this activity, Ss discuss ethical dilemmas that they have faced.

Group work

1   Books open. Explain the task and go over the sample language in the speech balloon. Give Ss a couple of minutes to remember a personal dilemma they faced. Then put Ss into groups of four or five to share their dilemmas and the ways in which they chose to deal with them. Have Ss say if they think they handled the situations well. Encourage Ss to ask follow-up questions and say what they would have done in the same situation.

2   Have a few volunteers share their story with the class.

Optional activity: *Role play*

Time: 15–20 minutes. Ss continue discussing ethical dilemmas from the perspective of another person.

1 *Group work* Books closed. Write three or four dilemmas on the board, such as:

> 1. *Street children ask you for money. You know that they will only be able to keep a small percentage of the money. The rest of it will be passed on to adults for questionable things.*
>
> 2. *A politician you like is working on a campaign against poverty and is asking for money. People have been saying he is using the money to build a mansion.*
>
> 3. *The love of your life is a very complicated person. If you get married, you might have very unhappy moments. If you don't marry, you might never meet someone you love again.*

2 Assign each S a role to play: teenager, teacher, religious person, student, mother, elderly man, farmer, judge, etc. Tell Ss they will discuss some dilemmas and that they should try to respond in the character of the role. Put Ss in groups of four or five. Have Ss introduce themselves saying, for example, "I'm Carlos and I'm a farmer." Then have Ss choose one of the dilemmas you've written on the board to discuss. Have groups discuss the dilemma they've chosen while you circulate to help Ss stay in their roles.

3 Have the class talk about the experience and share the high points of their discussion with the class.

Telling the truth

reading In these activities, Ss read an article about "little lies" and discuss whether honesty is always the best policy or if some dishonesty is needed for social politeness.

A Pair work

1 Books closed. Write the title *Little Lies* on the board, and have Ss call out what they think the article might be about and what little lies might be. Accept all answers at this point.

2 Books open. Explain the task and have Ss read the list of questions. Then put Ss in pairs to discuss them. Encourage Ss to give detailed answers and to ask and answer follow-up questions.

3 Have Ss silently read the text to compare their ideas with the author's. As Ss read, have them underline any words they don't know. Then put Ss in pairs to help each other with their vocabulary questions. Circulate to help Ss guess meaning from context where appropriate.

B Group work

Books open. Explain the task and have Ss read the questions. Then put Ss in groups of four or five to discuss them. Encourage Ss to give reasons and examples to support their answers. Have selected Ss or volunteers share answers with the class. Lead a class discussion as appropriate.

Students review noun clauses containing relative clauses; noun clauses beginning with question words, *whether,* and *if*; the future perfect and future perfect continuous tenses; gerunds as the objects of prepositions; expressions for adding information and showing conclusions; and conditions with *if, only if, unless,* and *even if* to make complaints, express preferences, describe irritations, predict the future, describe hypothetical situations, and give advice.

Noun clauses containing relative clauses

In these activities, Ss review noun clauses containing relative clauses to describe personal preferences.

A

1 Books closed. Write on the board: *Something that . . . , One thing that . . . , The thing that . . . .* Ask Ss to call out a personal preference of something they either really like or dislike while you write them on the board. Then have Ss put the personal preference together with one of the phrases on the board, producing a sentence such as "Something that I love is jumping into the ocean when I'm very hot." Have Ss use the preferences on the board to make sentences with *Something that . . . , One thing that . . . ,* and *The thing that . . . .*

2 Books open. Explain the task and have Ss look at the picture. Ask: "What is the man trying to do, and how does he appear to be feeling? Why do you think this is?" Have Ss call out their answers. Then have them read the example sentence and the five questions. Check that Ss understand the following vocabulary:

> **to intrigue** to interest (someone) a lot, especially by being unusual or mysterious
> **to inspire** to cause someone to want to do something or try harder at something

3 Have Ss write answers to the questions. Then have selected Ss share their sentences with the class.

Possible answers

> 1. Something that annoys me is children who are noisy, especially when I am trying to read.
> 2. One thing that I really like to do on the weekend is sleep late in the morning.
> 3. The thing that scares me the most about the future is watching my parents get old.
> 4. Something that intrigues me about my parents is how they've managed to continue working so hard for so many years.
> 5. One thing that inspires me is seeing how people who suffer crises in their personal lives pick up and keep going.

B Pair work

Books open. Explain the task and have Ss read the model dialog. Point out the follow-up question and advice. Explain that in some cases Ss might have advice, whereas in others they may just want to ask for more information. Put Ss in pairs to take turns talking about their personal preferences and asking and answering follow-up questions. Circulate and give advice where appropriate.

Optional activity: *Different types of personal preferences*

Time: 10 minutes. Ss continue talking about personal preferences.

Pair work Books open. Tell Ss to write one more statement about a personal preference with each of the following verbs: *annoys, scares, intrigues,* and *inspires* – but with blanks where the verbs should be. Put Ss in pairs, and have them exchange papers. Tell Ss to fill in the blanks on each other's papers and then to return their papers to have them checked. Ss could then ask and answer follow-up questions about each personal preference. Have selected Ss share any surprising or particularly interesting personal preferences with the class.

Noun clauses beginning with question words, whether, and if

In this activity, Ss review the use of noun clauses beginning with question words, *whether,* and *if* to talk about things that puzzle Ss.

1 Books open. Explain the task and have Ss read the example. Ask Ss to underline the noun clause (answer: why some people are always getting into fights). Point out the statement word order of the noun phrase. To further review the word order, have Ss convert the example to a question (Why are people always getting into fights?).

2 Have Ss complete the statements with things that puzzle them while you circulate to observe Ss' progress. Then put Ss in pairs to compare answers before having selected Ss share answers with the class.

Possible answers

1. I'd really like to know why some people are always getting into fights.
2. I'd like to find out how I can get along better with my family.
3. I always wonder whether or not I give a good impression when I first meet someone.
4. I can never understand why people like to watch scary horror movies.
5. I often ask myself whether I should go to graduate school or not.
6. How people can continue smoking when they know the health risks is a real mystery to me!

Future perfect and future perfect continuous

In this activity, Ss review the use of the future perfect and future perfect continuous to talk about people's lives in the future.

Pair work

1 Books closed. Write the following on the board: *By the time I finish this course, I will have learned enough to go on to the advanced course. In two years, I'll have been studying here for five years.* Ask Ss to compare the structure (answer: the first sentence uses the simple form, and the second sentence uses the *-ing* form) and the difference in function (answer: the second sentence emphasizes the duration of the action) of the two sentences.

2 Books open. Explain the task and have Ss read the example.

3 **Optional:** Have Ss call out time phrases commonly used with the future perfect and future perfect continuous, such as *after ten years, by that time, in ten years' time, within ten years,* while you write them on the board.

4 Have Ss write two sentences for each of the people listed while you circulate to observe progress and help with vocabulary. Put Ss in pairs to tell each other their predictions about the future. Encourage Ss to ask each other why they made those predictions. Have volunteers share the most surprising predictions with the class.

4 Gerunds as the objects of prepositions

In these activities, Ss review the use of gerunds as objects of prepositions to talk about their travel experiences.

A

1 Books open. Have Ss look at the two photographs and describe what they see. Then have Ss read the model language in the speech balloons. Ask Ss to underline the phrases that come before the gerunds *making* and *relaxing* (answers: in charge of, looking forward to). Remind Ss that gerunds follow various expressions containing prepositions.

2 Explain the task and have Ss read the three questions. Have Ss individually answer the questions.

B Pair work

Books open. Explain the task and put Ss in pairs to share their travel experiences. Circulate to observe Ss' progress and to encourage Ss to ask and answer follow-up questions. Have selected Ss share any particularly interesting or surprising information about their partner's trip with the class.

Optional activity: *More about your trip*

Time: 10–15 minutes. Ss continue using gerunds as objects of prepositions to talk about their trips in more detail.

Pair work Books open. Write the following expressions on the board: *be afraid of, be excited about, be interested in, insist on, look forward to, worry about.* Put Ss in pairs and tell them to take turns making statements about the planning of their trip and the trip itself using each of the phrases on the board. Remind Ss to ask and answer follow-up questions.

5

Adding information and showing conclusion

In this activity, Ss review the use of conjunctions to add information and show conclusion to talk about important issues.

Pair work

1   Books closed. Write the following conjunctions on the board: *in addition*, *therefore*, *consequently*, *furthermore*. Have Ss categorize them by function (i.e., adding information and showing conclusion). Have Ss call out their answers.

2   Books open. Explain the task and have Ss read the four issues. Check Ss' comprehension of the following:

> **hate crimes** crimes committed against someone of a specific race, religion, or ethnic group

3   Have Ss individually complete the sentences. Then put Ss in pairs to compare answers. Have selected Ss or volunteers share sentences with the class.

Possible answers

> 1. Consequently, there will have to be more health-care services in the years to come.
> 2. Therefore, there is a need to educate people to be tolerant of others.
> 3. In addition, the TV programs are more violent than before.
> 4. Furthermore, it is an irritation to nonsmokers.

Optional activity: *More on issues*

Time: 5–10 minutes. Ss continue to practice adding information and showing conclusions.

Pair work Books open or closed. Tell Ss to make up two more statements expressing issues similar to the ones in Exercise 5. Put Ss in pairs to tell each other their issues and to add information or make conclusions regarding their partners' issues. Have selected Ss share one of their partner's issues and the information or conclusion they added with the class. Lead a class discussion about the ones that most interest other Ss.

6

Conditions with if*, only* if*,* unless*, and* even if

In these activities, Ss review the use of conditions with *if*, *only if*, *unless*, and *even if* to talk about hypothetical situations.

A

1   Books closed. Write the following on the board: *unless, even if, if, only if*. Ask Ss to rank them from 1 to 3 in order of likelihood, with 1 being the most likely (answers: 1. if; 2. only if, unless; 3. even if).

2 Books open. Explain the task and have Ss read the example and the four questions. Have Ss individually answer the questions while you circulate to observe progress and offer assistance when requested.

Possible answers

> 1. I would drive my car over the speed limit only if it were a matter of life and death.
> 2. I would go skydiving even if my friends told me not to.
> 3. I would audition for a role in a movie only if I thought no one else would find out about it.
> 4. I would avoid working two jobs unless I had no other alternatives.

B Group work

Books open. Explain the task and put Ss in groups of four or five to take turns sharing their answers. Circulate to offer help and listen to Ss; encourage group members to ask and answer follow-up questions. Have selected groups share their most interesting answers with the class.

Annoying customers

In these activities, Ss review the language of personal irritations and complaints regarding public transportation.

A

Books open. Have Ss look at the picture and describe what is happening. Then ask Ss to say how the bus driver might feel. Ask Ss if it is the driver's fault that the bus is late. Explain the task and have Ss read the model language in the speech balloon and the list of five employees. Have Ss individually answer the questions.

Possible answers

> One thing that annoys bus drivers is when people complain about the service.
> One thing that probably annoys flight attendants is passengers who don't listen to their instructions.
> Customers who complain about the food is one thing that bothers restaurant staff.
> Something that irritates salesclerks is customers who don't have enough money to pay for what they want to buy.
> Passengers who make a lot of noise is the one thing that annoys taxi drivers.

B Pair work

1 Books open. Explain the task and have Ss read the model dialog. Point out how the bus driver resolves the complaint. Put Ss in pairs, and tell them to share their list of annoyances with their partners. Then have Ss take turns playing the roles of customer and employee for the different complaints.

2   Have selected pairs perform one of their role plays for the class.

Optional activity: *Guess the job*

Time: 10 minutes. Ss continue practicing language of complaints.

Group work Books closed. Tell Ss to think of a common employee complaint in a profession not yet mentioned. Put Ss in groups of four or five, and have them take turns role-playing their employee expressing the complaint. The other group members try to guess the employee's job/profession. The S who guesses correctly role-plays the next complaint.

---

8   ## The service was terrible.

In this activity, Ss review the vocabulary used to talk about problems and advice.

Group work

1   Books open. Have Ss look at the photograph and describe what they see. Explain the task and have Ss read the model dialog. Tell Ss to circle the complaint and underline the suggestions in the model dialog. Then have Ss read the list of useful words. Check Ss' comprehension of these words, and review as necessary. Ss can find the definitions of most of these words in Exercise 6A on page 92 of the Student's Book.

2   Put Ss in groups of four or five to tell each other about consumer problems they or a friend of theirs has had recently. Other group members offer suggestions about how to deal with those complaints. Have groups share a particularly interesting complaint and suggestions for dealing with it with the class.

---

9   ## The safe tourist

listening

In these activities, Ss continue to practice giving advice and listen for both general and specific information.

A Pair work

Books open. Have Ss look at the photograph and say where they think this person might be. Explain the task and have Ss read the model language in the speech balloon. Put Ss in pairs to talk about tips to remember when planning a trip abroad. Circulate to listen to Ss' ideas and observe fluency levels. Have selected pairs share their tips with the class.

Possible answers

> You should try to travel light so you aren't carrying around heavy suitcases.
> You should put all your important papers and money in your carry-on luggage in case your suitcase gets lost.
> You should try to learn a few important phrases in the language of the place you are visiting.

B

1. Books open. Read the instructions and then have Ss look at the chart to make sure they know what information they need to complete it. Remind Ss to complete the chart in note form.

2. **Optional:** Pre-teach any of the following vocabulary that you think will help your Ss:

> **wrinkled** having small lines or folds in it
> **"gotcha"** I understand, I got your point (informal spoken English)

3. Play the audio program. As they listen, have Ss complete the chart by writing in note form. Then have Ss compare answers with a partner. Replay the audio program as necessary before going over the answers with the class.

Answers

Who's giving the advice	Advice being given
Terry's mother	fold clothes properly carry traveler's checks separately from receipts carry wallet in front pocket have name tag on outside and inside of suitcase

Transcript

Listen to Terry getting advice on the preparation for his trip abroad. Who's giving the advice? What does she say?

Mother: Hey, anybody home?

Terry: Very funny. Hi, come on in.

Mother: How's it going? Have you almost finished packing your suitcase?

Terry: Yeah, almost.

Mother: I can't believe you're leaving tomorrow. All the way to Tokyo.

Terry: Yeah. I can't wait.

Mother: Be sure to send us a postcard when you get there. And don't forget to write us a letter or two.

Terry: Mom! I'm only going for three weeks!

Mother: I know, I know. But you'll still have time to write your family, won't you?

Terry: Look, I'm going to be busy. We've got Japanese classes in the morning and then field trips in the afternoon. . . . You know, it's a really busy program. . . . Hey! What are you doing?

Mother: Just checking your suitcase. . . . Terry, this is a mess!

Terry: What's wrong with it?

Mother: You can't pack your clothes like this! You have to fold them properly. Oh, here, let me do it. All your clothes are going to get wrinkled. . . . Where are your traveler's checks?

continued

Terry: They're right here on the table.

Mother: Do you remember what they told us at the bank?

Terry: Yes. I should carry my checks separately from my receipts. That way, even if the checks are stolen, I can order new ones easily.

Mother: That's right. Now don't forget those checks when you leave tomorrow.

Terry: Don't worry. Look, you can just keep on folding those clothes, OK? Don't worry about anything else. . . . It was just a joke.

Mother: Well, ha-ha. Terry, you have to be prepared to travel abroad. You also know that you should always carry your wallet in your front pocket.

Terry: Yes, it's harder for someone to take it if it's in your front pocket.

Mother: And your suitcase . . .

Terry: Mother!

Mother: Well, you can never be too careful! You should always have a name tag on the outside and on the inside.

Terry: On the inside, too?

Mother: Yes, just in case. If the tag on the outside is accidentally pulled off, your suitcase can still be identified because you've got your name on the inside as well.

Terry: Gotcha.

Mother: I know I'm probably annoying you, but I'm your mother, and I want you to have a great time in Tokyo. And to be safe.

Terry: I know, Mom.

Mother: What time is it? . . . Oh, it's almost ten thirty! You'd better get to bed. You've got a big day ahead of you!

Optional activity: *Different attitudes*

Time: 5 minutes. Ss listen again for details, to make deductions, and to evaluate Terry's and his mother's attitudes.

1 Books open. Write the following questions on the board. Ask Ss to try to answer these questions without replaying the audio program.

   1. How old do you think Terry is?

   2. Has Terry traveled abroad before?

   3. Where is Terry going?

   4. When is Terry going?

   5. What does Terry's mother want him to do that Terry doesn't seem to want to do?

   6. How does Terry feel about the trip?

   7. How does Terry's mother feel?

2 Replay the audio program for Ss to check their answers and to answer any remaining questions.

3 Put Ss in pairs to compare answers before going over them with the class.

Possible answers

1. He's a teenager.	4. tomorrow
2. Probably not because his mother seems concerned and is giving him a lot of advice.	5. write to them
	6. excited
3. to Tokyo	7. worried

10 *Do the right thing.*

In these activities, Ss practice explaining how they would solve personal dilemmas.

A

Books open. Explain the task and have Ss read the situations and the options. Then have Ss choose an option, or write their own, for each situation.

B Group work

Books open. Explain the task and then put Ss in groups of four or five to take turns explaining their answers. Groups try to reach a consensus on the best solution to each dilemma. Tell Ss to discuss each option, asking and answering questions that will help them agree on the best solution to each dilemma. Then have groups present their solutions with reasons and examples to the class while you tally responses on the board to use as the basis of a class discussion.

Optional activity: *What's the dilemma?*

Time: 10 minutes. Ss continue talking about dilemmas and solutions.

Pair work Books open or closed. Put Ss in pairs to write a dilemma and three or four options for solutions, but tell them to write the dilemma on one slip of paper and the solutions on another. Then have pairs exchange their solutions with another pair. Tell Ss to write what they think the dilemma is. Have pairs return their papers to check the answers. Put pairs together to discuss them.

Friends and family

Lesson A What kind of person are you?

Exercise 1

1	avoid	1	enjoy
1,2	can't stand	1,2	hate
1	dislike	1,2	like
1	don't mind	1,2	love

Exercise 2

2. Roy and Yuko avoid <u>going to museums</u>.
3. Lisa likes <u>going for long walks/to go for long walks</u>.
4. Adam enjoys <u>spending time with his family</u>.
5. Sam hates <u>working on the weekend/to work on the weekend</u>.
6. Celia is interested in <u>taking some art history classes</u>.

Exercise 3

Answers will vary. Possible answers:
2. I like to be busy all the time.
3. I dislike being the center of attention.
4. I love trying new restaurants.
5. I don't mind traveling alone.
6. I can't stand to talk about my feelings.

Exercise 4

A

Answers will vary. Possible answers:

Positive	Negative	Neutral
adventurous	impatient	ambitious
organized		reserved
practical		sympathetic
romantic		talkative
sociable		

B

Answers will vary. Possible answers:
2. I'm somewhat impatient. I can't stand waiting for anything.
3. I'm very organized. I always keep my room neat and know exactly where everything is.
4. Sometimes I'm reserved, especially in unfamiliar situations.
5. I'm usually sympathetic to other people's problems. I'm a good listener.

Exercise 5

A

1. My mother is very adventurous.
2. My friend John always says what is on his mind.

B

Answers will vary.

Lesson B Every family's different.

Exercise 1

Dear Diary,
   I love my family — all of them, my parents and my four brothers and sisters. However, sometimes they drive me crazy. There are good and bad things about coming from a large family. One of the advantages of coming from a large family is <u>that I always have someone to talk to</u>. Unfortunately, one of the disadvantages is <u>that I never have any privacy</u>. And of course the biggest problem with not having any privacy is <u>that I never have any space I can call my own</u>. Our house is big, but sometimes not big enough!

Exercise 2

2. The best thing about having my own room is (that) I can do whatever I want.
3. A problem with always being late for family outings is (that) my relatives get angry with me.
4. An advantage of having a family that loves to celebrate holidays is (that) we have a lot of great parties.
5. A bad thing about being the most mischievous person in my family is (that) my parents get upset.

Exercise 3

Answers will vary. Possible answers:
1. An advantage of having strict parents is <u>(that) you learn discipline at an early age</u>.
2. A problem with living in a noisy household is <u>(that) you cannot concentrate on your homework</u>.
3. The best thing about being the most sociable person in your family is <u>(that) you get to talk to everyone all the time</u>.
4. A disadvantage of living in the same neighborhood as your family is <u>(that) your parents can drop by unexpectedly at any time</u>.
5. The worst thing about having parents who both work is <u>(that) there is no one at home when you come home from school</u>.

Exercise 4

2. mischievous	5. generous	8. patient
3. sensible	6. strict	9. adventurous
4. inexperienced	7. active	

Exercise 5

A

1. c   2. b   3. a

B

1. False. Brother-brother pairs are the most competitive.
2. False. When parents treat each child differently, the children become more competitive and aggressive.
3. True.
4. False. Children take sides in arguments that their siblings have.

Lesson Ⓐ How can schools be improved?

Exercise 1

2. Students who receive a <u>failing</u> grade should go to summer school.
3. There should be more <u>extracurricular</u> activities offered to students, such as theater groups and sports.
4. In addition to <u>academic</u> subjects, students learn important life skills in school.
5. Going to school is <u>compulsory</u> for young children in the United States.
6. Schools should teach students how to be <u>organized</u>.

Exercise 2

2. Students ought to be aware of their graduation requirements.
3. Schools should teach students to appreciate art and music.
4. Teachers shouldn't force students to speak in class.
5. Grades ought to be based on more than just exams.

Exercise 3

Answers will vary. Possible answers:

2. should be given
3. ought to teach
4. shouldn't give
5. should be offered
6. ought to help
7. should be provided

Exercise 4

Answers will vary. Possible answers:

2. Computers are necessary in today's world. Schools should buy computers for every classroom.
3. There are too many exams. Students shouldn't be forced to take so many exams.
4. School uniforms are not necessary. Students ought to be allowed to wear jeans to school if they want to.

Exercise 5

A

Sentences that support the topic sentence:

1. The teacher can't give each student enough individual attention.
2. It's difficult for students to concentrate with so many others in the room.
4. Students at the back of the room can't see the board clearly.
6. There are often not enough textbooks.

B
Answers will vary.

C
Answers will vary.

Lesson Ⓑ What's the best way to learn?

Exercise 1

1. A: The only way to learn new words is by <u>memorizing</u> them.
   B: I don't agree. I think the best way is to <u>write</u> them down on vocabulary cards and to <u>use</u> them in conversations with native speakers.

2. A: A good way to learn to pronounce words correctly is to <u>listen</u> to songs.
   B: Really? I've never tried that. My teacher told me that a good way is by <u>watching</u> how native speakers move their mouths and then by <u>practicing</u> in front of a mirror to see if I can move my mouth in the same way.

Exercise 2

Answers will vary. Possible answers:

1. A good way to develop public speaking skills is <u>by practicing first in front of friends and colleagues</u>.
2. A good way to memorize important information is <u>to say it aloud again and again until you remember it</u>.
3. One way to learn how to play the guitar is <u>to buy a book and teach yourself</u>.
4. One way to develop good manners is <u>by watching what other people do in certain situations</u>.
5. The best way to learn about another culture is <u>to go to the library and read a lot of books about it</u>.

Exercise 3

2. I signed up for some dance classes in order to stay in shape.
3. I bought a new computer in order to have easier access to the Internet.
4. I took a cooking class in order to make more interesting meals.

6. I plan to enroll in Spanish classes so that I can study in Mexico next year.
7. I signed up for a public speaking class so that I could get experience speaking in front of others.
8. I'd like to take a music class so that I can learn as much as possible about classical music.

Exercise 4

1. realize
2. achieve
3. completes
4. reach
5. fulfill

Exercise 5

A
Answers will vary.

B
Statements the author would agree with:

3. The use of new technology is positive.
4. Corporations should get involved.
6. Education is important for people of all ages.
7. The fact that schools will change is positive.

Lesson Ⓐ Fascinating destinations

Exercise 1

Dear Mom and Dad,

Greetings from Maine, <u>where the water is too cold for us to go swimming</u>, but the scenery is beautiful. We're having a great time, and we've enjoyed every place that we've visited.

This week we're in Bar Harbor, <u>which is a lovely island town</u>. The place is absolutely full of tourists!

Tonight we're going for a ride on a boat <u>that will take us to one of the nearby islands</u>. James, <u>who has been here before</u>, has already taken me hiking and to the Bar Harbor Music Festival. It's been fun!

That's it for now. I miss you.

Love, Sarah

Exercise 2

2. Tourists, who visit Washington, D.C., in the spring, can see the cherry blossoms in bloom in April.

3. The cherry trees, which were a gift of the Japanese government to the United States, are admired by everyone.

4. Thousands of years ago, the people of present-day Mexico began to grow corn, which continues to be the most important food in Mexico today.

5. The tortilla, which is a thin, flat bread, is typically eaten in Mexico.

Exercise 3

Answers will vary.

Exercise 4

2. scenery   4. cuisine   6. customs
3. architecture 5. nightlife   7. historical sites

Exercise 5

A

2. New York City is a great place for art.

3. Many artists live and work in New York, but they often can only support themselves by working more than one job.

4. the night market in Chiang Mai `

5. Chiang Mai is a city in Thailand that has a wonderful night market.

6. I love spicy Thai food.

B

Answers will vary.

Lesson Ⓑ It's my kind of city.

Exercise 1

1. Honolulu is <u>a beautiful island city with fabulous beaches</u>.

2. Paris is <u>a wonderful, old European city with many cafes</u>.

3. Hong Kong is <u>a modern trading center with huge skyscrapers</u>.

4. Montevideo is <u>a charming capital city with fascinating old buildings</u>.

5. Chicago is <u>a large, modern, industrial city with a beautiful lakeshore</u>.

6. Orlando is <u>an exciting tourist destination with world-famous theme parks</u>.

Exercise 2

(left)   an old fishing village with a charming harbor
(middle) a crowded city with lots to see and do
(right)   a picturesque resort town in the mountains

Exercise 3

2. Despite the serious crime problem, it's still a wonderful place to visit./It's still a wonderful place to visit despite the serious crime problem.

3. Although the shopping malls are crowded, people aren't buying much.

4. Even though it snows a lot, I still like living here./I still like living here, even though it snows a lot.

5. My city is on the ocean. However, the water there is too polluted for people to go swimming.

6. The city center is very picturesque. Nevertheless, there's not much to do.

7. The town I live in is pleasant enough. Just the same, I wish I lived in a more exciting place.

8. There's a lot to do here at night. On the other hand, it's a very noisy neighborhood.

Exercise 4

Answers will vary. Possible answers:

2. The worst thing about <u>Miami</u> is <u>the heat and humidity</u>. Nevertheless, <u>it's a fun place to live</u>.

3. The best thing about <u>Tokyo</u> is <u>having a variety of stores to choose from</u>. Just the same, <u>a lot of the stores are overcrowded</u>.

4. Even though <u>Moscow</u> has a lot of <u>snow in the winter</u>, <u>you can still get around the city by subway</u>.

5. The weather in <u>San Francisco</u> is <u>cool and foggy in the summer</u>. On the other hand, <u>it's a nice break from the hot summer weather in other cities</u>.

6. <u>Seoul</u> would be a great place to live. However, <u>I don't speak any Korean</u>.

7. Although <u>the Grand Canyon</u> is a favorite tourist destination for many, it also has its problems. For example, <u>it can be hard to get a good hotel room during the busiest season</u>.

Exercise 5

A

2. public transportation   4. auto emissions
3. a landfill

B

1. ❶ & ❷   4. ❶ & ❷
2. ❷   5. ❶
3. ❶   6. ❷

Lesson **Your energy profile**

Exercise 1

2. Whenever I need to wake up, I go for a jog./
   I go for a jog whenever I need to wake up.
3. As soon as you start to feel stressed, you should relax
   and count to ten./You should relax and count to ten
   as soon as you start to feel stressed.
4. Before I start/Before starting a really busy day, I
   have a good breakfast.//I have a good breakfast
   before I start/before starting a really busy day.
5. While you are studying/While studying for a big test,
   you shouldn't listen to music.//You shouldn't listen to
   music while you are studying/while studying for a
   big test.
6. I watch TV until I fall asleep.

Exercise 2

Answers will vary. Possible answers if false *is chosen:*
2. False. As soon as I get home, I start to prepare
   dinner.
3. False. I can't think straight in the morning until I've
   had a bowl of cereal and a glass of orange juice.
4. False. I like to straighten up the house while I'm
   watching TV and the commercials are on.
5. False. After I fall asleep, the only thing that can
   wake me up is my alarm clock.

Exercise 3

Answers will vary. Possible answers:
2. Whenever he has trouble falling asleep, he counts
   slowly from 1 to 100.
3. He always talks on the phone while watching TV.
4. She can't wake up in the morning until she's had a
   cup of coffee.
5. He always sleeps in his parents' bed whenever there's
   a big storm.

Exercise 4

A
1. People's sleep needs change as they go through life.
   a. Just right   b. Too specific   c. Too general
2. People's energy patterns change according to the
   time of day.
   a. Too general   b. Just right   c. Too specific
3. In the U.S., vitamins are a big business.
   a. Too general   b. Too specific   c. Just right

B
Answers will vary.

Lesson **Sweet dreams**

Exercise 1

1. Unless   4. Unless
2. Even if   5. Since
3. Provided that

Exercise 2

2. I always feel great in the morning, provided that I've
   slept well the night before./Provided that I've slept
   well the night before, I always feel great in the
   morning.
3. My neighbors don't wake me up, since I sleep very
   soundly./Since I sleep very soundly, my neighbors
   don't wake me up.
4. I never oversleep in the morning unless my alarm
   clock fails to go off./Unless my alarm clock fails to
   go off, I never oversleep in the morning.
5. I never take a nap, even if I feel tired in the
   afternoon./Even if I feel tired in the afternoon, I
   never take a nap.
6. I almost never use an alarm clock, since I
   automatically wake up at six o'clock every morning./
   Since I automatically wake up at six o'clock every
   morning, I almost never use an alarm clock.
7. I fall asleep easily unless I have too many things on
   my mind./Unless I have too many things on my
   mind, I fall asleep easily.

Exercise 3

Answers will vary. Possible answers:
2. I snore unless I'm sleeping on my stomach.
3. I sleep like a log all night, provided that there are no
   loud noises.
4. Even if I've had a busy day, I'm usually wide-awake
   when it's time to go to sleep.
5. I don't sleepwalk unless something is on my mind.
6. Even if I've had eight hours of sleep, I'm usually still
   sleepy when I first get up in the morning.
7. I need eight hours of sleep a night because I have a
   very stressful schedule.

Exercise 4

2. I had a really <u>vivid</u> dream last night.
3. If you take a <u>long</u> nap, you might feel drowsy when
   you wake up.
4. She had a <u>horrible</u> nightmare and woke up
   screaming.
5. His insomnia is <u>chronic</u>.
6. Does <u>loud</u> snoring wake you up?

Exercise 5

A
1. weight gain; the throat muscles lose their tone so that
   they vibrate as air passes over them (2 causes)
2. A person with sleep apnea actually stops breathing
   for several seconds and wakes up breathless.

B
Answers will vary. Possible answers:
2. Kate should sleep on her stomach or side because
   most snoring occurs when people sleep on their backs.
3. Rick should avoid alcohol because it disturbs sleep
   and contributes to snoring.
4. Angel should drink coffee or soft drinks an hour or
   two before going to bed because the caffeine will
   make his sleep lighter and his snoring less intense.

278

Lesson **What's typical?**

Exercise 1

2. While
3. In contrast to
4. While
5. except that
6. Unlike
7. except that
8. except for

Exercise 2

2. While most people my age take the train to school, I usually drive.
3. In contrast to many people my age, I don't like hip-hop music.
4. While many of my classmates have traveled abroad, I haven't.
5. Unlike most students here, I don't have a part-time job.
6. I have a lot in common with my friends except that I don't like to eat out.
7. People in the United States and people in my country are similar except for their eating habits.

Exercise 3

Answers will vary. Possible answers:

2. Unlike Marie, I don't like loud music. I prefer mellow jazz music.
3. While Donald is interested in politics, I'm interested in sports.
4. In contrast to Luis, I'm not a fashion designer. I work in marketing.
5. Both Luis and I enjoy reading books except that I prefer romance novels to books about history.

Exercise 4

A

1. More and more Americans are living alone.
2. People are living alone because of divorce or the death of a partner, or because they choose to.
3. Twenty-five percent of all households in the U.S. are made up of just one person.
4. The typical person living alone is neither old nor lonely.
5. A quarter of the 23 million single people in the U.S. are under the age of 35.
6. The majority of these people have chosen to live alone, and they are responding to decreasing social pressure to get married and have a family.

B

Answers will vary.

Lesson **B** **Topics of concern**

Exercise 1

2. Most (of the) people are optimistic about the future.
3. About half (of) the people are worried about pollution.
4. The majority of the people are concerned about the economy.
5. Hardly any (of the) people are interested in politics.

Exercise 2

Answers will vary. Possible answers:

1. Most of my friends are concerned about <u>deciding on a future career</u>.
2. The majority of <u>my friends are concerned about getting good grades</u>.
3. Quite a few of <u>my friends are concerned about dating</u>.
4. Hardly any of <u>my friends are concerned about making new friends</u>.

Exercise 3

2. surprising
3. heartening
4. alarming
5. fortunate

Exercise 4

Answers will vary. Possible answers:

2. If schools had more money, they could buy computers.
3. If the city hired new police officers, the crime rate would decrease.
4. If motorists drove more slowly, there wouldn't be so many accidents.

Exercise 5

A

Answers will vary.

B

1. False. More and more Americans are living alone. This is a dramatic change from the extended families of just a couple of generations ago.
2. False. There is decreasing social pressure to get married and have a family.
3. False. People can maintain one-person households as they get better jobs and become financially independent.
4. False. People who marry are marrying at a later age.
5. True.

Lesson A Making conversation

Exercise 1

Answers will vary. Possible answers if different *is chosen:*

1. Different. In my culture, it's customary to wear your shoes inside a home.
2. Different. In my culture, making eye contact when talking to someone is impolite.
3. Different. In my culture, it's typical to shake hands when meeting friends and relatives.
4. Different. In my culture, arriving 30 minutes late for a dinner party is inappropriate.

Exercise 2

2. It's polite to ask people how they feel.
3. It's customary to ask people what they do for a living.
4. It's inappropriate to talk about religion with people you don't know well.
5. It's impolite to ask someone his or her salary.

Exercise 3

2. Asking people how they feel is polite.
3. Asking people what they do for a living is customary.
4. Talking about religion with people you don't know well is inappropriate.
5. Asking someone his or her salary is impolite.

Exercise 4

im-	in-	un-
impolite impossible	inappropriate	uncommon unimportant unusual

Exercise 5

Answers will vary. Possible answers:

2. When you receive a present from someone, it's common to say "Oh, you shouldn't have!"/When you receive a present from someone, saying "Oh, you shouldn't have!" is common.
3. When you walk into your office in the morning, it's polite to say "Good morning" to everyone./When you walk into your office in the morning, saying "Good morning" to everyone is polite.
4. When you take a message on the telephone, it's appropriate to say "May I take a message, please?"/When you take a message on the telephone, saying "May I take a message, please?" is appropriate.

Exercise 6

A

Bad Brother	envious
Bobby's Girl	hurt, angry
Doubtful Dad	proud, worried

B
Answers will vary.

Lesson B Personal secrets

Exercise 1

2. I asked her if she <u>had been</u> on a date with him.
3. She asked me why <u>I was</u> asking so many questions.
4. Then she told me <u>not to</u> tell anyone.
5. I said I <u>would</u> promise not to tell.
6. She said that they <u>are</u> in love.

Exercise 2

2. He asked her <u>if she'd heard about Paulo Alvaro</u>.
3. She said that <u>she hadn't</u>.
4. She asked Mark <u>what had happened</u>.
5. Mark said that Paulo <u>had gotten a promotion</u>.
6. Sandra asked Mark <u>when it had happened</u>.
7. He said that the official announcement <u>would be made soon</u>.

Exercise 3

Answers will vary.

Exercise 4

A

2. concealed   4. abolish   6. seal
3. devalued   5. intimacy

B

2. f   3. a   4. e   5. c   6. b

Lesson Ⓐ Storytelling

Exercise 1
2. Afterwards
3. Before that
4. As soon as
5. The next day
6. Before that
7. Later

Exercise 2
2. opened; gave
3. had not been
4. had been
5. waited
6. saw; felt
7. received; began
8. had never seen

Exercise 3
Answers will vary. Possible answers:
1. The moment I saw him, I smiled and said hello. He was surprised to see me. Later, we went to a nearby cafe to have a cup of coffee together.
2. Before that, I'd never lost anything so important. As soon as I realized it was gone, I called the police. Afterwards, I reported it to the embassy.
3. When I was assigned the project, I felt anxious. Until that time, I'd never worked alone on a project. I had to stay late and work hard. Finally, I finished all my work. Later, I felt relieved and proud.
4. Up until then, I'd never gone swimming in the ocean. At first I was nervous, but when I got in the water I felt fine. I had a great time. The next day, I went scuba diving again.

Exercise 4
A
A. 2 B. 4 C. 1 D. 3

B
Recently, I was walking home from work late at night <u>when</u> I heard someone walking behind me. I looked back, but it was too dark to see clearly. <u>Until then,</u> I had felt very relaxed because it was Friday evening – I had the whole weekend to look forward to. <u>As soon as</u> I heard the footsteps, however, I started to feel nervous. I began to walk more quickly. <u>Just then,</u> I could hear the person behind me walking faster. I was being followed! I got scared and began to run. <u>Until that moment,</u> I hadn't really noticed that a woman carrying a shopping bag was walking slowly in front of me. <u>The moment</u> I began to run, she screamed, dropped her shopping bag, and turned to face me with a look of terror on her face. She thought I was chasing her! <u>When</u> I saw this, I stopped running and tried to smile at her. <u>At that moment,</u> the person I thought had been chasing me walked by, looking curiously at both of us. I picked up the woman's packages and apologized for frightening her, but I didn't try to explain. I was too embarrassed, and she looked very annoyed.

C
Answers will vary.

Lesson Ⓑ What's in the news?

Exercise 1
2. grammatically correct
3. Police <u>have arrested</u> several gang members so far this year.
4. Burglars <u>stole</u> two paintings on Monday night.
5. Several observers <u>have seen</u> a rare butterfly in Central Park over the past week.
6. grammatically correct
7. The stock market <u>fell</u> sharply the other day.

Exercise 2
2. were trying
3. were preparing
4. heard
5. searched
6. located
7. was hiding
8. were removing
9. escaped
10. jumped
11. was standing
12. were watching
13. applauded
14. smiled

Exercise 3
2. robbery
3. hijacking
4. natural disaster
5. political crisis
6. human-interest story

Exercise 4
Answers will vary. Possible answers:
2. A bank robber has stolen <u>$1.5 million in the daring daytime robbery of a downtown bank</u>.
   The bank was closing for the day when <u>the robber entered the bank. He was wearing dark clothes and sunglasses. He made everyone lie down on the floor while he was robbing the bank.</u>
3. Passengers on Flight 200 were enjoying a meal when <u>two men stood up and announced that they were hijacking the plane</u>.
   The hijackers have demanded <u>that the airplane change course and fly to a different destination. In addition, they have asked for $1 million each.</u>
4. Most people were getting ready for bed when <u>a strong earthquake hit the California coast</u>.
   The earthquake has damaged <u>many buildings and roads. Fortunately, no one has been killed. The cleanup operation began a few hours ago.</u>

Exercise 5
A
Answers will vary. Possible answers:
Steven Lee was unsuccessful because he tried to escape by climbing over a fence into the state prison.
Stan Smith was unsuccessful because he used a dryer that made too much noise.

B
1. Stan Smith
2. Stan Smith
3. Steven Lee
4. Steven Lee
5. Stan Smith
6. Stan Smith

Lesson A   Growing up

Exercise 1
Answers will vary.

Exercise 2
Answers will vary. Possible answers:
2. I shouldn't have cheated on my exam.
3. I wish I'd paid attention.
4. I wish I hadn't talked with my friends in class.

Exercise 3
Answers will vary. Possible answers:
1. Tim shouldn't have had so much money in his wallet.
   Tim wishes he hadn't put his wallet down next to the phone.
2. Laura wishes that she'd left her house an hour earlier.
   Laura ought to have taken a taxi.
3. Charles shouldn't have gone to the movies with his friend.
   Charles wishes he'd studied for more than 20 minutes.
4. Janine wishes she'd called her mother.
   Janine should've left her friend's house earlier.

Exercise 4

Verb	Noun	Adjective	Noun
discipline	discipline	compassionate	compassion
forgive	forgiveness	courageous	courage
persevere	perseverance	honest	honesty

2. persevere
3. honesty
4. forgive
5. compassionate

Exercise 5
A
I am glad that I learned the value of work when I was young.

B
Answers will vary.

C
Answers will vary.

Lesson B   The wisdom of age

Exercise 1
Dear Editor:
   I read with great interest your article on today's society. Although I don't agree with everything you said, <u>it is apparent that</u> some of the points you made are true. For example, <u>it's a shame that</u> young people don't try to learn from their elders. <u>It's obvious</u> we all have a lot to learn from each other, but you can't tell young people that! <u>I hope</u> my children don't grow up without learning from others, but <u>it is sad to say</u> I won't be surprised if they do!
                                        Sincerely,
                                        Madeleine Wright

Exercise 2
1. It's untrue that people in modern society have no solid values.
2. It's a shame that some older people don't have much faith in the younger generation.
3. It's obvious that kids grow up faster than they used to.
4. It's fortunate that many people can look forward to an active life as they grow older.

Exercise 3
Sentences containing noun clauses:
3. I <u>guess</u> that everything will be all right in the end.
4. I don't <u>imagine</u> that future generations will romanticize this one.
5. I <u>suspect</u> the next generation won't be much different from this one.
6. I <u>hope</u> it's OK.

Exercise 4

Certainty	Uncertainty
believe	guess
be sure	hope
realize	imagine

Other verbs of certainty:
  know, think
Other verbs of uncertainty:
  suppose, suspect

Exercise 5
Answers will vary. Possible answers:
2. I think it's important to be open-minded and optimistic. If you're too negative, you will miss out on many new opportunities.
3. I don't think I will work as many years as my parents have worked. I will make more money and be able to retire earlier.
4. I guess that my priorities will change as I get older. Right now, my studies are my first priority, but that will probably change.
5. I imagine that people today are more tolerant than they were in the past, but I'm not sure. Nowadays, the world isn't perfect, but at least people talk about difficult issues openly.

Exercise 6
2. set   3. give   4. make   5. have

Exercise 7
A
1. The *generation gap* refers to differences in opinions between the younger and older generations. The generation gap was discussed a lot in the sixties and seventies.
2. differences in appearance (long versus short hair), the civil rights movement, the antiwar movement, the environment

B
2. extreme hairstyles   3. hair   4. the United States
5. the civil rights movement, the antiwar movement, the women's movement, the environment

Lesson Ⓐ Exploring creativity

Exercise 1

Answers will vary. Possible answers if disagree *is chosen:*

2. Disagree. I don't think patience is the most important quality for anyone who is learning a second language. Enthusiasm is more important than patience.
3. Disagree. The best thing a person who is starting a new job can do is listen closely and watch what other people are doing.
4. Disagree. Someone working with children needs to be very patient and a good listener.

Exercise 2

Answers will vary. Possible answers:

2. Anyone wanting to be a doctor has to study for many years.
3. Someone trying to find a job in the arts should do volunteer work in that field first.
4. People working at home need to be very disciplined.
5. A supervisor having too much work to do should delegate some of the work to others.
6. Anyone employed by the government has to do a lot of paperwork.

Exercise 3

Adjective	Noun	Adjective	Noun
curious	curiosity	patient	patience
decisive	decisiveness	resourceful	resourcefulness
determined	determination	sensitive	sensitivity
intelligent	intelligence	thrifty	thriftiness

Answers will vary. Possible answers:

2. Intelligence is the most important quality for a math professor to have./A person working as a math professor must be very intelligent.
3. Sensitivity is the most important quality for a counselor to have./A person working as a counselor must be very sensitive.
4. Curiosity is the most important quality for an archaeologist to have./A person working as an archaeologist must be very curious.

Exercise 4

Answers will vary. Possible answers:

2. A person wanting to be a construction worker has to be strong and know how to use different tools.
3. A person wanting to be an interpreter should be a quick thinker and good at languages.

Exercise 5

A

Answers will vary. Possible answers:
determined, resourceful

B

First paragraph: If you drive a car, this probably has happened to you, but I certainly never thought it would happen to me. . . .
Second paragraph: I was about to call the police when I got an idea. . . .
Third paragraph: The next day, I went out and got two sets of spare keys made. . . .

C

Answers will vary.

Lesson Ⓑ Ideas that work

Exercise 1

1. It only moves at about 20 miles an hour, which means we need to leave now.
2. The buses are even slower, which is why people avoid using them.
3. The office is a short distance from here, which means it shouldn't take long.
4. Yes, but then you'll have to breathe in the exhaust fumes from all the cars, which is why there are so few pedestrians.

Exercise 2

2. New diseases are being discovered all the time, which means (that) researchers have to work even harder.
3. People enjoy listening to music wherever they go, which is why the Walkman has become so popular.
4. Traffic congestion is becoming a major problem in many cities, which means (that) new types of public transportation will have to be developed.
5. Some companies have branches worldwide, which is why they use E-mail to communicate.

Exercise 3

Answers will vary. Possible answers:

2. Air travel has become easier, <u>which means (that) more people than ever are flying</u>.
3. Laptop computers are easy to carry anywhere, <u>which means (that) more people are taking them along when they travel</u>.
4. Pollution has become a major problem in many cities, <u>which is why people are moving to the suburbs</u>.

Exercise 4

1. found	4. found
2. organize	5. analyzing
3. explored	6. find

Exercise 5

A

reading, writing, and mathematics

B

1. a   2. b   3. a   4. b

Lesson   That really bugs me!

Exercise 1

2. Water dripping in the sink at night is the thing that keeps me from falling asleep.
3. One thing I can't understand in the supermarket is why people push in front of me in line.
4. The thing that really irritates me when I go out to eat is waiting a long time to be seated.
5. Being interrupted by someone in the audience is something that annoys me when I'm giving a speech.
6. Something that bothers me about my computer is how complicated it is to use.
7. People making noise on the street is the one thing I can't stand about my neighborhood.

Exercise 2

Answers will vary. Possible answers:

1. The thing that really irritates me when I go out to eat is having to listen to people who talk loudly at a nearby table.
2. Thinking about what I have to do the next day is the thing that keeps me from falling asleep.
3. One thing I can't understand in the supermarket is why so many items do not have their prices clearly marked.
4. The fact that all the stores close at 5:00 P.M. is the one thing I can't stand about my neighborhood.

Exercise 3

Answers will vary. Possible answers:

2. Something that bothers me when I'm in the park is seeing people who litter.
3. One thing that gets on my nerves in the library is when people make a lot of noise.
4. The thing that irritates me the most on the subway is passengers who take up extra seats.

Exercise 4

Answers will vary. Possible answers:

1. People who smoke in crowded places is something that annoys me because everyone else has to breathe in that smoky air.
2. People using cellular phones in public is something that often gets on my nerves because you are forced to listen to someone else's private business.
3. The sound of car alarms late at night is the one thing that really bothers me because I have trouble falling asleep.

Exercise 5

A

Order of paragraphs: 2, 4, 3, 1

B

a. 2   b. 1   c. 4   d. 3

C

Answers will vary.

Lesson   Let's do something about it!

Exercise 1

2. I wonder <u>if the city will build any new schools this year</u>.
3. <u>Whatever the planning board decides to do</u> will help.
4. <u>Why people are not concerned about the crime rate here</u> is a mystery to me.
5. I don't really know <u>whether or not others are concerned about the pollution problem</u>.
6. <u>Whether the budget passes or not</u> will depend on the support of people like you and me.

Exercise 2

2. I'm not sure what <u>we can do to get better health care for everyone</u>.
3. I have no idea why <u>the government can't reduce taxes</u>.
4. It's hard to say whether <u>(or not) more people will get involved</u>.
5. I know what you mean. I wonder if <u>anybody really cares</u>.
6. I don't know, but I'm going to try and find out how <u>people took care of these problems in the past</u>.
7. That's a good question. I don't understand why <u>more people don't vote in the local elections</u>.

Exercise 3

Salesclerk: bargain; discount
Customer: guarantee
Salesclerk: refund
Salesclerk: deposit; bill

Exercise 4

Answers will vary. Possible answers:

2. I'd like to know <u>if they can build more parking garages in the city. There aren't enough parking spaces on the street, especially downtown.</u>
3. I wonder <u>why taxi drivers are so rude and often lose their way. They need to give taxi drivers more training before they start working.</u>
4. I don't understand <u>why trash collection is such a problem. The trucks come by at odd hours and make too much noise.</u>

Exercise 5

A

Answers will vary. Possible answers: funny, trivial

B

2. dominates
3. get it off your chest
4. see red
5. sense

6. tempting
7. Get over it!
8. unique
9. bug

Lesson A Culture shock

Exercise 1

2. True.
3. False. By September 2011, they will have been attending school for one year.
4. False. By June 2024, they will have graduated from high school, but not from college.
5. False. By this time next year, they will have been traveling for only one year. They will not have finished traveling around the world.
6. True.

Exercise 2

2. Paul is interested in meeting new people.
3. Paul is afraid of flying.
4. Linda is looking forward to speaking a foreign language.
5. Linda is interested in tasting different kinds of food.
6. Paul is worried about feeling lonely.

Exercise 3

Answers will vary. Possible answers:

1. I'm looking forward to seeing all the famous buildings and taking a river cruise.
2. Yes. I'm excited about leaving the tour group to explore some interesting neighborhoods on my own.
3. Yes. I'm afraid of getting lost and not being able to find my way back to the hotel.
4. I'll insist on having a room with its own bathroom, not a shared one.
5. Yes. I'm counting on making new friends. I'm very friendly and make friends easily.

Exercise 4

A

Answers will vary. Possible answers:

Advantages of international travel

learning about the world
seeing how people in other countries live
trying new foods
doing things you couldn't do at home
having new experiences

Disadvantages of international travel

getting homesick
dealing with the food
figuring out the exchange rate
feeling lonely

B

Answers will vary.

C

Answers will vary.

Lesson B Globe-trotting

Exercise 1

1. c   2. a   3. e   4. b   5. d

Exercise 2

2. had prepared
3. had made
4. would be staying
5. would not have caught
6. had brought
7. wouldn't be sneezing
8. had bought
9. had followed
10. wouldn't be having

Exercise 3

Answers will vary. Possible answers:

Characteristics	How it would affect my life
open-minded	accept new ideas easily
self-assured	give a speech in front of a large audience
self-motivated	start my own company

2. If I were more open-minded, I would be able to accept new ideas easily.
3. If I were more self-assured, I would be able to give a speech in front of a large audience.
4. If I were more self-motivated, I would be able to start my own company.

Exercise 4

Answers will vary. Possible answers:

mountain climber: self-motivated, self-reliant, self-assured, nonconforming
businessperson abroad: culturally aware, culturally sensitive, nonjudgmental, open-minded

1. The mountain climber has to be self-motivated because <u>there is no one else around to do the work for her. If she doesn't work hard, she won't make any progress.</u>
2. If the mountain climber weren't <u>self-assured</u>, she <u>would be too afraid to even try.</u>
3. The businessperson abroad should be <u>nonjudgmental because he's dealing with an unfamiliar culture and should try to understand it.</u>
4. The businessperson abroad <u>needs to be open-minded so that he can negotiate with people from different cultural backgrounds.</u>

Exercise 5

A

take a course in anthropology
talk to someone who has lived abroad
learn about culture shock itself

B

2. Stage 1   4. Stage 1   6. Stage 2
3. Stage 4   5. Stage 3

Lesson **A** Public concerns

Exercise 1
1. Thus
2. Consequently
3. Furthermore
4. Therefore
5. In addition

Exercise 2
2. Teachers should be given more respect. In addition, they should be given better salaries.
3. Smoking is a costly habit. Moreover, I find it to be an offensive one.
4. The stock market has dropped dramatically. Thus, people are feeling anxious about the economy.
5. The roads are in terrible shape. Therefore, repair work needs to begin immediately.
6. Skydiving is an expensive sport. Furthermore, it is dangerous.

Exercise 3
2. It's being towed away.
3. They're being cut down.
4. It's being torn down.
5. It's being painted.
6. It's being repaired.

Exercise 4
1. pessimist
2. fatalistic
3. optimistic
4. fanatic
5. skeptical

Exercise 5
A
1. Mom and Dad
2. Michael

B
2. P
3. M
4. P
5. M
6. P
7. M
8. P
9. P

C
Answers will vary.

Lesson **B** How honest are you?

Exercise 1
1. only if
2. even if
3. only if
4. unless

Exercise 2
Answers will vary. Possible answers:
2. I sincerely feel that it's OK for parents to lie to their children. Children should be protected from news that will hurt them.
3. I'm absolutely convinced that employees should always report problems. Everyone should follow the same rules.
4. I still maintain that young people shouldn't live alone. It's too expensive for a young person to have his or her own apartment.

Exercise 3
Answers will vary. Possible answers:
1. I agree. I wouldn't let a friend copy my test paper even if he promised never to do it again.
2. I agree. I would tell my parents even if my brother asked me not to tell anyone.
3. It depends. I wouldn't lend my best friend a lot of money unless it was truly an emergency.
4. Really? I'd call the police only if I thought it was a dangerous situation.

Exercise 4
Answers will vary. Possible answers:
2. I would make up a story about being too busy to see friends if I were too tired to go out.
3. I would lie about why I was late for work only if I had to do it to keep my job.
4. I wouldn't lie about my age to someone I was dating unless I felt uncomfortable with the situation.

Exercise 5
A
the website of a TV program

B
1. You should use The Hottest Gossip because it's totally secure.
2. You should send us documents or photos to support your story.
3. You shouldn't worry about fingerprints because we always photocopy the originals to protect our sources.
4. You should never call us from home or on a work, mobile, or hotel phone.

C
keeping their advertisers happy